We Are the Murder Victims

Who Lived

A Survivor's Truth on Sexual Assault

S.K. Menelle

We Are the Murder Victims Who Lived
A Survivor's Truth on Sexual Assault

Published in the United States of America
S K Menelle
Copyright 2021
ISBN: 9798987136416

"While this is a memoir and therefore a work of non-fiction, names of people and places have been changed for legal reasons, with the exception of historical and famous characters.

Although containing true events and real recollections of the author's life, details have been omitted and/or modified for privacy. Any resemblance to real persons, living or dead, is entirely coincidental."

We Are the Murder Victims Who Lived

S K Menelle

Dedication

My dearest Bethesda, you are a light at the end of the tunnel.

My almighty God, thank you for restoring this downtrodden soul.

My mother and father, when the road was too far and too long, you carried me.

My beloved sister Lauren, you are everything that life promises you.

My Elio, my love, may you one day understand these words when you grow up.

Lastly, to the people that have given me a home: in you I see that home follows you around and also waits patiently for your return.

To the survivors, you make me brave.

And to the little girl I once knew, may your life be ever the fullest.

Foreword
Revisions: August 1, 2022

Hello again.

It's been two years since we last spoke.

And I must admit that it has taken me more than long enough to put this book back out. But as so many of us have learned, while we are busy living, life hits. And in the past two years, life hit us all in more ways than one.

While I stepped away from my words late last year, I've returned with a new vigor for the pen, and a desire to tell you about what brought me here. It will always be so important to me.

What started out as the reexamination of my book, soon lended itself to me pencilling in the addition of a few new chapters. This then transformed into a full-fledged reinvention of the original manuscript which was published in March of 2020. Six additional chapters.ages. New edits, new notes. New stories unearthed from the archive of my life.

It feels like I've waited an entire lifetime for this. A lifetime to tell my story. But the comical and perhaps even bitter irony, is that I wouldn't mind waiting a few hundred more. I wouldn't mind every and any lifetime which follows this one, passing me by without mention of this book. Because that would mean that what happened to me would have never happened.

And these words would never be, because no life would have ever been breathed into them for them to exist in the first place.

It's a foolish dream, a simple reimagining of history. It is the invisible and impossible hope that a past which I cannot erase, would one day leave me without a trace.

But it is a past which stands in both the physical realm just as much as it stands in the spiritual and emotional realms, and therefore has proven impossible to scribble out, paint over, cover up, and shove aside.

So what have I done instead? Knowing that this story will never go away? I have brought it to you.

I quickly managed to toss in the new adaptations within weeks.

I added brand new chapters at the speed of light. Any spare moment which I could claim for the book, went right to the keyboard. I typed out words like my life depended on it. I wrote all winter. The words poured out of me liberally. I had so much to say. I remembered everything, just as the way it was.

Then one day, spring came. And then summer. And the words just simply stopped.

Suddenly, the sentences which seemed to flow out abnormally well, became my stumbling blocks.

I waited for months to finish the one last chapter that remained. It was the very last piece of the puzzle. Just a few more pages and then fin; complete. If only I finished that chapter, then the new, re-imagined version of the book would be complete. It was my chapter about closure. And it was the one thing standing in the way of my book remaining hidden on my laptop and finally making it's way to shelves. I couldn't stomach it.

Perhaps I feared that with my novel no longer for sale, I was safe. So maybe I wanted to prolong my hiatus for just a bit longer. Perhaps I feared that once it was back, there was nothing more for me to hide.

Now that my words are in public view, I have nothing left.

I have been emptied out like a well. The splashing pale of water sloshes side to side and gives me motion sickness. There is not one drop left.

Is that such a bad thing though? To be emptied out in this

sense has been rather cathartic.

To purge the words out my body and out of my very being, and to displace them on to paper has given me both a sense of fear and relief.

I am scared of how these words will be received. They are blunt, brutal, and perhaps maybe even graphic at times.

Nothing of my story has been leveled out for the comfortably of others, not one brilliantly bright color bleeds into the next. I wanted to be sure of it. No murkiness, no grey. Even if it makes us sit in a place that we don't like.

That is the power in my story. It is the truth, plain and simple. It is that which may appear ugly, out in the open for you all to see. But to find my voice within ugliness has been empowering. To hear myself speak after all this time of feeling helpless to the sound of my own voice, is purely miraculous.

I've waited for a long time. But I think that time cannot fully be measured by what makes us ready, or how we are ready or when we are ready…or even why. But simply time is measured by the easy going fact that when we know, we know, and that is enough. So now I know that I am ready.

Ready to embark on this journey again.

Ready to produce and ready to give, to learn and to grow. Ready to be seen and heard, ready to see and hear in return.

Ready to hand over this work to those of you who are willing and emphatic enough to understand, who have perhaps been where I stand.

Ready to make full again what is now emptied out onto these pages. Ready to revive something and someone who has been on hiatus, ready to bring these words back to life.

Every day away from all of you was a day too long.

And so, I present to you: the second addition of my book: WE ARE THE MURDER VICTIMS WHO LIVED, with six new chapters, a new cover, and other edits.

Here's to healing.

S.K.Menelle

Preface

"Rape is one of the most terrible crimes on earth. And it happens every few minutes. The problem with groups who deal with rape is that they try to educate women about how to defend themselves. What really needs to be done is teaching men not to rape. Go to the source and start there."
-Kurt Cobain, 1991

Sometimes, I am so sick of writing about real life. Ernest Hemingway once wrote that, "all you have to do is write one true sentence. Write the truest sentence that you know." I concur that that the world has been entirely built on untruths, operating on the lies which we tell ourselves, and the manipulation that humanity has managed to offer us. So many of us are grasping at dangling strings and all the wrong things, one lie more painful than the next. It would appear that writing the truest of true statements should or could be the easiest thing for a writer to do. Write what you know, write what you see. It is a simplified, elementary, and unembellished concept at its core.

But sometimes writing the truth is the most painful part. And sometimes it feels safer to write nothing at all. But if I had never written these words-never shared these factual truths with you-where would I be? Even if the pages were not looking directly back at me in black font, it would still be my story: a massive jumble of invisible ink and floating words in my brain, just waiting to be reined in and penned down. The story would still be there, still trapped in my memories, but it would not be here, for all of you. And although truth is pain, it is also freedom.

Kurt Cobain. I cannot think of any other male musical artist so outspoken about women's issues, a rarity amongst an entertainment industry that seems to have fostered misogyny and sexual violence in its very foundation. Grunge legend Kurt Cobain, gone far too soon, and far ahead of his time. Cobain is famously known for his diehard support of women and desire to dismantle rape culture more than twenty-five years ago, a culture that becomes more exposed by the day. He was an advocate for the harrowing idea that rape is worse than murder because the victim lives.

That is enough to send a knife into my spine, the weapon that never pulls back out but instead turns in my side ever so slowly. This knife did not kill me and kill with it all memory of the pain, but instead remains in me for the rest of my life because I survived.

Ultimately, we are the murder victims who lived.

And so, I write this, sometimes with the strength of one-thousand warriors, and other times feebly, leaving all the lights on. I write all through the night when I cannot sleep, or sleep when I cannot face the cruel darkness of what I am writing. It seems, sometimes, that this job is too vast for one mere mortal. To pen it all down is pain. It is also a necessity, an empowerment, and a freedom. To me, there is no other option now.

If I think of myself as the murder victim who lived, I feel bold.

And yet, how unlucky am I to carry this unwanted title?

You cannot win in such a case as this, but in these ever-changing times, you are perhaps promised just one thing: a chance.

Cobain realized the monstrosities of a backwards system when his female friend explained that she was in self-defense classes at a rape crisis center. When she looked outside of the window at a football field of boys playing sports, she told herself, "They should be in here getting schooled." That is how I have often felt over the past three years. Why am I the one having to learn karate, having to practice how to wield a purse knife and pepper spray, having to listen to the speech about never traveling alone at night? Why am I the one that has to compensate for a disastrously evil culture, why am I the only one who has learned a lesson here?

I have become hyper-aware and educated on these "unspoken's." Meanwhile, I tell myself that men should be at the head of the line for these discussions…they should know what is inherently right and wrong. But if it is just "that grey" then they should be told, again and again. Boys should be raised not to rape. Instead, girls are raised on how to avoid it.

But if your common sense tells you not to kill, then where in the hell is your common sense telling you not to rape?

Do I really have to tell you why you should not have done this to me?

It is for the same reason that we are taught as children about basic values, the ten commandments if you will: do not murder, do not steal, do not lie…the list trails on. Do not to take another life into your hands. Do not take a life. Do not decide that your life holds more value than another, that you are worthy of living and someone else is worthy of dying.

"Well of course, I would not murder someone," you say wryly to yourself, already questioning what I am getting at. But would you take no for an answer? Would you pressure your significant other? Would you take advantage of someone who was passed out or too drunk to agree? If the lines between each of these three sentences were blurred for you, then perhaps you truly have in fact decided that you were the one worthy of living and of deciding for others, of choosing when another could not. If once upon a time, you decided that your life was more important, more superior, and more salient, then you have murdered, just in another sense of the word. You have killed a part of someone that they will never get back.

The time is now. I am impatient, yet hopeful. People are speaking up with their voices heightened, yelling at the top of their lungs, throats scratched and words on fire. We are on the mountaintops: are you listening? No longer voiceless or powerless, yet we are still fighting a crime committed to make the victim feel both of these inadequacies. Sexual assault is a complete, corrupt abuse of power, it is the taking of what we can never have back, it is the invitation we never gave you.

I was a virgin planning for love. Maybe I really did think life would work out ever so perfectly for me. Maybe I would fall in love, and he would be the only one and the first for everything. That was before. Reality brought me to nothing of the sort. There were no butterflies, no fireworks, no first times and "I Love You's". There was no spontaneity, delicacy, and naivety that comes with young love.

The Hollywood depictions of a candlelit romance, and a forbidden love such as that of The Notebook, were merely joking points for me of how far off the movies were from real life. There was nothing warm or fuzzy feeling about my pants being ripped off me so suddenly that I felt as if my body were made of ice. Or maybe stone. To feel like a block of immovable stone is certainly not the kind of feeling consensual sex evokes.

The light-hearted, joking phrase "the morning after" has its very own profound and deeply painful meaning. I envision an eighteen year old version of myself, waking up bloodied, with bruised arms and dried puke on my blouse sleeve. As the years fade, I can no longer so harshly taste that morning after, but I remember everything. Coming to in complete confusion and utter pain, like I had been shot in the ribs. My bones were paper thin, I could feel my insides cracking. And yet, my body pulsed with denial.

What happened? I kept asking. What the hell happened to me?

I was too young to withstand something like this. I felt as if a part of me had been stolen and I would have to accept that I would never get it back.

I was a house robbed of all furnishing and all of my most expensive artwork, and some valuables could never be replaced. The rest would take years of the hardest, deepest, and most aching work I had ever known to earn back for myself. My journey meant that I was called to fill in the gaps where there was once empty space and to accept that some empty spaces would never be filled.

Determined, I knew that my house would be filled once again, but it would not look the same.

After I escaped my assailant, splotches of black cloud my memory as fragments of what happened next continue to rock me to my core. I found myself alone in the bathroom of my friend's house and the whole room had gone woozy. The memories would come back in waves over the next week, maybe even months or years, but I could have gone fifty lifetimes without the unwanted information of what happened to me.

Victims of murder do not get woken up, they do not stumble awake the next morning, aching in pain, confused what happened the night before or how they made it out. They do not walk around living with the pain of what has happened to them, in the unforeseen and unknown. They are not told "do not worry, the worst is over." They do not have to deal with thoughts of hating and then forgiving their attackers. They do not have to relive their deaths day by day…

They never make it out, and damn it I did, so in this I remain strong. It is the only thing that kept me going these past three years when the weight of knowing, seems too much to bear. Knowing every detail of what happened is enough to kill. Mourning a loss, time, and the life you will never get back, is enough to send someone into the darkest of bottomless spirals.

Unwanted, invasive touch, of any kind, sexual violence of any kind, abuse of power of any kind, assaulting and abusing of any kind…is ultimately a grieving of what has died. That which has died by no accidental or unplanned death.

So, while we-the ones that were supposed to die that day-still live on, there is promise in this mere fact that we live on.

I pray you see it.

I pray this story conveys itself solely as a story of survival.

When it becomes too hard of a pill to swallow, take a moment and take care of yourself. I took careful time in writing this book, but when the words flowed out, I did not stop. I have omitted some details, but many remain my unchanging truth. I am scared you will be caught off guard, I am concerned you will look away or skip pages. I worry that you will not want to find yourself in that bathroom with me. But I owe it to myself and to others to tell the whole truth, no matter how uncomfortable. My sole mission is to inform and to raise awareness, even if it raises eyebrows. Because I will not feel any more shame for something that was done to me by someone else. I will not feel guilty for another's wrongdoing. My story is my story.

It can never be too much to tell the truth.

The truth is what I will always tell.

If given the chance, he will lie.

He already has.

He will never say sorry.

His story went from "I do not know her" to "I just kissed her." My story went from "you know what you did" to "you know what you did." Disastrous, messy, broken, harsh. Then fulfilled, recovered, and whole. That was my story then, and that is my story now. Unchanging. I have no other choice for my own sake then to speak truth. That is all I have in this depraved universe.

I have been telling the truth for three years, squashed down and ostracized by the other side, but my story remains unchanged. My truth is unwavering, always.

I pray that you take gentle care of yourself, that you are healing or healed. My wish for you, is that you may feel emboldened, no matter your story, no matter the truth it holds.

I pray that this book is a beacon of hope in a fickle world that gives up on us too easily, shuts us up without seeing that we are too big to be ignored. I pray that when you, dear reader, read this, you are able to digest down some of the details you wish you could unread, but also comprehend the redemptive qualities my story-and many stories like mine-hold within our pages.

Long ago I quit running and started writing instead. It was most important to love me more, but I could only do that if I was being honest with my spirit.

I celebrate in small victories: the simple getting up out of bed in the morning. I celebrate reclaiming my body, my mind, my soul and my spirit. I celebrate the days I drag myself to yoga, and I can feel myself finally reconnecting with my limbs. I celebrate looking at myself in the mirror and liking what I see. I celebrate art and love and breathing life into dried lungs again. I celebrate weddings. I celebrate birthdays. I celebrate the warmth of long hugs. I still celebrate. I celebrate survival. I celebrate the fight, the race that will one day be won, even if it is a win I will not see in my lifetime on earth.

I celebrate.

Victim, I am not. Survivor I am.

I still live, and live, and live…

"Morning P! Started reading your book…I read the preface so far. I am gathering up courage to read the rest and I am afraid of what I will find. However, you lived it and are still dealing with it, so I am here to continue on this with you—whether behind you to hold you up, next to you so you can lean on me, or in front to gently guide you forward. I will be brave as you are brave and ready to share in the full knowledge of your attack and aftermath. I am glad you sent the book—glad you wrote it—it is part of the survival. I pray Jesus will continue to fill you with His strength and peace and wisdom. That you will not be defined by the event—although it has certainly shaped you—and that you will conquer in all aspects of life and be aware that you are still here. You are still here to experience love and beauty and joy and relationships and fulfillment. I love you most deeply, Papoi-"

-Text sent from my father (nickname Papoi) the morning of Monday January 27, 2020, 9:53 am//

Chapter One

Dear New York Times,

During my winter break, I submitted an OP-ED piece via email to the New York Times opinion section titled "I Can Wear What I Want."

I waited with the anticipation that this would either be nothing or something, knowing fully well that it was most likely going to be not a thing. There was a typical time window of waiting three days for either a reply or no reply. If three days passed and I heard from no one, maybe I would start out on smaller platforms. Or maybe I would just keep writing this book. Either way, I was determined to be heard.

It was too late for me, but maybe it is not too late for us. I was told that I waited too long, but the truth is that the odds were never in my favor. This crime is "too hard" to prove. It becomes a "he said, she said". The part that burns, is that it feels like "he" always wins.

And so, I never sat in court and faced my assailant; I never got the justice here on earth that I can only pray God may divvy out. I never got physical edification or admittance that this crime actually happened. I never went to the police or the hospital the next morning, but even if I had, would that really have put him behind bars? (Don't even get me started on our justice system...) Why is this a fate of defeat that we have come to willingly accept for our sexual assault survivors within society? Why hasn't this barrier been ripped in two?

Pretend a clothing store chain was robbed for every bit of merchandise they have, and somehow the whole thing goes unnoticed. It never makes news, never hits the media, and only a few friends of the employees hear about it. So, it just sort of lives on in a small circle by word of mouth. But no arrests are ever made. People say "man, that business must have really suffered," but no media outlets ever cover it. So technically the crime was never committed in the face of the law. These grey and murky waters are where I so often find myself. here Somedays it feels as if my existence has become one big old question mark.

My crime was never a crime acknowledged by law. My rapist is probably out drinking with friends right now. And I am here, sitting beside my mother as she snores, hands flying on keyboard. I am only in my parents' home for one more week, and it took coming here to start this, so I assume that I may just finish it by the time I go.

I write while he does God knows what, but I have not thought about what his life must be like in a while. I try not to think about it, because I am determined to have a daring and beautiful life. I would say my life already is beautiful, despite it all. Regardless of what his life paints itself to be, I know what my life is. I admit that there is still beauty to be seen everywhere, even at the times when I can't see a thing.

I am home on Christmas break writing as my mother sleeps beside me. Her soothing presence is an embrace of warmth. Just being in her envelopment settles me. Quiet company is a powerful thing…to exist with someone in the silence, to feel all their love and safety and comfort without even sharing a word, is to know one another. That is just one innate power held by mothers.

Writing, to me, is the equivalent of that same unspoken peace. I don't have to say a word, and yet I pour it all out in the stillness. Writing to me, means pure unabashed freedom. It reminds me that my story is my story, and it is truth, because it really happened, like so many of these stories really. did. happen.

A male friend of mine was raped by another male. Late one night in August he disclosed this to me, revealing what happened in the springtime when we had parted ways for summer break. He had spent all summer submerged in the pain of what he had survived.

He had gone back to his date's house after wine and a candlelit dinner. And that was where it happened. This was why he never stopped punishing himself-it was his date, he went back to that apartment willingly. Why do we think that means we deserved this?

We've sat at dinner tables and shared meals and conversations and drinks with our rapists…we have gone on dates with the ones who will so wittingly impact our lives in a way we never could have imagined or wanted. Some of them may even be in our family, the abusers we could never escape. And others are mere strangers, evil encapsulated that wreak havoc on our lives without even giving us a name or face to put that very evil to.

When my friend told me, he didn't so much tell, as he did blurt it all out like a child uncensored. Maybe it was the alcohol talking. He wasn't drunk, but he was on his third glass. I stood at my kitchen counter, pouring a second round for our friends. We were all joking about something, but I can't remember what. I suppose that doesn't really matter now. What matters was what he said next. I recall him looking at me goofily, laughing the words off before they even escaped his lips, and saying "wow, and I was raped!"

If I could encapsulate that feeling it would be like the wind going out of me when I fell backwards in first grade. Or the rug being pulled under my feet as if by some magic trick. Truthfully, I hated that word, I abhorred it so passionately. I couldn't believe that some people used it so casually, so flippantly, and even jokingly. It was grim and grimy. Within one word, there was the ability to turn an entire room dark. And indeed that kitchen seemed to suddenly feel so dark.

I am not sure that many of our friends heard or noticed what was going on. Or maybe they saw the way his eyes seemed to haze over from the wine, so they dismissed it. While they ignored the words had stumbled out of his mouth, I was stuck on those words, confused and concerned for what was to come next.

My smile turned dim, and I looked at him narrowly, stunned. He was looking back at me with the most pained, puppy dog eyes, as if reality had just centered back into focus. No one said a word, standing in the discomfort together. Our friends struck up their conversations again as our eyes remained locked in to one another.

"Wait, what? Are you serious?" I stared deep into him, as he bore his eyes back into mine gravely.

His lips parted in an attempt of a smile, "yes, but I'm fine!"

He snapped out of it, shrugging off the shock factor with a dry laugh. I furrowed my eyebrows with concern. His denial, his processing of this most recent and painful memory, was to joke it off as if it never happened, as if it didn't hurt in the ways which it did night after night. There was no manual that we had been given for this. No one said, "you might actually make a joke about one of the worst nights of your life." No one told us this probably was not going to be a good sign, but there was also no proper way to do this. No black and white path to living. So, we might not say the things we really want to in the ways which we so desperately long to say them, we might even add in a sarcastic laugh to ensure that we are unphased.

We might not process in the healthiest ways, but we never wanted this to process in the first place. And when it all becomes too much to bear, we might just spit out word vomit in all the worst ways, we might cry out for help and attention at the most random of moments.

My dear friend's truth spilled out at the wrong time, as I found mine often did too. What I deciphered was that there never actually was a right time.

Sometimes I would just blurt it out because I wanted people to understand, or perhaps, I just craved for a human to accept me. Or maybe I wanted the pity. Either way, it never came up in the way that I wanted to. I'm not sure I ever wanted it to, but like an old unwelcome nemesis, it always did.

It was boiling over in me and I didn't even realize it. Therapy helped me to see what I had been blinded to, and writing helped me to permanently vocalize it. The words were dying to come out.

"Why are you joking about it?" I remember asking him, so confused, pulling him off to the side hallway.

He gazed back at me hopelessly, as if to say, "What else can I do?"

He was trying to 'un'-victimize himself, trying to let the world know that he was just fine. Trying to make light of his traumas like so many of us do, to mock them in order to feel in control of them.

I gave him my "me too" pin and reminded him that we would fight this together, that he would never have to be alone ever again.

It was not a badge of honor, but rather a battle scar. No one had asked for this, but we would make it out of war.

I realized harshly that assault doesn't just happen to women. His story is the most recent I have heard. I remember how harshly and suddenly it struck me that people needed to know. How is a social justice issue that is so disgracefully common and real, still so taboo? This crime is one that does not select based on race, gender, or sex. It simply selects out of opportunity. Evil people see a chance and they take it. This happens to men, too, more men than I even realized until the stories amongst friends continued to come out during my years in college.

This crime thrives in dark corners of night, in shadows, in doubt, in disregard. This crime gets excused with "are you sure that's what it was?" and "what were you wearing?"

There are statutes of limitation placed on this crime, expiration dates for rape, and theories that maybe it was consensual. The victims are met with open-ended questions, instead of open arms. As if we have not experienced enough that makes us fearful, we are yet again made afraid that no one will believe us. We are reassured of this long held belief that victims will never be believed, through all the speculations and criticism that we endure. Perhaps it is even the squirming or wincing of discomfort we see in others when they hear our stories which is enough to keep us quiet.

This crime plays out daily and hardly a quarter of what should be done, is done. The "unprovable crime" has now found a time where it will be proven, because it is real for so many of us—too many of us—and it happens as sure as you and I wake up each morning.

Now, the world is paying attention.

We are all so sick of living in a clouded grey world, where our truth is very much black and white. We should not have to narrow ourselves down to the outfit we put on that night or how many drinks we ingested. We should not be limited into a category that files us away as victims, without ever really letting us speak.

Frankly, we are fed up.

So, I wrote. I was fed up and I was writing and suddenly I felt myself both angered and then at peace, both fulfilled and then emptied out all at once. I was speaking now, but I just needed to be heard, I needed to find an audience that would listen. So, I began writing this book and never looked back.

I waited for the three-day response to arrive, and it never did. Three days came and went. The New York Times was not interested in my op-ed. I mean, who was I, anyway? I was a no-name to them. But I had something to say.

People needed to listen! They simply had to, I assured myself. Soon enough, it was 4 a.m. and I had typed up fifty pages of thoughts and feelings that I began to organize into chapters and topics. Pretty soon, I couldn't stop. In writing, I found therapy. At that point, who listened or when stopped mattering so much. Saying it aloud began to help piece me back together.

I had been writing since I was a little girl. Some things never change.

I grew up in a home that encouraged practicing your cursive and journaling. I still harbor a hefty collection of crinkled pages and old diaries. By the third grade, I was waking up half an hour before my dad would come in to get me up for school. I would rise with the sun so that I could work on my fictional stories about mythical fairies and mice. My dad would come into my room at 7 a.m., but sure enough, my bedside lamp was already on. I was already writing on various bits of printer paper scattered around the bed and floor, spreading out pages over my blankets and throwing unwanted words on the rug. I worked like a madwoman when it came to my writing. That was just the third grade. That same drive is mirrored in me today, as I type away on these pages so rigorously while the house sleeps.

I realized that the more I write, the more the thought dawns on me that I have so much more to say than I have ever even realized. Enough to fill up hundreds of pages of paper.

I wrote on and on for the next week to come, writing when that was all I could do, stepping away when I could not say any more. I would read over and over my words, sometimes skipping over the one's that I didn't feel like dealing with that day. But no matter what, I wrote down everything I remembered word for word, peeling through old diaries and journals, copying down each word I had so painfully scribbled out in black and blue pens while the world had unknowingly continued.

So, this is how my book began.

We do not get to choose which stories we write, only that we chose to write them at all.

This was not the story about mythical fairies named Esmerelda and Lilac that I had spent my entire elementary school existence writing about. This was not the story I was scribbling away at before my father came in to wake me. This story was not one that I wrote in the early morning hours of childhood, but rather in the late-night hours of adulthood while the world wandered on. This story was far less dazzling, but perhaps more daring, then any bit of fiction

I had managed to write in my entire twenty-one years. This book is just one of many books I have written, but the first I have ever finished. I was more determined, more hard-wired and strong-willed than I had ever been for anything else that I had poured out from mind to page. This labor of love had done the one thing none of my other books could: it told my story-completely and totally even name for name. It could tell the truth, mask off.

This story was one I had not chosen to write, a topic I had not picked out of a hat in creative writing class. This story began and ended in a little black and white tiled bathroom right off a college campus. This story had more or less chosen me, and I had never asked for its selection.

As Robin Williams says in one of my all-time favorite movies-Good Will Hunting, "no one can possibly know the depths of you."

People will read this and they may not understand, and that is okay. This book doesn't encompass every bit of who I am. It doesn't describe the ways in which I have lived out some of the greatest memories of all time and laughed so hard I thought my stomach might burst.

I didn't include the nights I spent sleeping under the stars with my best friend, or the nights I watched Law and Order and Golden Girls with my mama because we could not sleep. I didn't tell you in great lengths about all the hugs and the arguments and all the life lived. Just know there was a lot of it, always a small silver lining that made the bad a little less ugly. Looking back now, I see that it was always there. There was always some amount of clear sky that made the gray a little more bearable.

This book doesn't go into great detail of my travels, my adventures, my summers, and the moments I wish I could live inside of forever. But just know, those moments are there, and they happened.

My story doesn't detail in great depth the nights I cried myself to sleep, or screamed into my pillow, or hid under the covers and watched movies until the sun came up. I didn't want to talk much about all of that. Just know that it was there, because it happened, and everything unsaid is as much a part of this story as what is being said. Read between each line. I promise you, there has been far more than I could ever explain.

"I can't learn anything from you unless you want to talk about you, who you are, then I'm fascinated, I'm in, but you don't want to do that do you? You're terrified of what you might say," Robin Williams continues in one of my favorite movie scenes of all time. Then he looks at a young Matt Damon as he leaves him on that park bench with these lasting words: "Your move."

Your move, I tell myself every time I sit down in front of this computer screen, rubbing both palms together. Unless, of course, I am terrified of what I might say, which I am. But I will choose to say it anyway.

This is just one prime example of how movies helped me through when writing dead ended itself. They made me cry during the months where I had grown hardened and cold. They made me laugh when I needed my spirit to be lifted. Well-written movies gave me the guts to keep writing my very own script. The right movies didn't glamorize the pain, but instead interpreted it, and I was interested in what this would illuminate in my very own playwright. To no coincidence, Good Will Hunting has been a childhood staple for me but was produced, of course, by none other than Harvey Weinstein, the very name threatening to taint every bit of good in the movies he helped dispatch to the public.

Truth be told, my story has threatened my sanity. It's tugged at memories of worn-through friendships and burned bridges and reminded me of all my reasons to be depressed and miserable. It forced me to look backwards, which is a place often times none of us would like to go.

And then…

And then it all took a surprising turn, casting me toward the ones I love as a reminder to soak them in for everything they are and everything they have done for me. This story of trauma turned me towards thankfulness. Before I knew it, within these recollections of darkness which conquered page after page, I found myself saying thank you, thank you, thank you. Thank you, mom. Thank you, dad. Thank you, sister. Thank you, friends. Thank you, colleagues. Thank you, classmates. Thank you, strangers. Thank you, warriors. Thank you, survivors.

Thank you, Sophia. You have done so well, do you know that? Pretty soon, my thoughts of despair turned towards promises and acknowledgments. I had been gifted good humans and the opportunity of a limitless future. I had not bowed my head in defeat. I had not become like my aggressors: Endlessly insecure, spiteful, and hateful. I hadn't become jaded and bitter from the world.

I was not out for revenge, to ruin lives. I was determined, instead, to rebuild mine. I had become resilient and rock hard, not stone cold. If I had made it through, then I could tell other people that it was possible. I could hold someone else's hand and say, "together, we will do this thing." Or, "stop this thing." Whatever it was that I was meant to do, I knew I was meant to do it. So, I wrote vigorously. I wrote evening after evening. I wrote in the middle of lecture classes and in the middle of the night.I wrote because I was writing for hundreds of thousands of other humans.

I write now because it's not just my story. It's my mother's story, my father's story, and my family's story. It is the story of my friends—both male and female—and the stories of friends I have never met and may never meet in this lifetime. It's the story of the ones whose shoulders I lay myself down to cry on. It's the story of both survivors and their supporters. I write because one day I want my children to know and I want them to understand, although it may be difficult. I write because I don't want this to happen to my daughter's and my daughter's friends. I write because I want the discussion to continue unendingly.

I write because if not now, then when?

I write because I can. I write because I have the freedom of speech, and the freedom of undeniable truth. I write to inform, explain, shed light, share hope, spread peace. I write for any and every reason and any and every emotion I have experienced in these three years of processing and healing and crying and mending. I write because I am not broken, I am whole. I write because it's all I have ever known, and some concepts remain unchanged. There is so much in me that was once a part of the little girl in third grade. The one that did this to me didn't take away that little girl from me, didn't turn her dark and hopeless. I write because I am triumphant, because I win. Because although I am bruised and battered, I am still charging forward, never stagnant. My attacker does not win.

The ones who take and take from us will one day fall. The ones who thrive on others' failures and pain will one day break. I will still be standing while they fade away. I will be at the top of my mountain, grazing fingertips with God, and they will be at the foothills, unable to imagine how it looks so high up.

I write because I have never stopped and never plan on stopping. I write because I want you to hear this. I want you to know. I write because all these words have been trapped in the confides of my brain for far too long. I write because I can wear what I want, and so can you, and it doesn't make us willing or consenting. I write because I have to. I must.

And it is time for you to listen. You must.

Chapter Two

Look How Far We Have Fallen

We are now living in a world of the "Weinstein Trials" not the "Weinstein Company." The movies that preceded his name have faded away. The voices of survivors are much louder. As the Harvey Weinstein trials have come to a resounding close, I find it ironic that it has taken decades to prove a guilt that I thought was already so obvious. I think that the world was divided into two: the ones who cared because it meant something so personal to them, and the ones who paid little mind. All the while, I peered in through a dusty window on a world so painfully familiar. And yet, observing from a distance. During the trials I did not watch the news, not once. I also don't pay for cable, so I suppose that helped. My mother and I got off the phone today talking about how strange it is to watch a movie and see the Weinstein Company's name pop up on the title sequence. It is almost as if he has ruined the movie before it even started. I wonder each time…what horrors went into the making of this film? What darkness thrived behind the scenes? What personal hells were being painted over and glamorized for the sake of film?

Please, I pleaded quietly the first night of the trials, staring out at a dark night with buildings glistening on to water through my apartment window, please let this not be Brett Kavanaugh and Brock Turner trials, part three.

So far, Weinstein has been found guilty on lesser charges, but perhaps this is just the beginning. He has been found not guilty for the charges that would have put him away for life, but further allegations face him on the West Coast. Maybe for now this is the only bit of justice us survivors will ever receive from a terribly warped system—it is the partly achieved kind of justice, the grey between guilty and not-guilty that offers little more than closure. It is justice found in a guilty verdict on lesser charges, and an acquittal of the most serious charges. It is a drop of water in a desert, but never the ocean you dreamt about.

Harvey Weinstein, you son of a bitch, deserve to go down, for preying on the hopeful and vulnerable, for taking advantage of talent and warping art into something ugly, for overshadowing the art and influence of movies and performance with your perpetual predatorial behavior and insatiable sexual appetite. The damage that has followed you around for decades is nearly irreparable; however, we are stronger than you, we stand taller, we speak louder.

During the forty-eight hours that I spent in New York in mid-January of 2020, I sort of completely by accident stumbled right on to the front steps of the New York Times. The sun was golden and blinding, the scaffolding metal and glass glistened. I had never come into direct contact with this sacred place before. I think about how we might not be here at all, if it were not for two NYT writers who took years to burst a story through the waters, a story that took minutes to shatter lives so many years before. It was a story long overdue, that not many would have the courage to pursue and yell to the rooftops.

Coming out and into the light can be a powerful thing, a terrifying thing, because the damage can be both concurrently freeing, yet uncanny and inconvenient.

While in New York, I sent early copies of my book to a few friends.

My best friend Bethesda's first words were, "I'm crying, Sophia." As I walked through the Upper East Side, I realized that I thought the scariest first step was the writing part. In reality, writing was much easier than I thought it might be. The most terrifying of all would not be in the writing of this, but in the sharing of it. I told myself, was this not why I wrote in the first place? These words didn't just belong to me. I had intended to spread them long before my fingers even connected to keyboard.

While in New York, I found a different sort of appreciation for myself. New York made me love me more. It forced me to be a single human being in a crowd of thousands and to hold my own and be alone with myself. As I stood looking up at the New York Times revolving doors, I said a silent thank you.

Thank you, Jodi Kantor and Megan Twohey, authors of "She Said," who broke the story to front-page headlines. Before them, thank you Rose McGowan and Ashley Judd and countless other young, beautiful, talented faces who are now the grown faces of survivors. My neighbor downstairs offered me "She Said" and "Catch and Kill" by Ronan Farrow, and I must say, I devoured each page. I was fascinated to watch the detective work unfold.

I pray that in twenty years, sexual violence isn't so prevalent, so silently taboo. I pray for the hearts and souls of the ones that feel so alone, and I offer this book up to them.

Every particular instance when people would ask me ever so casually, "what is your book about?" I would shy away, and say "oh, you can read it when it is published."

Eventually, my answer became a somewhat censored "mostly about me…and other people…and uh, a Kurt Cobain quote."

"Oh, which quote?"

The one about rape…

So, even in writing this book, it took me some time to understand the magnitude of such instances and such words as these. The intimidating, frightening, painful pages of truth packed in between small bits of hope so that it may not all be "so dark."

It took me a while to break through this level of self-consciousness and accept that this book was not meant to be written and left untouched, but instead meant to be read, as all hard-hitting books should be.

The entertainment industry has long held a culture of misogyny, manipulation, quid pro quo harassment, and abuse of power. Take it from someone who received her degree in the arts: it is everywhere. Even when it is under the surface, it is still there. For both men and women, boys and girls, our mentors, trusted advisors, bosses, and directors can at any moment unveil themselves to be a predator. One never knows until they find themselves alone with the person who stood at the front of the room just hours earlier, auditioning them by the hundreds.

How badly do you want the job? You're so talented. Manipulation mingled with insult. You need me. Threats mixed with promise. I can make or break you. Lastly, the words in our industry to end a career: Do you want to be blacklisted? Say no and you'll never work again.

Choreographers, producers, casting directors, network executives. It becomes hard to distinguish the good from the bad guys until it feels too little, too late.

Harvey Weinstein has been found guilty of third degree rape and a count of criminal sexual act in the first degree. He was found not guilty on two counts of predatory sexual assault, so goodbye to any hopes for a life sentence. However, having been remanded, it is likely that Weinstein may very well die behind bars. Staring the sixty-seven year old sex addict in the face is a minimum of five years and a maximum of twenty-nine for crimes committed decades ago. Some crimes can't be charged against him, so not every victim will get their total and complete well-deserved justice. His female attorney defends that many of the "victims" remained Harvey's "friends" …that, as well as her mockery of the Me Too movement, was her argument.

I swallow hard and think about how far we have fallen. Manhattan district attorney Cyrus R. Vance Jr was quoted saying, "this is the new landscape for survivors of sexual assault in America. This is a new day." This gives me hope that maybe despite how far we fell, we are beginning to climb.

Donald Trump was impeached but acquitted by the Senate, and now we wait to see about a re-election. I can't say that the world looks lovely, because it doesn't. And it only takes the click of a few television channels to see this. All I can say is that I am living to see it all, both good and bad, and perhaps to contribute to the change, and that is more than any victim of murder can say for themselves. The murder victims can't speak; I can. I will speak for every voiceless person, both dead and alive.

The "Just World Hypothesis" is a doozy I learned in my "Psychology of Evil" class, during my final few months of college in Pittsburgh. The "just-world-er's" are the ones who live by the saying "everything happens for a reason" until it happens to them. Their ideology is fairly cynical and unsympathetic, and it reminds me of a certain set of brothers I encountered in my teenage years (you will meet them later in the book.) They are the perpetuators of classic victim-blaming, the "well then it must be your fault," "you should not have been walking alone at night," "what were you doing there?" and "maybe you're confused."

That is their mantra until the day their sister gets raped, or their father dies from cancer, or their mother drowns in the ocean. Suddenly they can't process the facts of life and they are left shattered with the fact that their beliefs don't line up with the real world. It rattles them when their mantra is dismantled. I don't think that they heal well.

Harvey Weinstein's female attorney sounded like she exists within a "just world hypothesis." I think she should just be glad that her daughter never met Harvey.

The facts are this: good things don't just happen to good people and bad things don't always fall upon bad people. Life comes for us all. The bad aren't always punished and the good aren't always rewarded. I believe our world is not black and white enough for that. I suppose that the gray area leaves gaps that no one can fill in, so the "just world-ers" decide to do that themselves. I choose instead, to keep going, because I must. And so do you.

If our lives are pre-destined, and fate or God or both are real, then why this? Is it because if nothing were horrible, nothing could ever be wonderful? Is it because God doesn't give us anything that He knows will be too much for us to handle? Is it because good and bad go inseparably hand in hand, and without one we cannot have the other? Is it because I was chosen to tell this story to save another boy or another girl like me? Is it because Eve ate the apple? Is it because human nature is innately bad? Are we born to be good, and then influenced and shaped over time? Are we all without hope?

Harvey Weinstein was held responsible in a court of law for his sins, and I think maybe, just maybe, there is hope. Our legal system still has a long way to go, and so do men and boys and the human academy in general—a real long way.

Weinstein's defense attorney, Donna Rotunno, questioned the Soprano's actress Annabella Sciorra with the following questions:

"Did you call 911?"

"Did you hit him?"

"Try to poke him in the eyes?"

"Did you go to a doctor?"

"Did you ask to see footage of him entering the building?"

"Did you scream?"

"Why didn't you tell your family?"

"Why didn't you tell your friends?"

Every question deserves one universal response: "Why did he rape me?"

Harvey Weinstein is once quoted saying this: "I wanted to do something inspirational for my children."

He has four daughters.

Goodbye. We are shutting you off our television for the last time.

Goodnight, Harvey.

Chapter Three
Before...

It is actually incredibly unfair to chalk one's life up to a chain of events, but for me I can see a time line very clearly.

On a long line, there is to the left side, the "before", the shimmering yet vague prelude. A childhood littered with good and bad, a wholesome family but a lingering teenage depression. Artistic expressions and passions. Lessons learned, voices raised, and many hugs. It was not perfect, but it was something special.

Following the good old before, comes the dot, a big black circle in the center of my time line that so harshly divides two lives in half. It is a stark detailing of a Sophia "then" and a Sophia "now."

Then, there is after.

One event that alters the course of your life and you never asked for it.

Before:

If I could describe the "before" it would be explained in this single journal entry from October 2016:

"I am legal! Before my eighteenth birthday, I did a hell of a lot, mostly adventures shadowed in secret. I was seventeen, underage, still lived at home...we were sneaking into clubs twice every week of the summer until we had befriended the owners. I went to different parties every weekend. We stayed out till four am. Now that I am eighteen, so much has changed. But I do feel like I have grown in a sort. Graduated from baby to adult. I've always grown up fast. I have always been one step ahead, even if it didn't work in my favor.

I have always been a little wild, ever since I was a kiddo, but I feel like now I have changed into everything I ever wanted to be. And I am growing upwards and onwards."

That was three years ago. That was before...

My older sister Lauren, or Lo, is four years ahead of me but as the years advance, the age gap seems to diminish. She is a licensed speech pathologist with a heart that could fill up the ocean, a heart for helping people quite literally find their voice. Lauren has been in love and been burned, but she still loves hard. The world has not managed to win the war on her. She still laughs, still opens up her brimming heart to others, still loves so entirely and wholly that it reminds me of everything good and pure and untainted in the world.

I have a rarity from childhood, a mother and a father who are still married and still the best of friends. I am convinced that if they could spend time with one person for the rest of their lives and no one else, it would be each other.

Mary Kathryn and Michael met at university, the way we all thought we would meet our future spouse. Having familiarized myself with every aspect of their love story growing up, I was convinced that my destiny was to meet my husband at age nineteen in a lecture hall at college and to be married by twenty-one years of age.

Both of my parents came from similarly struggling family backgrounds, which is perhaps one of the many reasons as to why they were a perfect match. They were able to meet each other where the other was at, with all of their brokenness and all of their traumas.

Together, the two have built thirty-plus years of life, love, and healing. To this day when I think about how I still have not met my person-and I am now older than my mom was when she met my dad-I chalk it up to the fact that my parents really needed each other. And together, they made it through years of tribulations that would have made any average individual seek a way out. Marriage is hard.

Marriage is a perfectly imperfect picture of our humanness; it is flawed but beautiful. Any worthwhile relationship is challenging, it is listening when you want to speak, it is apologizing when you want to hold your chin high, and it is loving unconditionally even when the world tells us that love holds limits.

I never needed a partner in the way that they had needed each other. I already had a family, but they would become each other's own.

My mother's father Bob died when she was seventeen. He was an avid alcoholic who left when my mom was just a little girl. Sometimes parents leave and sometimes people are so broken that they never grow up past their own childhood. Like my grandfather, generations of children turn into adults who, unequipped to heal, are tortured their entire lives. This is part of her story, and so many others.

My mother always warned me against drugs and alcohol growing up, as a result of her scarred childhood. She never had any interest in getting drunk or in indulging in all sorts of youthful mischief. Those behaviors had damaged her family, taken her father, and broken her home. She instilled so much fear into me over these things, and rightfully so.

I think that was why I lied to her for so long about all my high school habits. I was terrified that she would magnify the underage drinking as something so much more. I wish I had told her, but it would take time, piece by piece.

My mother bailed her brother out of jail before I came along, and this was just the tip of the iceberg. The intervention they held for him failed, he came close to death and paralysis from a spinal infection due to contaminated heroin needles. My mother was put through hell and back for the older brother who used to lock her in her closet as a little girl. I think that my mom always deserved the best older brother that she never had, she deserved to be daddy's little girl, to be the spoiled baby sister and the princess.Men play an integral part in our lives as females, whether in our relationships with our fathers, brothers, partners, or friends. My mom deserved the right kind of men in her life that never existed, but in the end, she had my dad...and Joe.

And then there was Joe. Joe was imperfect, but he was perfect for my grandma Betty. Joe reminds me that fatherhood, and parenthood, is not defined by DNA. Joe had already raised his kids but went for a second go around the block when he saw my grandmother working at the clothing store that she owned inside of the mall. And once Joe got to know Betty, there was no turning back.

My mother was so young when her father left the family, and barely even in college when her father passed away, that Joe was the man to walk her down the aisle on her wedding day and to hold my baby sister when she was born. Joe was the glue, he was the peacemaker, he was a quiet voice of reason and sense of understanding. He took the spark plugs out of my mother's car when she wanted to meet up with her bad boy D.J. boyfriend at a bar in a snowstorm in the a.m. He would slide her a twenty dollar bill when she begged for a five. He would remind my grandmother to remember the keys to her house and the key to her shop.

"I won't always be here to remind you," he would say.

I never knew him, but I always knew my grandmother to have a set of keys clenched tightly between each ringed finger, the metal clanging against her jewelry, unwilling to set them down. Now I know why. It was Joe, it was always Joe. Perhaps I have known him my entire life without ever once hearing his voice or seeing his face.

Betty and Joe are finally together again after all this time, pain free and dancing together like they used to on a Friday night. And if I could have met my mother's step-father Joe here on this earth, I would tell him thank you. Thank you for being the dad that my mom needed, and thank you for choosing my grandmother, because she deserved to be chosen.

My father was abused by his very own father, an angry Italian who I grew up adoringly calling my Papa. Much was shielded from me as a child, with bits of darkness slipping in through the cracks as I grew older. There was dysfunction, anger, unhealed traumas, and codependency rooted deeply and twisted inside of a generational curse that I was not privy to as a young girl.

In hindsight I can understand that as the first born grandchild, my older sister bore the brunt and was far more exposed to the overall generational toxicity and messiness of our extended family, than I was.

I was always so jealous of Lauren, the eldest and golden grandchild, the perfect picture of maturity and brains. I was jealous of the way our relatives welcomed her into some sort of inner circle that I, as the second born, was not welcomed into.

She spent the most time with them out of the two of us, she held the privilege of sitting at the adults table at thanksgiving, and my grandma would ask her about boys. Meanwhile, little Soph was always tagging along like an afterthought, questioning my invitation with my own extended family.

So much of who we become as adults begins at the integral ages of our early childhood development. Our very core ideas of trust, shame, guilt, autonomy, doubt, belonging, independency and dependency, safety, and control stem from our experiences beginning as early as infants. We learn a sense of either pride or inferiority in our accomplishments in the early school years of our youth. Our sense of identity is questioned in our teenage years. And as we become young adults, ego psychologist Erik Erikson proposes that our sense of intimacy and isolation are defined where we believe that "success leads to strong relationships" and "failure results in loneliness and isolation."

I can suppose that none of these occurrences in my childhood with my extended family played any role in who I have become as a woman today, but I would be strong in my wrong if I offered this false narrative to you.

Sure, I saw my grandpa get angry. What I did not know was his much darker side. My father's father was "always right", never wrong. Always starting fights, always finishing them. My dad grew up with the mentality that being a man meant punching through a wall when drunk. The beatings suffered on my father's behalf still put a chill through my body. My dad has healed and moved on. Sometimes I think it bothers me more than it does him.

His parents wanted to get divorced on their honeymoon, and my grandma ended up accidentally pregnant with my dad instead. I saw her for the first time in six years. And as we sat on her back porch-long thin cigarette dangling from her lips-she explained to me that she missed her chance in life. She had not been ready to become a mother let alone a wife, had wanted to travel and have a career instead. She felt cheated by life. But why did it have to be too late for her? Why couldn't she fall in love again or chase after that career that she wanted as a twenty-something?

I wanted to never think that it was too late. I did not want to be seventy-eight and wishing I "had not done" or "had done". I did not want to be defined by my "what if's" and guilts. I suppose her regrets in life had led her to becoming a mother, and given me my father, so I must say thank you for how fate worked out for us.

And yet I admit that my grandmother and I shared one prominent sentiment at the time: fuck men.

Somehow two broken homes came together and made a completely whole one, so full of overwhelming love. I do not know how my parents did it, but here we are. In this family, we accept without option, we love recklessly, we laugh wildly, we talk about our feelings, we believe in mental health.

My parents did the best possible job that they could, to build a home with no roadmap or manual on how to make it to where they have arrived.

And indeed, the most at home I will ever feel is in my mother's and father's house.

It is a house brimming with life, barking dogs, flickering candles, saturated artwork on the walls, photographs in the hallways, homemade pasta sauce.

I would say my parent's love story could have a movie made from it.

When my mom laid her eyes on my dad, she ran back to the dorms and told her roommates with such conviction that she saw the guy she was going to marry in art history class. She did not even know his name.

From the first time Kathy laid eyes on the back of Mike's head in a lecture hall auditorium full of hundreds, she knew he was the one. That shit blows my mind.

Later she said she caught a glimpse of his name when he dropped his folder under his seat (of course my dad had neatly printed first and last name on the top corner of his folder…God love the man). Now, she had a name to go off, and that would begin the journey of my mother finding her soulmate. She would do plenty of research to figure out they had friends of friends, which sounds like something I might do nowadays, except she had no technological benefits.

Six months after Kathy saw her future wrapped up in one single stranger, she met him.

My parents were officially introduced on my dad's 21st birthday.

My mom was nineteen, almost twenty.

I was eighteen almost nineteen when it happened to me.

That was three years ago.

My family had seven dogs at the time and now we have 5. I lived with my parents and went to community college, now I live in the city four hours east.

I have been a twirling little twinkle toes since my mother first put me in tap at the age of 3. Dance was my sanctified safe-haven and sanity. It was my refuge and recluse, both my expression and my escape.

It then became my major in college, where I was immersed in a conservatory of performing arts.

I was born in Orlando. We moved around a lot. I would consider my childhood to be very wholesome, but I was always the new girl at school, so I didn't have many friends. All that changed in the sixth grade when I met my lifelong best friend Bethesda (insert fireworks here). A decade long friendship incomparable to anyone I've ever known. My rock in the worst of places, she kept me steady. This is what a best friend does for another.

When her father passed away from cancer in 2015, I thought life couldn't get much worse. It seemed we could never quite catch a break. Now my best friend would have to live without her best friend. Death shifted our world entirely. We were velcroid at the hip, the inseparable pair who leaned on each other for sanity. I think in those days, I needed her just as much as she needed me. It was hard for her to be alone in the house, crying at night, grieving. Two years later, and she would be the one wrapping me up while I cried.

We often tell each other we do not know where we would be without one another. When the whole world seemed to fall away right from under us, we were the balance the other was so desperately seeking. We recognize each other to be incredibly strong and we know both of us could have done it all alone without any help, because we are just that independently stubborn. But we did not have to

There was never any need for that, for being alone...what was the point when we had each other?

Besides, the worst possible state to be in is alone in your pain.

I love my parents. I love my parents. I love my parents.

That is pretty much it.

They have shown me the proper definition of grace. They have taught me I am never alone in my suffering. They are a perfect portrait of redemption, second chances.

They have my heart. They have shown me theirs.

I am grateful, ever and overwhelmingly grateful, for the light they have bestowed upon me. Our family is one woven from strength, scarred from battle but molded beautifully. We are a force of four, and when one falls, we all do.

We are in and out, up and down, inside of and around, together, through it all.

I would say perhaps that alone surpasses any timeline of before and after's that I could produce for my life

So…onward…or perhaps backwards.

Back in time, back to that night, back to that place which I never wish to see or feel again. Because in order to grow and to thrive, in order to plunge onwards and into the bright light, we must continue to trace our steps back to that shadowed "before."

You will never understand me unless you understand this.

Chapter Four

April Fools

*Trigger Warning: Rape/SA

My entire world was thrown upside down on April Fools.

I walked into March 31st as one girl, and the next morning woke up as somebody else. I didn't know who she was, but I knew that I would be stuck with her for a very long time.

I never went to the hospital the next morning. It was April Fool's Day and I was panicked. I kept telling myself it was just a sick, cruel joke that the universe had played on me. It must not have been the actual, real thing, because I got away, so I'm fine...right? April Fools.

We were on the University of Dayton's campus bouncing around from frat party to a bar named Flannagan's. It was a squat hole in the wall pub near the Speedway on the intersection. The sidewalks are etched into my mind, the paths we took from house to house to bar to eventually that condemned little white house on the corner where it happened to me.

I met a red-headed boy, and his degenerate friend was the bartender at the Irish Pub, so he poured us drinks all night. I question whether I was drugged, why I had never felt that sort of "drunk" before, and if it was because I was not drunk at all, but rather had been poured some other unknown substance. I question a million things; unanswerable open-ended remarks have become my reality.

I was eighteen, spending another Friday night with my friend, Olivia, who is no longer my friend, and two other girls: Roommates Marie and Allison, who were never friends.

They were friends with my rapist, two females who sided with a predator and shamed me into saying I wanted it and that I was "all over him all night."

I had met him once before in passing, weeks earlier, the day I had gotten my nose pierced. I took Marie over to that dingy home since it was just a block away from her own rented house, and I stood in the corner while her coke dealer separated bits of white dust with a credit card on his desktop. We were in the attic bedroom of the house; the string lights had a blueish hue and he had a poster of Kanye West above his bed. I told them I was going home; it wasn't my scene.

I was in his room. It had been him and I had never known.

Run, run fast.

It was a black and white checker-tiled bathroom, situated right off the kitchen of the same, small house off campus.

Perhaps these details will be too much for you, but they were also too much for me. If you need to step away from the heaviness of these words, return in the morning. I am okay with that. Are you?

Before the naysayers ask, "what if it was consensual?" and "what if he didn't know what he was doing?" consider this: Would you want your first time to be experienced in a dirty bathroom at 2 a.m. with a person you aren't even attracted to?

He was in that cramped, damned bathroom off the kitchen, washing his hands in the sink and I walked in because I had to pee.

So many nights I have spent with my own thoughts, agonizing over why I had to go into that bathroom in the first place. Why in the hell did I walk into hell? Did I do this to myself? Was it my fault? Had I given him reason to think I wanted it? Why did I flirt at the bar? Why did I let his friend pour me all that fireball? Had I wrongfully entertained and misled him?

Except I never gave permission. More than that, I yanked away.

I remember the room was moving into slow motion, and he closed the door behind me and grabbed me and started kissing me hard. He was biting me—hardly kissing—ravaging rather, and I yanked away. We had kissed at the bar, but not like this.

I watched as if I was out of my body, looking down below on two people in a cramped tile bathroom. I saw everything; therefore, I remember everything, too.

I looked down. He had ripped my pants down around my knees.

No, no, no! My mind was racing. I pushed him away but it felt like moving a one thousand-pound weight. I had never felt this way before and I had been drinking since I was fifteen. There was something so, so wrong happening here.

I got pushed up against the wall. He was standing behind me.

"Just take it," my mind said. "It will soon be over. I guess this is just how it is going to go down."

Word for word, that was exactly what was racing through my mind amid the pain.

As if a train were coming to a screeching stop, about five seconds later, I realized this was not how it was going to go down.

"Snap out of it!" my brain yelled, coming to its senses. I was inwardly screaming at myself to wake my body up and revolt.

And with that, I drew back an elbow, and I gutted him in the stomach. He fell backwards and we both toppled onto each other, hitting the tile floor hard.

I scrambled over and sat down on the toilet to check and see blood.

He shoved himself into my mouth as I sat on the toilet, and I threw up. I puked all over his member and all over my blouse sleeve.

I yanked my pants up and pushed him back from me.

"Move."

But he was not listening.

He grabbed me and pushed me over to the sink, trying again.

"Just kiss me, keep kissing me," I begged, trying to think of a plan as my mind wavered. He could not go inside of me ever again.

I felt foggy, so foggy, so clouded.

"Go get a condom," I said suddenly.

And that was my way out.

That was it, my escape.

He lived in an attic bedroom upstairs, this gave me enough time to get out the back door off the kitchen.

"OK," he stammered, confused, as I pushed him away with all the strength my loose limbs got muster and unlatched the door and ran.

I ran and never looked back.

I passed through the kitchen, where the three girls stood. They stood there, just feet away from where it had happened to me, and they had done nothing, not checked on me, nothing. I never realized how much they had betrayed me in that moment, never once making sure I was okay that night, or any night after.

As I buttoned my pants in the kitchen, I panicked. I felt the room closing in.

Marie mumbled, "get out of here, you're an embarrassment." She was probably thinking that I was the whore who just had sex with her coke dealer in a dingy bathroom just feet away from where she was sipping her Coors Lite.

She told her friend Alison to take me back to the house, but I was already running, running out the back porch and through the backyard, down the sidewalk, where I felt my stomach lurch and cave in on me. I hit my knees in the grass, and wretched into the dirt.

You were surrounded by some of the worst humans that night, I tell myself today.

I went back to Marie and Allison's shared house down the block, where I ran into the upstairs bathroom and hurled my guts out.

I was crying, on my knees, as Olivia helped wipe off my makeup with toilettes.

"I didn't want that. I didn't want that," I said, and would continue to repeat the next morning, and every day after.

The last thing I remember was sitting cross legged on a beach towel on the bathroom floor, as Olivia patiently tried to feed me tortilla chips, warning that I needed to eat something for my empty stomach.

She got me into bed that night, but I have no memory of it. I knew something was terribly wrong, since I always remembered everything. I woke up with blood stained underwear, telling her we needed to get out of the house.

Over the past three years, I have learned that next morning of denial is perfectly normal. Who the hell wouldn't want to chuckle and say, "oh yeah, last night was one for the books!" instead of saying what. really. happened. Women have enough to deal with. We don't want to be victimized, ashamed, slut-shamed, made dirty. Somehow all those grimy garbage bags chock-full of pain end up on our shoulders, not theirs. It is their fault. Not ours. So why are we the one's that feel like we did something wrong?

I ask myself, why didn't you speak up sooner? Then I remind myself of the opposition I was faced with just the next morning, and by fellow females at that.

I sit here, swallowing hard at this memory, wondering if it might be too much for people to read, wondering about the look on my parent's faces.

I woke up the next morning beside my friend, Olivia, in Marie's tiffany blue bedroom, but Marie was nowhere to be found. She pulled an all-nighter at the boy's house, having a dandy good old time in the company of my rapist and friends, as if nothing bad had ever happened to me in that house.

Who took off my makeup? I wondered to myself, seeing a pair of false eyelashes sitting neatly beside me on the bedside table.

I shuffled to the bathroom, pulled down my underwear, and there I saw it.

The dried blood that I stared at so woozily has forever imprinted itself into my memory. That image has burned itself into me, it is now my scar.

The rush of memories came back in a panic, and the room began to close in on me yet again, like it had the night before.

I woke up to two texts from the person who had not just taken advantage of me, but had taken from me, stolen from me, disregarded me as a human being, even.

He had put my number in his phone earlier in the night and texted himself off it.

"Where are you?" 3 a.m.

"Come back."

Reading over the messages from the night before made my stomach lurch. Did he not see? None of it made sense.

Knowing nowhere else to go, I dialed up my best friend Bethesda who was away at Ohio State. The conversation was a blur, as I was still in shock, but I remember her saying "you know what that's called, right?"

Certainly, could not happen to me, I told myself, no way. I remember I was so traumatized that I could not even call it the one word that it was.

The next morning Olivia and I drove to her bridesmaid's dress fitting for her sister's wedding. I was utterly numbed, told her to go ahead without me while I waited outside the woman's alterations shop.

I recall sitting on a bench outside in the early spring air, the cold swiping at my cheeks as I dialed up my best friend.

"B…" I stammered, "something's happened."

I remember at that moment I began to cry hysterically, desperately. I was spluttering out the words "but, but…are you sure?"

"Yes, Sophia, I am sure."

Her words were steady and even. Her tone of voice was grave, yet centered. She wanted to know who and when and where. What was his name? She was almost too calm. She might kill someone.

I needed her with me. There was only so much to be said over the phone. My heart ached; my body was dull.

She was right.

How had she done that…brought me back to reality when no one else could? Of the entire conversation, I still remember those words, "you know what that is called right?"

I just knew I had to see her.

I had barely any money in my gas tank or my bank account, but unflinchingly I made the drive to Ohio State University to see my best friend, to feel her arms around me, to have her voice in my ear saying "it'll be okay Soph, I got you."

Sometimes that is all any of us need, what we truly crave, the people that say, "I got you" and mean it. If it were not for her steady voice, I don't know where I would be.

I was battling so many other voices at the same time, and not just the ones that were in my own head. Here are actual words I was told right around the time I was still reeling from what had just happened:

"you were all over him all night."

"you're so embarrassing."

"if you're here to cry rape, I don't want to hear it."

"what happened is between you and him. I don't really care."

"you know how flirty you can be."

This was one side. The hateful, ignorant voices of the ones who I thought I could trust but took my attacker's side instead.

The second side was one of many questions.

"should you go to the police?" I don't know.

"should you tell your parents?" Not right now. (I wish I had but I can't change that)

"how much do you remember?" All of it.

"are you sure?" Sure as the sky is blue.

"did you feel drugged?" Never felt that way in my entire life; maybe I was.

Then there were the voices in my head, reliving, reeling, the subtle victim blaming mingled with pure shock and confusion:

"how did you get here?"

"what is going on?"

"I hate him."

"how could this happen?"

"my mom and dad…"

"no one believes me."

"I wish I never went out that night."

"I want to wake up to a morning where this never happened."

"I am another statistic."

"I am the girls I've watched on Law and Order."

"I wish I had never started drinking."

"You always promised your parents that you would be careful, and you let them down."

And then there was the voice of my best friend. It sounded something like this.

The first step: "Tell me everything."

The reassurances: "You're so brave."

The loyalty. The one who would go to bat for me: "I will kill him for you."

Arms engulfing me in warmth and safety.

"It's okay, Sophia."

Tears cried for me and with me.

"We'll get through it together."

A promise that tomorrow would still come.

We sat inside of an empty study room on the same floor as her freshman dorm, and she made me walk through every painstaking detail, how it happened, when and where and who, and what we needed to do from this point forward. I think of her as my hotline, my guidance counselor, my survivor's advocate. Without her, I probably would not have processed in the way that I did, or I would have spent a decade in denial and then the following decade in a depression when the reality hit. I will never forget the beige of that room, the empty chairs and sofas, the late-night hour where it was just her and I together in the quiet, my heart spilling out on the brown carpet floor like blood.

While the world slept, I was game planning on how to survive. But I could not have done it alone. Every survivor needs that one someone who picked them up piece by piece and held on every step of the way forward, reminding them that they are brave, that they have always been brave, perhaps even from the day they were born

Chapter Five

The Little Girl with the Big Eyes

My inner child is broken. Let that sink in-say it again. Say it with me.

"My Inner Child is Broken."

I am afraid that I do not know her anymore, not even a semblance of what she once was. In searching and in unpacking that which has been stuffed into a dusty attic, I wish to find her again, and to know her, in the hopes that she will meet me where I am at.

I had a happy childhood. My life was always accelerated. I was a "gifted" child. I excelled in literature, I received the highest testing scores and the best graded paper for any fourth grader. I started preschool early and ended high school the same way at the age of sixteen. I stood at the front and center of any dance studio, unfaze by the floor-to-ceiling mirrors glaring so unkindly back at me. Dark audiences, shadowed faces, and filled auditoriums I faced with an eagerness. I was bursting with energy, passion, and curiosity. A lot of the rest I forget.

My therapist has since encouraged me that there is no sense in attempting to remember that which the body has blocked out for protective purposes.

While sometimes I find a sense of calm and closure in digging through the "Archives of Sophia", I also realize that in most cases there is nothing left for me back there. No point in rehashing what has been long buried and buried for a very valid reason at that. I have done the best to protect myself my entire life, and I vow to continue to do so. It has gotten me here thus far.

I realize now that I have not quite figured out how to mother my old self, how to encourage her, how to show her grace and forgiveness. My parental protective instincts never want to see that little girl get hurt, knowing full well that she does. And my survival mechanisms wipe it clean to protect her from ever having to see it again.

I wrote once that I hoped my child would never cry in silence in the shower the way I used to when I was a teenager, holding it all in and away from the ones who loved me. I realize now that I battled depression long before I was assaulted, but I did not quite understand that level of verbiage until my late teenage years.

I had a textbook "good" life. Often times I was guilty that I was ever unhappy, because after all what reason did I possibly have to be unhappy? My mother and father were married, I had a roof over my head, and my parents sacrificed so much to pay for my dance lessons.

Toxic positivity tells us that no matter how difficult the circumstances, we must trudge through with a smile because it could always be worse, couldn't it? The emotional invalidation that this brings about causes feelings of denial. Suddenly we feel bad for being unhappy or for struggling.

"We don't mean to complain," we apologize, suddenly feeling stupid.

The excess of positivity minimizes the natural ups and downs that come hand in hand with the human experience. Sometimes, we cannot simply just "get on with it" or remind ourselves that "other people are suffering more."

I now understand that I have had depression and panic/anxiety disorder for quite some time. Perhaps it was the toxic positivity that is so ingrained into our culture that caused a chain reaction of long held denial in my adolescence.

I realize now that an emotionally unregulated child becomes an emotionally unregulated and imbalanced adult. And I was a very angry child. I held it all in, even when my thoughts were traveling at the speed of light. I was unequipped to communicate for fear that people would see me differently. As an adult, I have attempted but failed at healthy romantic relationships where I soon realize that either a) I am trying to make it work with the wrong person or b) I am terrified of exposing myself to hurt, so when the chance comes to say how I really feel, I say nothing. In turn, said person has been chased off by my unhealthy habits.

One of my most important questions right now is why a certain idealism has rooted itself into my consciousness in terms of love, relationships, men, and loss. The sentiment is this: "love me, don't leave me." I am confused as to when-and why-this started, and when it will end. My therapist tells me that she is not so sure she has an answer to this question for me just yet, or where this deeply rooted fear of abandonment even stems from. If my parent's never left as a child, why am I always so terrified of people leaving me?

Perhaps it is time to acknowledge that more repressed traumas exist within these walls than just a singular moment of sexual violence.

Always the new girl, always the one trying to make up for lost time.

Nothing about my growing up or attending school was ever linear. We lived in apartments deep in the Midwest, houses in the country, and condos by the beach. We bounced back and forth between Florida and Ohio undecidedly.

I finished high school at sixteen, but I didn't start college until eighteen.

My one constant, though, was dance. I always managed to find her no matter where we moved, and I believe that it was because we moved so much that I latched on to my art so heavily, and thankfully so (everything happens for a reason, am I right?).

Even so, I transferred to the conservatory of my dreams at the age of nineteen, a year late into the program, and yet again scrambled to find my place. I attempted to scurry my way in to where cliques and groups had already been formed, where professor-student relationships in the dance department had already been sealed.

As I grew older, I became the girl who was dependent on the safety of running away, the now woman who burned bridges in cities that she convinced herself she would not have to stay in. Hence why I used the prior term "escape plan." In the back of my mind often lurked the thought that I could leave remnants of damage wherever I went, because I would in the end, yes you guessed it…leave.

What once began as the "pick me" need to fit in, warped and manifested itself into the need to be loved as an adult. And not so much a need, but a sickness. It was my crippling insecurity to be chosen, needed, and loved, that left me choosing the wrong people, places, and things.

I would not be the woman that you left, cheated on, passed over, or shut out. And yet time and time again, I found myself slapped in the face with these cruelties.

I realize now, looking back on that little girl with the glimmering chocolate brown eyes, that so many of these deep rooted complexes and identity crises', planted themselves securely within me by the time I was only ten years old.

As we fast forward through the years, it should be no surprise that as I grew older, I became more obsessed with being chosen, and with the concept of staying.

Being the new girl more times than I can count has built me, truly. But being the one that leaves has also developed an unwanted pattern in my relationships that there must be an escape plan at all times.

Truthfully, this chapter is hard for me. I struggle because my childhood was not "bad" to an outsider's perspective. It was "normal." But what is normal? Is there even a standard for normal anyhow?

In dialectical behavioral therapy, we learn that two opposites can still be true: I had a good childhood and a good family, but I also had an imperfect childhood and an imperfect family, just like every other human on the planet.

As kids, we mirror the behaviors that were displayed for us. We do what we know, and we act out what we see acted out before us.

Healing your inner child does not mean you were parented poorly. Although sometimes true, this is not always the case.

Yes, our parents are not perfect. But truthfully, life establishes patterns, biases, and harmfulness in us as children whether or not by our parents or by the world. It is inevitable that life will mold us, as we cannot stay sheltered from its affects forever.

Often, we linger on our parent's core beliefs as we grow older. Each teachable moment of our youth becomes a clearly defined characteristic in our adulthood.

I was always so hard on myself, so unforgiving.

I masked my insecurities well, but that did not make them any less real. I held the ability to pick myself apart into pieces so small that they could float away. My inner battle of self-acceptance has been a life-long journey, one that does not discriminate with age or time. I was just a kid then.

Now, some of that little girl still remains. That spunkiness, that sassiness, that strong-willed stubbornness, the need to do it all myself, and that innate understanding and knowing of who I was so early on.

But the pressure of being gifted-of being great-built my expectations mountain high so that I began to expect nothing less than the best. Straight A report cards meant that I had to make my parents happy at all times and then maintain that happiness. Being talkative and bubbly in grade school was my best attempt at getting everyone to like me. They had to like me.

And why won't these kids play with me at recess and why doesn't six year old Collin with the ear piercings and spiky hair like me?

Am I not pretty enough, am I not good enough?

What is your earliest recollection of thinking or feeling that? How old were you? Four, ten, thirteen? Does it simply span your entire life with no distinct beginning or end?

For me, it was the first time that I can remember moving with my family. First grade.

How I dreaded those sit down talks at the kitchen table that came every few years. It was the big announcement: "girls, we're moving." I came to expect it, but I did not know how to label it at the time. At the time, I would shrug and accept that "this is just how it is" (but always with a pouty lip and maybe some tears). Now, I would label our family's constant need to uproot and move around as a direct result of my dad's overly ambitious and zealous search for the next best thing in his career. He would say that, too.

As a little girl, I was always the new girl. I was always the one who was trying so hard to show why I was a good friend to have around, to prove why I belonged.

And every time we moved away, I would get out a gel pen and my little address book with the tabs, and I would jot down my friend's house phone number, their mom's email address, and their address.

Will they ever want to talk to me again or am I burden since I am going away? Am I irrelevant because I'm leaving, will they even make the effort to talk to me if we are not going to school with each other every day?

Will I ever see them again? Did they ever even like me to begin with?

We all know these two phrases well:

"You must be doing something wrong."

"It is your fault."

These untruths go hand in hand with our unwillingness to accept ourselves. We are so often fearful that others will be the ones who will not accept us.

The worst victim blaming any victim can experience is commonly the blame of one's own self. We are our harshest and cruelest critics, and we offer ourselves very little leeway.

The fact is, I have been blaming myself since even before I was raped.

I look down at the black and white photograph of me smiling on the beach. Cross-legged in the sand, crooked smile, long windblown hair, bangs dangling into my face, and an undeniable light permeating through my eyes and into the camera lens. I was only five years old. My therapist has asked me to bring in any childhood photo that I can find for our next session. She tells me to "sit with this girl" and take some quiet time to acknowledge her, to remember. Who is she? Who is Sophia? And what parts have gone away and what parts have innately stayed ingrained within my DNA? What do I have to tell her? What do I forget, what can I unearth?

Digging back through the past is tricky. It is sometimes painful and other times uneasy, it is both enlightening and terrifying. So many memories look lovely on the outside. But all it takes is to remember, to really remember the way it was and not just the way we have held it in our brains as being. To look back at the images from those days, to dig back into the home videos and the photographs and the journal entries, is to dredge up the actual feelings that we sometimes glaze over as the years do us in.

I remember how angry I was as that little girl; how angry I still am. Maybe I've always been angry, and all it took was one night to be robbed of something, to bring that anger out in me that had been laying dormant. Perhaps I was already susceptible to the anger that he had pulled from me, and maybe I was always going to be that fiercely independent and often argumentative and incorrigible little girl.

Maybe there are parts of me that will never change. After all, so many of my qualities have been with me since my youth, as if they were built into me from my very beginnings. From the second I came into the world as a screaming baby with the lungs of life, I have had a certain "Sophia blueprint" that I cannot erase. But whether my anger is inherited from my father, whether it is situational, environmental, or trauma-induced, I cannot call her my friend forever. She has run her course through me.

Being angry is so tiring. There are so many people, places, spaces, and things to be angry at.

I set the photograph down on the carpet in front of me and lean back against my dresser, blowing out a sigh. Being alone with this little girl is harder than I assumed. I gather up the photo albums and shoe boxes that I dragged out from the back shelf of my closet, and begin to stack them back up one by one. To sift back through all of these in one day might take more time than I have for now. When I'm ready, I'll return.

If I close my eyes, I can see her face, I can talk to her because I know her better than anyone. I was once that little girl with the big eyes. I had a short, neat little bob with bangs cut straight across my forehead, Brooke Shields eyebrows, and a scrunched up potato nose when anything displeased me.

I was fiery, stubborn, introspective, and thoughtful. I have always possessed an innate knowing of how to think and care deeply. I study what others overlook; I jot it all down. I watch. Pick up on other's energy. I over think, I worry too much. I hide in my own head. So did this little girl.

I believe my inner child to be incredibly gifted, but incredibly misunderstood.

Unknowingly, I have been so hard on my inner child my entire life, and she remains with me to this day, so it is about time I accept her.

I set the photograph on my bedside table, the black and white one from the beach. It is time that I extend to her the permission to forgive herself. And instead of feeling a guilt that I have let her down, instead of shaming myself with the responsibility of offering her love and forgiveness, perhaps she has something for me.

Maybe I learn to lay my anger down and to see the world through the eyes of a child.

To not be afraid of where that little girl has been or what she grew up to be, but rather to be proud that she is here.

It is time that I learn to love her again. To stop saying sorry. And in turn, maybe I will know what it is to love myself more.

"And if I could say anything to that little girl with the big eyes, it would be this: your feelings are valid, you are worthy of taking up space, you are loved beyond words, you will have no problem finding your place in this world. Your anger is not unfounded, your need for greatness is not unrealistic. But life gets easier. Remember, you are Sophia. And most importantly: good job, kid."

Chapter Six

I Call This My Denying Phase:

Carrying on is hard to do when most of your world doesn't even know your story. I call this the denying phase.

How are you supposed to go on living a fabulous life if you have been whittled down to "victim status"? I was unaware that I was a survivor, completely unaware of the word itself. Instead, I longed so desperately to just pretend it never even happened. The thing about these "things" is that, since they did happen, they will all come back to us eventually.

You can manage to try and hide your truths from the world, but the world will never let you forget.

Soon enough and nearing around the bend, it would all resurface on my behalf, and I would have to do the one thing I was currently refusing: to face it all. I was terrified to turn away from my denial and start dealing. The fact is that there is no right or wrong way to go about one's own process of healing because it is different for all of us.

But I can say with certainty that I was wandering aimlessly through the dark. Instead of looking at my struggles as a symbol of heroism, a sign of impossible strength and willpower, I was shamed into painting over the bad. I didn't paint over it with good, I just painted over it all, as much as I could. I combated my pain with drinking, going out, faking confidence, never talking about my assault as I should have been. I was the girl kneeling near the toilet of the bathroom inside the club and puking on the sidewalk. I skated a fine line. I was nervous that something might happen to me again, so I stayed suspicious and clung to my friends. At the same time, I wanted to forget so desperately, that I drank until there was no more to be had.

Just a few years have passed since, so the healing process I assume will continue until I die, probably. But I think one day I will be able to wake up, and I won't think about it, not once. I will get up out of bed, shower off the night, wake into the sun, and I won't think about him. I think that day is coming; soon, in fact. I called these phases that I went through, my "after-the-fact phases."

At first, nothing changed. I wore whatever I wanted and went to the clubs a lot. It was a big "fuck you". I was hot and no one could have me. I thought I could still have fun, so I was certainly in denial, because nothing about that time in my life screams even a sliver of "fun". I relied greatly on the company of my girlfriends, to the point where they became my crutch. And since my parents knew nothing of what was really going on, my home life suffered greatly.

Just prior to the attack, I had finally gone on medication for my anxiety and depression, and thankfully so, or else my story would look much different. So many days I just wanted to stay in bed forever, maybe crawl into my mom's bed and lay there with her into eternity. And some days the words were on the tip of my tongue, and I wanted so badly to say it, but I never did. Where even to begin? And how? "Hey mom, I need to tell you something…" I wish I had.

I wish I had told you. I wish I had run away from that bathroom sooner. I wish I could punch him in the face more than just that one time in the club.

I wish I could float away like a balloon. I wish I could paint the sky in all of the colors of the rainbow just to make myself happy again.

I wish you could see me for who I am, not what I have seen. I wish that you would understand without hearing a single word fall from my lips. I wish I wouldn't cry. I wish the tears which cascade like waterfalls would freeze mid-droplet, like a river in winter. I wish that she never whispered in my ear, "me too". I wish that he never left me. I wish I never met you. I wish that my life were like a garden growing in full bloom, brimming with growth and color and newness. I wish that my life were as bright as the piercing yellow moon in mid-October that I watch from my car. I wish that I did not feel so heavy, so burdened by a thousand pound chains. I wish that I could fling myself out to sea, and that the water would catch me and hold me up, not let me drown. I wish that gravity worked in my favor. I wish that I could run and not grow tired.

I wish that I could forget the way it all smelled in my mind-the smell of him in that bathroom from hell, the smell of you and that little red car, my jeans, the grass after it rained the night before, the smoke, the salty lake, the summer air.

It is a lot to wish for what never comes, praying for a relief that never reaches for my hand. Why?

Questions that always go without answers and explanations that we never ingest.

It would take me an entire year post-attack to form the sentences. The words were there, but they wouldn't come. If you stuff it all deep down, you think to yourself, "maybe if I'm lucky, the words will never come."

When I think back to my eighteen year old self, I often ask rhetorically: "what were you looking for?" If I could ask her anything, it would be that. I think although the answer is fairly clear, it wasn't so plain at the time. I believe myself to have been too lost to even be able to identify why I did what I did, or for what purpose.

It is apparent to me now, as certain as a stoplight changing from red to green. It is this: to be loved.

But why? That damn three letter word greets me again. I am still working on unpacking that one. Who knew one word could be so heavy? Why did I want so desperately to be loved? I was already loved by so many, what gap was I possibly trying to etch in? Perhaps it is innately built within us to want to be loved so desperately, even if we were raised lovingly growing up, even if we saw what an undamaged version of love looked like. We could be loved, but still feel as if we did not have it. Sometimes I just felt so unlovable that it was easier to pretend. To deny, to cover up, to patch up, to trace around, to escape, to lie my way out of…to forget without ever actually gaining the luxury of true forgetfulness.

If I can pretend that nothing ever happened to me, then so can you. That was easy enough, right?

This mythical thinking was reinforced with the standard of men that I was introduced to throughout my college years: they loved denial! They were all in denial! We could be in denial together, how perfect. Unable to commit, crippled with toxic habits, bound to past mistakes, chained up by failed relationships. We were drinking too much, too scared to grow up and too scared to be alone. Together we were terrified of our very selves, frightened by the quiet. I was unwilling to face a picture of stillness and contentment, of what it meant to settle and to slow down for a second, to stop the madness.

Denial was fun, denial was easy. And we did it well. We were good at living like this, friends with the nighttime of nothingness called denial. It was life laced with the absence of acknowledgement and a plethora of lies.

So, in my maddened state of insanity (repeating those same patterns and thinking this time would be different) I had sunk deep down into the comfort of denial with anyone willing enough to stay down in that falsified reality with me.

I went out every weekend and thrived on the routine "forgetableness" of the same music, the same club, the same alcohol, and strange faces. Everything became the same after a while, even the people. We were no strangers to one another and no stranger to the night.

I would do my makeup religiously at 10 pm, fake lashes and all. Always eyeshadow and lipstick and contour, hair curled or straightened. I spent so much time skipping around as if nothing was the matter, perhaps because I thought that was what people expected of me. All dolled up always with somewhere to go. Never the one who couldn't make it out of bed in the morning or leave the house at night. I refused to let my trauma lead to a narrative of seclusion and separation. What I realize now is that I was always secluded and separated during that time, and not from others but from my own self.

I didn't want the people which I encountered to catch on to the sadness in my eyes, especially if they didn't know why it was there in the first place. There was nothing about the situation which I enjoyed explaining.

I had to smile and fake it, so that they would still see me as "me."

If I was not thinking about the elephant in the room, my life would not become a circus.

Today I might swipe on some mascara and be lucky if I even manage to brush my hair. I realize that underneath the surface, when we take away the temporary façade of vanity, when we tug away at the disguises, the right people will always see us.

The right man will always see me. I wish I had known that then, but I know that now.

The nighttime now feels different to me than it once did. I enjoy the company of after hours, I always will. I still love the moon; I still love going out and grabbing drinks. I will always be a human craving connection: I will always love the feeling of catching up with old friends and welcome the chance to make new ones. I still love the dark, as opposed to fearing it.

Turning twenty-one years old for me was more of a segue into adulting than a segue into drinking. The doorway had long been open for me into that world, especially since a pretty face often gets you what you want but not what you need. Sometimes I felt as if I had nearly seen it all and done it all by the time that I hit seventeen. Much has changed.

My rational and reasoning was one of any eighteen/nineteen-year-old, and I can't help but think that I was doing the absolute best I could have done, the best anyone in that unwanted situation could have done. I did my best, but wow it was still all so screwed up, so messed up, so messy and dirty and heavy.

I was running, always running, and never looking back because I thought maybe I could get away with it. But what happens when you stop to catch your breath? In that moment when you are hunched over, paused and out of air, you look back to see how you got there. Glancing back at that distant yet near place which you have seemed to come so far away from begins to sting. You often feel not empowered by the journey, but rather discouraged at the exhaustion of the distance.

When I looked behind my shoulder, I didn't like what was waiting for me.

You mean, I must carry this? I kept thinking to myself. I didn't ask for this. I didn't want this. This is too heavy.

And then, a silent voice in my head, a steady whisper: Give it to me.

But in my stubborn nature, I was convinced that I could do it all alone. I can take this on, I can bear it. Let me do it alone, I've got this.

Now I don't care if you believe in Jesus Christ or the power of the stars, but my faith is what carried me through the most impossible of times, and I would be remiss if I didn't mention that in this book. My saving grace was in a force greater than I. As you can probably tell from prior chapters, I relied heavily on the hope-and promise-of tomorrow to survive today. It was all I had.

Now, I am still the same resilient girl which I have always been, but that girl has since grown up and still has so much more growing to do.

I can look at myself in the mirror and I can smile. Before, it was hard to even look. I still carry the painful feeling that I am being watched, always. That men are looking at me for every wrong reason. I make eye contact with them as their eyes fall to search my body. I want to spit in their face. Sometimes it seems that there is absolutely nothing I can do. I feel hopeless and full of range. I deny it so it doesn't hurt, I act unfazed and unbothered so that you still think I'm lighthearted and vivacious.

But I admit, I am not angry in the way that I used to be. I was quick to throw a drink in any man's face, punch someone for bumping into me, or smack them for spilling a bit of beer on my shoes. I was not just gutsy, I was angry. I was boiling over. It came out in physical swings and punches. I was angered and my anger was justifiable. I was broken and rightfully so. I had a reason to despise men, so I did. All men.

The club was not the place for me to deal with my anger or hatred towards scummy men, yet Saturday after Saturday I ended up back there, standing on the dance floor with no place to go.

It was as if in some ironic and bizarre self-fulfilling prophecy, night after night, week after week, I continued to surround myself with that which I abhorred the most.

10:59 p.m., April 12, 2017, just a few weeks after the night of my nightmares, I scribbled this out in my journal:

"There are simply no instructions, not one. People deal with these incidents in all sorts of ways. And sometimes they self-destruct. And other times they desperately try to find the light.

But it is so hard to find, and darkness is so easy to fall into, because it is comforting and dangerous all at once.

And to live in that kind of darkness is to feel nothing and face nothing.

But you cannot run forever.

I wrote once, to let light be what I seek. But how do you find that when you are lost? How do you lift up your head without shame, or love without bitterness, or smile and truly feel that happiness for more than just a fleeting moment?"

Reading that makes me proud. It had only been seventeen days and I was still reeling. But I was also writing and reflecting. That is a powerful thing. Reading old journal entries gives me hope that maybe I was not denying all along. Maybe it was just my form of coping. I always knew, even when I did not.

When I was not voicing it, I was writing it.

This year, it will be three years in March, and I don't particularly care to drink very much these days, especially not in the way I used to. I would rather drink a glass of wine with friends or create something meaningful, like these words. I would rather dive into my art, which has become a sort of solace for me. I would rather do something today that fructifies for my future self. I would rather look out for her, the woman waiting in tomorrow.

And I would rather make memories in the light than to live out a night so forgettable.

Since that night, I have taken slow steps to come back out of my shell, to be certain in where people's loyalties lie, in whom I can trust. I have put down the bottle I used to cope. I have cut off ties with the people who do me no good. I have deleted the habits that serve me no purpose.

I would rather have an Amaretto Sour at the little bar downtown where I can sit quietly and write while the bartender slides me another. Served with foam and an orange and a black cherry. And good conversation and the safety of good company.

Or maybe no drink at all. I don't think I need it anymore.

How many times I wanted to bury myself with the bottle. To me, the bottle was always broken. I knew that college kids did it for fun, but I was scared that with me it was not that.

I was terrified of my realities, and willing to capture whatever alternative universe that I could escape into. There are so many things I do not need anymore. Thank God.

Maybe a night in, time with myself, time to write this story. Time to be alone, to be able to breathe in the once uncomfortable silence. Time to appreciate me, time to feel safe, time. Time to recall the little girl that was writing stories on top of her bed every morning before school, and to remember that we are still one. Together, her and I work on it.

Yes, that sounds wonderful to me.

Chapter Seven

I Wish Perhaps, It Had Been You

I no longer felt like me, but rather a shell of myself, and I was so desperate to fill what had been emptied out of me like water running dry.

Rewind the tapes. Take it back. Two years before.

Almost five years behind me now.

Lewis.

We met the night of senior prom in the basement of the massive mansion after party. It was very cliché prom. Odd enough, I still remember how it felt, a memory so tangible I can taste it, and I still get a smile out of that memory.

The big house, the big basement, dancing, drinking, a swimming pool, a bonfire, an indoor basketball court (yes, you read that right), dim lights. After prom was flooded with this sort of excitement that we were all young and bold, living out the days we could never get back.

I had opted out from drinking that night, had never been kissed, and was staying out past my curfew. Bethesda and I had made a pact to be designated driver buddies. Since one had to drive, the other would ride passenger, and both would not drink.

I was sixteen years old. It would be my first kiss.

He was senior captain of the soccer team, eighteen years old and brooding. Bethesda's dad was still alive. We were fun and fearless and free back then.

Perhaps the only three things that taint my memory now are:

1) Lewis is engaged (I imagine showing up at his wedding which is coming around the bend, just for the shock factor, not because I particularly care anymore).

2) The afterparty was held at Harris's house, Harris who would later tell me I was crying rape (but that chapter's coming).

3) we snuck back into Bethesda's house at 4 a.m. that morning to avoid her father catching us, just three months before we lost him from this earth.

Lewis smoked American Spirits in the pale blue pack. He had striking green eyes and a deep voice that I obsessed over. He also had a dry, rude sense of humor, and I soon developed a sore spot of insecurity for his words. We argued a lot, both stubborn and fiery, but our habitual fights with one another were laced with toxicity.

For me, Lewis is synonymous with my growing up. He represents the standard I set for myself at the time, which was rather low. He showcases my need to be noticed back then, my will to chase and chase and chase until I got what I wanted.

I played a good game and it turned out, I got played.

Some people fit like missing puzzle pieces and others just repel, and boy did we repel.

Bethesda and I were driving in the car with our friend Meredith after prom. We were changing in the backseat. I switched to converse and a jean jacket and Meredith to a tie-dye t-shirt. We ditched the sparkly dresses for leggings and pulled onto the street of the after party. The neighborhood was packed with lines of parked cars along each curb, and I could feel the post-prom excitement—to be around people, to be out late. I was sixteen doing sixteen-year-old things, but sober as a skunk.

"Sophia, you'd like Lewis," Bethesda pointed out, as we prepared to climb out of the car.

"Oh my gosh, he's your exact type," Meredith echoed. "Get him Sophia!"

"Who?" I scrunched my eyebrows together, wiping off my plum lipstick from prom and applying pink gloss instead.

"He wasn't at prom. He didn't have a date," Bethesda noted, looking back at where I sat in the center backseat. "But he'll be here."

"Kiss him tonight," Meredith winked, as I felt my mind go blank.

I didn't kiss people…

"Make him the mission!" Meredith continued as Bethesda laughed.

"You don't have a ride home unless you do it."

"Yes, yes, you have to!"

And so, April 2015 and the game commenced. I had no inkling that the "game" would continue for the next three years to come, a spiral of up and downs that I never could have predicted in the street that night.

We hopped out of the car and waited while Bethesda changed. She scrambled out the back just in time for a group of laughing teenagers to pass us right up, holding on to crumpled water bottles that most definitely did not contain water.

There were mostly girls and maybe three boys, they smelled like booze and giggled as they breezed past us.

"Oh sorry," one boy laughed hazily, as he looked back at me.

"You're fine," I waved him away, he had barely bumped into me, if only gotten just a little too close.

"Who are you?" he said suddenly, as if I was the one that had gotten into his space. "I've never seen you before…" Our eyes locked.

"Come on!" one girl named Kourtney dragged him away before anything else could be said.

"Oh my gosh, that's him!" Meredith exclaimed with excitement in my ear as he disappeared down the neighborhood.

"What?"

"That was him. That's Lew, that's the mission of the night!"

"You just met your man," Bethesda laughed as she motioned us to head towards the house.

"You guys have got to be kidding me," I rolled my eyes with a chuckle, but let my sight trail after him all the way down the cul-de-sac. The group was congregating in a field at the end of the road, wandering around and laughing and maybe smoking.

I was curious, so curious, and my eyes followed after him, watching until we headed for the house. Lewis, they said, soccer player.

Maybe this could be fun.

That girl from the street, Kourtney, always seemed to have her eye on him, but about halfway through the night, I realized that just maybe he really did have his eyes on me.

We played a game of basketball on the indoor basketball court and somehow ended up slipping and toppling over each other and ending up on the ground laughing our stomachs out.

Somewhere along the course of the night we sort of just lost each other and got separated in the crowds of conversation.

I was dancing in the basement with the girls, when I saw him around the corner.

"Oh my gosh!" he looked at me with wide eyes, stunned. "There you are! I really thought I dreamed you."

I laughed incredulously, sitting down with him on the couch. "I guess that would make me the girl from your dreams."

Our kiss was underneath the porch light of the side door near the garage. It took me by surprise, but I never paid an ounce of attention to the people that passed by us giggling. For all I knew, it was just him and I, bubbled in this little pool of light on this little corner porch of this mansion of a house on my prom night.

A lot of kids are losing their virginity at prom but that was never my style. I did, however, get myself into something a little stickier: my first, official situationship. I define a good old "situationship" as one step away from a relationship. While lacking all the titles, it still harbors every bit as much drama.

He was the first guy that I let in, and my first real broken heart.

You don't have to love somebody to get your heart broken by them, this I know for sure. And you don't have to get your heart broken by the one you love even when it doesn't work out. There are a lot of tricky ins and outs that no one really accounts for, plenty of in-betweens in the black and white.

When the night came and went and the party died down like embers in a fire, we just weren't ready to go home. About seven of us relocated to Bethesda's house where we parked our cars in the dark of early morning and hung around in the cool spring air.

My favorite last memory of the night: Lewis and me, laying under the stars, looking up at the moon on a golf course in front of the lake, the lake we would later swim in on the fourth of July.

"Kiss me," he asked, and I remember I was saying, "No, you're drunk," to which he responded, "I'm sober now," to which I interjected, "there are people watching."

"No, they're not," he reassured me, cupping my face in his palms. His eyes were looking intently back at me. I didn't know what to say.

I look back now and laugh at how times have changed so drastically. I grin at how shy I was to give a goodnight kiss in public, or to kiss at all, how I thought I might be bad at it, or bad because it was an improper thing to do.

Nothing is nearly the same as it was, so innocent, so fragile and pure. Simplified times, delicate naiveties, memories that we made late at night when our parents thought we were sleeping. Somehow, we were always doing these beautifully harmless things, creating these moments that any teenager would look back on and chuckle.

But all I can do is look back and think about how that Sophia doesn't exist anymore.

I got my guy, succeeded in my mission, secured my "ride home" that night with a kiss, and yet never kept him.

I have a very distinct memory from the Fourth of July 2016. Bethesda's mother was in Africa for three weeks and her father had been passed away for almost a year. We spent those three weeks being seventeen and eighteen-year-old free little birdies, running around the backyard together with the water hose, sunbathing on the balconies, eating plenty of takeout, hosting all our friends at night.

Fourth of July and we had everyone over as long as they paid at the door (a brilliant, commendable business move on our part). We went swimming in the lake and set off fireworks, our bare feet dipped in and out of water and grass.

He was taking a shower upstairs in B's room where I was changing out of my white swimsuit.

"Get in with me…" he hastened with a goofy laugh.

"No," I said with a grin. I was terrified to have sex.

As the years continued past us, and Lewis ended up with someone else, I could not help but punish myself in a way. I always used to think that if I had said yes all those times, would the path have changed, would the course have bent a little differently for our story? Would he be with me today if I had given him that? He was with her now…

I think of all the no's I said to guys when the opportunity was just a thin piece of paper away. And how they always backed off and respected my choices to abstain.

So, for the less-than-human that violated me, there are no excuses.

I think about my story with Lewis, reminiscing over the way I thought we might in fact work out. But then I recognize that our story was pretty much not a story at all, just a string of episodes clumped together over a couple of years, a rollercoaster of fighting and making up, weaving in and out of the line of friendship and way past this boundary, to the point of no return.

Never dated, never called him my boyfriend. But he hurt me in a way that no one had before.

I realize now, as I examine my inner child and her innerworkings, that I have always been this way. Lewis did not make me this way. I have always existed in a self-fulfilling prophecy of "love me, don't leave me" where I drive the other person away with my crushing need to be loved.

I do not think I loved him, but perhaps this was my first encounter with "love" of any sort.

Even if it was the puppy kind, it was an attachment, nonetheless.

And even though he did not choose me, not once, I believe that my constant draining desire to be chosen held me onto him for so long.

The scary part? These behaviors were already engrained and etched into me well before that night at my senior prom.

They simply manifested themselves into an undefined situation with a boy who was incapable of loving me, and that is in part why forgiving him is so easy.

It has only been five years, but it might as well have been another lifetime ago. I was naïve and impressionable, soaking up every ounce of attention that I could possibly grab at. I needed to be liked, accepted, and chosen.

Lewis and I spent a lot of nights together, but I never had sex with him. We slept side by side, but we never really knew each other. In fact, he was my first in a lot of ways, but none of those ways really meant anything to me or mean anything now.

Chapter Eight

Part Two: What Once Was...

The best part about being young and dumb is you get to get it over with when you're young. The worst part about being young is feeling the pain of mistakes far too early.

Also, willingly drinking a black cherry four loco.

It is funny, now I could never imagine myself with someone like him. I can't even begin to comprehend that I put up with that much from someone for so long.

A year after prom, the next summer. 2016.

Our mutual friend, Jacob, held his 21st birthday on a large piece of land, referred to as the "barn party." The night started out with rounds of beer pong and shots of fireball inside of a friend's refurbished barn, and ended up with Lewis and I bumping along in my little white jeep back to Jake's house, back to the guest room we always ended up in. I remember he was holding my hand, and we were laughing and telling stories.

"Goodnight," I whispered, rolling over on my side.

"Goodnight." He yawned, turning the other way, a pillow placed in between us. But then we both rolled over in the middle of our sleep, and then it happened, and we kissed, and it felt like it was the first time, because this time it was more real.

He looked confused, staring up at me in the dark, his voice laced with disbelief that it was us, again.

"Sophia?"

"Yes?"

My mistake was in thinking that it would always be "us, again…"

The next morning, we got dressed wordlessly and pulled our cars out of the drive, making it down to the stop sign at the end of that country road. That exact morning is engrained in my mind. It was unusually bright, cool in the transition to summer.

I took a right and he took a left, and we never even said goodbye.

But there was no point, because every time we parted it was always a "I'll be seeing you" until one day it was not, and he would get engaged and I would move away.

All he would become to me, and all that he needed to be, was a ghost.

Fast forward from this night in May. The year was now 2017. The day was June 10.

He had gone from sitting beside me underneath the moonlight at the lake to sitting beside me in my 2006 Jeep Liberty and singing along to every song as we laced our way through the country. He was the one riding passenger with me on St. Patty's Day, holding my hand and sitting next to me in the backyard hot tub. He was the one standing beside me on the rocks that we cliff jumped from forty feet down into the waters as the sun set.

Now he was sitting beside me on the carpeted floor of the same guest bedroom from years earlier, except nothing was the same.

We were leaned up against closet doors in the light of a single lamp, my head leaning on his shoulder as he handed me wads of tissue from a box.

As I cried in his arms that night, the last night we would ever spend together, I let my body collapse into his, my chest convulsing with tears, and I wailed like I never had before. I never cried in front of people, let alone boys.

But I cried, and cried, cried with the pain of what had happened to me just two months before. Cried with the pain that someone had done something so ugly and dirty to me, ripped a piece of me away that Lewis never knew. Cried with the realization that Lew had met someone else, and that in the past few months that I had inwardly been dying, he had been living. Cried at the knowing that I had lost so much, and now I had finally lost him too.

I cried because I had been raped, and I cried because the person whom I really wanted, did not want me.

I had neither the sanity nor the luxury to feel embarrassed or ashamed of my tears. I have never cried like that for or with anyone. I didn't care. It felt good. And it hurt.

I cried and then something amazing happened.

So did he.

He cried, too. With me and for me, his voice quivering and choked.

It broke me to hear his sadness. And it broke him to see me in pain.

"It hurts me to know that I'm happy…and you're not," he said.

But you aren't actually happy, I was fighting inside, you aren't really, are you? How can you be happy in a relationship with a girl that you say you don't even have good sex with? And are you even going to marry this girl that you hooked up with at some random party?

Everything I never wanted to happen, was happening, every bit of it happening only to me. Lewis, painfully so, would be fine. I would be fine too, eventually, but it would be without him.

I wish I could time travel back those couple years ago and tell my eighteen-year-old self that healing would come, that light would come, that time would fade away and this moment would too. But for now, all I could see was this: blurred eyes, the guy that wasn't coming with me into tomorrow, smeared makeup, and a mess of the life I had spent years piecing together.

I never intended for him to find out. In fact, he was the one person I never wanted to know. But his friends told him anyways, at least our "friends" that we had in common. It came from a good place I surmised, and I knew that they cared. Still, the mess would have been cleaner if he had never found out or if at least I could have been the one to tell him. And rightfully so, it was my choice and my decision to tell him, if ever. But people, no matter the intentions, do not always let you take control of your own narrative. They are far too interested in trying to "spice things up" at your expense.

As we sat in the room that we had spent so many late nights in, I realized this would be the last night for us. Over the past few years, I always figured this night would come, but I never painted it to look like this. He was saying that he respected me so much for how I had always said no to sex, that he wished he had never had sex, that his current relationship's sex life was so bad he would rather not even do it. Yet he was still choosing her, not me, and I never understood it.

"I considered dating you, maybe when I first met you…" he shrugged, looking deeply into me. "but it was just too far gone."

He was right. There was too much history there, too much. It was too far gone down the road, and we could not turn back. All we could manage was to move onwards without one another.

More than two years were spent playing hide and seek with him, and he has sex with a girl on the first night and now they're getting married?

I suppose this just proves to me that there really is never any right or wrong way to do it.

The only thing that matters most is that you chose in the first place, that you wanted to. And saying yes to sex, or no to sex, will not make or break a relationship if it is the right one. The point is that the consent is there in the first place, and that it is being honored.

I will never forget this night, this token offering from the stoic boy who rarely showed his true feelings. I will never forget the way he choked up and cried for me. I will never forget the way he showed me, for once and if not only that one time, his heart. I will certainly never forget the way that it closed off to me the next morning.

"You can hate me," he was telling me, "As much as you hate him. I hate him for you. I hate myself for how I treated you. I'm just as bad as him."

"No, you're not," I mumbled through the tears. And that was what bothered me the most, was that I could not get myself to hate him, and I thought maybe if I did it would have made getting over him a lot easier. Maybe that was why he said it, because he thought it would be in my best interest.

I wonder, even now, if that was just his copout, if he was hoping that it would be easier for me to hate him to move on. Was he trying to preserve me in some sense? Did he think I was more fragile or more broken than that which I really was?

Is it easier to hate the ones which we love, in order to get over them? In order to rid ourselves of them, must we first be angry, regretful, crippled with resentment?

What was the point in hating him? He was not the one I hated, and he knew it. I couldn't hate him anyways, not even if I tried. Not even if I rehashed all of the sordid details of our every argument and every fight in my mind. Not even if I relived the way that he had mocked me, embarrassed me, or played me. Not even if I managed to paint over every brightened moment with black. I still could not-would not-hate him. Besides, I don't think it would bring me back anything that I had lost.

Hours passed, while the others partied in the backyard outside, and the house went to sleep, and the lights went black, and I cried on.

What can be a worse feeling than being held by the one who doesn't want you?

What was the point of being here anyways? What was the point of knowing him? Or of ever meeting him at prom, phasing in and out of years of back-and-forth, games, and indecision? It was too late to go back now, too late to erase it. And certainly, it was too late to go home.

Soon he helped me into the left side of the bed and offered to stay and sleep on the floor.

We laid side by side, separated by bed and floor, but worlds apart, looking up at the ceiling.

"Be honest with me Lewis, I can take it." I remember saying suddenly. "It's okay." I stumbled through my words, eyes glassy. "Did it ever mean anything at all?"

"I can't..." I remember him saying to me, his voice cracking. I looked down at him, and his eyes were watering. "I can't."

I was angry now. "Why not?" The tears began to flow, and I wasn't trying to hide it. "Just say it."

Deafening silence.

"I can't."

"Why not?"

"Because I don't want to break your heart."

"It's ok, I'll be okay."

Silence, again, this time I could hear my heart pounding in my ears.

"It never meant anything. It. Was. Just. A. Game."

I nodded my head in silenced disbelief, top lip griping onto bottom lip, streaks of salt-water streaming down my cheeks. "Okay."

And silently, we turned away from each other. And cried ourselves to sleep.

While I had a small inkling deep down that his words were baseless, I decided to do the one thing I had never done with Lewis: Take him at his word and leave him at that.

No more reading in between the lines. If it was a game to him, then it was a game, and I was glad I never had sex with him.

Years passed and every time I always get the same answer: He was lying, you meant something to him, we all thought different, he was just saying that. But I always shake my head, rebuking it. "He said it, he meant it." I shrug.

That was years ago. It was years and nine lives ago. For the first time that night, I felt I was finally seeing him, and I was being seen—for who we were and what we had been and what we had done to each other.

And now we were "all growed up" as my mom would say, and finally outgrown of each other.

He was slipping away from me, if not already gone, gone from the moment we met.

Somehow, as we lay there in the darkness, we realized that our lives didn't look as perfect as we hoped.

I was now a victim—so messy, so heavy, and so alone—and Lewis was in a stable but dull relationship with a bottle-dyed silver-haired, bellybutton pierced girl who I suddenly found myself feeling jealous of. Later, I would hear stories about how she was always bossing him around, about how they were "as happy as they can be, I think." If anybody ever says that about my relationship, please encourage me to think twice.

The last night in June, I was hit with the realization that not only was this my current and forever reality-to be stuck with this burden of what had happened to me-but that it would never be him I was meant for, and it never was supposed to be.

"I wish it had been you," I remember muttering to him. "So many times, I have thought, if I would have just had sex with Lewis this wouldn't be my first memory of sex. I wish it had been you not him."

I wished my virginity had gone to Lewis, not to this piece of shit, but I was strongly mistaken. My virginity was not something that had gone or gone to die. It was not a gift to give. It was stolen from me because it had not been the experience I wanted or ASKED FOR, but I would reclaim my body as MINE and my story as MINE and my virginity could be mine again too. And one day I would share, not give, my body to someone that cared deeply for me, and valued me, and let me lead the way.

So, Lew didn't take my virginity, but neither did my rapist.

I could rewrite the narrative. My first consensual sexual experience would not be defined by my rape. This knowingness emboldened me, but in that moment, I could not see far enough into the future to feel any kind of hope, so I just sat there and cried in the lap of the one who didn't belong to me.

I could not help but ask myself that night, do we ever stop? Do we ever cease going further and further back? Is it over or does it just keep running on?

Except this time, it really was the last.

The next morning, he would close back off to me and we would get inside of our cars. I would take a left at the stop sign, and he would take a right and we would never have to say another goodbye to each other again.

We would meet one more time, summers later at your best friend's wedding. Your arms were wrapped around the miserable relationship that you had bound with a diamond ring. With an awkward hello, you leaned in for the hug that no longer felt like home to me, but rather a cold outline of what once was. As the party dwindled down and the bride and groom skipped off into their future, you picked your future bride up off the ground. Too drunk to walk, you helped your stumbling soon-to-be-fiancé to the car. I remember how you looked at me, with those eyes that lingered on a little too long, turning your back one last time. My wish is for you to be happy, you are, aren't you?

Chapter Nine

I Call This My Hiding Phase:

Next, the idea that the world was looking at me and through me, into me and into everything that I once was and now am, crept into my being with a haunting will power. I was completely naked and vulnerable, and nothing was off limits.

This is what being assaulted does to you. It strips you.

Suddenly, in a place where you once stood tall and unashamed, you now find yourself holding an unbearable weight that makes your knees buckle. Any space that you take up seems to be a mistake.

Perfectionism, comparison, overcompensation: "you will never be enough". The vague outlines of imposter syndrome have been etching their way into my life since perhaps my youth. Even before I was assaulted and made to feel like an imposter in my own skin, I have long felt like an imposter in the spaces I take up and in the interactions which have defined my adulthood.

Do I even belong? What is my worth?

These plaguing questions were only exacerbated by a singular life event at the impressionable age of eighteen that forever changed my outlook on the world and on myself.

Imposter syndrome is the "persistent inability to believe that one's success is deserved or legitimately achieved as a result of one's own efforts." It is the doubting of one's talents and accomplishments, the constant nagging and internalized fear that "I am a fraud."

This defense mechanism is one I know well. In being a high-achieving individual, I often question my worth. In being a victim and a survivor, these thoughts continue to anchor themselves into my consciousness even worse than before.

I am forever marked by inability to internalize success. My traumas will forever overshadow my accomplishments.

No, I must tell myself, change the narrative.

Tracing back to the beginnings of my journey, when my freshly inflicted wounds were more real than ever, we find ourselves in my "hiding phase."

So, this called for turtlenecks. Loose jeans. Oversized sweatshirts. Never too much leg. No low cut tops.

Walt Whitman writes in "Song of Myself" that, "I have said that the soul is not more than the body, and I have said that the body is not more than the soul."

I think that I had trouble distinguishing between my soul and my body. The two are so interconnected, but when one is assaulted, one's body becomes a foreign object. Survivors of sexual violence are left feeling completely outside of their bodies. We are so often unsure of what is looking back at ourselves in the mirror, or the lump of skin that we see when we look down in the shower.

I realized that without my heart, my bones were nothing but frail marrow, and that my mind was just a wandering container without my spirit. I came to understand that the two are deeply entwined. After all, what is a shell of a body without the soul which it contains and protects, or the soul that gives life to the body?

One without the other or separated far apart, are just two broken bits of human.

But I had not made it there just yet.

I was still in my hiding phase, in the phase where my outer body was clothed with excessive garments and baggy jackets and limbs that ached to get out of bed. My soul was also aching, but mostly brimming and brewing over with anger and an intense hunger for revenge.

There are so many things to hate about my story. I hated that my body had been used, I hated that being assaulted and invaded now left me with a neglected body and neglected soul.

There are places deep within me that are so far out of your reach, and you reached them anyways. I hate that.

No one should ever fully know me until I have trusted myself to them. I never trusted myself to you. I imagine you would not understand this because of what you did, what you took. If I could scream these words on the rooftop I would and I will. I am.

Do not chase after a heart just because you cannot have it, or a body just because you can.

Say it again.

Do not chase after a heart just because you cannot have it, or a body just because you can.

Do not take my body and leave my spirit behind. Do not bother fooling my heart to leave me worse off.

I am two in one, I am soul and bones, all belonging to myself. You must accept me for my everything, or you must leave and take nothing when you go.

And to the one that did this to me: I did not invite you here.

Time had passed since April Fools and June 10, both days imprinted in my memory as two coincidently painful instances that would take me more than just this out-of-state move to get over. It was the fall of 2017, when I had transferred colleges to a conservatory in Pittsburgh. Changing universities had been my plan all along, even since the "before." Thankfully, it was my out.

I had always been planning to leave that town even before I was assaulted and thank God for this, because leaving was my chance at living.

After my night with Lewis, where I was told that I never meant anything to the boy that I had spent so much time and energy and heart on-I had driven straight to my best friend Bethesda and never looked back.

In the hours that followed June 11th, I took drastic measures. "Drastic measures" for Sophia always involved a fun night out and a big dramatic haircut. Ten inches of hair gone and one concert in Cincinnati later, and life seemed to change for me in a mere twenty-four hours. The rest of the summer of 2017 was spent with my friends, diving headfirst into teenage adventures. I clung to my confidante and best friend, in a world marked on my timeline as "after." Together, Bethesda and I learned to adjust to a life where she had no father, and I had no safety.

We attended concerts, we spent sleepovers under the stars, we drank a lot of cheap gas station French Vanilla coffee, we drove a lot when we didn't feel like sitting in the house. Those days were simplistic, but they were healing. They were everything to me.

We managed to laugh, even when there was pain, even on the days where it rained so hard, that we could not see the road ahead of us. We found a new freedom in ourselves and a new comfort in one another. To this day, we are always laughing, because it is all we have.

Our sophomore year of college rounded the bend, and we wrote letters to each other before we parted, with the promise of seeing each other soon.

With a final curtain call bringing our warm summer months to a close, I moved to the city in anticipation that a fresh start, fresh friendships, and a fresh reputation were awaiting me downtown.

Nobody had to know me as the girl who got raped. Instead, they could know me as the girl who had survived it.

Or maybe they did not have to know about it at all. This was redefining for me to say the least. I began to explore the mechanisms of healthy compartmentalization. This does not mean that I was idealizing my life, although I did repress and deny much in order to stay afloat. While my journey to healing was not perfect in these early stages, I was still able to separate my traumas from my successes.

This played an integral role in my being able to still create art and to finish out college not just by the skin of my teeth, but through absolutely excelling. I was not crippled from making long-lasting friendships instead of trauma bonds, and I was able to decipher the difference. Although my trauma had the possibilities to be debilitating, I refused to let up. And although healing is neither linear nor neat, this is my power.

It would, however, still take a lot of work. Certainly, tripping up became my familiarity until I managed to get to a place where I could walk steady again.

The day would come where I could hold my head high and talk about it if I wanted to. If I wanted to. It was my story and no one else's. I could pick the time and place, the how and where. I did not owe anyone an explanation or a reason to pity me. I could talk about it as much or as little as I wanted. I could scream it to the news stations or whisper it into this book.

Do not ever let anyone who does not understand your story, guilt you into how you should or should not tell it.

I knew that there would be a safe and warm space in my life, a time where I could sit down and ever so determined, write this book with the sole purpose of saying "me too" to the ones I had never met. In the end, I controlled my story, and it took me the tolls of time to understand this.

I thought during those days that maybe moving to a new city would make everything better, make me forget. It freed me, but also inhibited me. I found myself boxed into a brokenness I never imagined, neglecting my own mental health and escaping reality as often as I could. I avoided ever going home, erasing the very thought of my hometown from my identity. In turn, this drifted me farther away from my family than I wanted, and I continued to wade further and further from the sandy shores of home that I had known as a girl. I did not even spend Thanksgiving Day with my family. I never made it back for more than a few days during the holidays. The very thought of being back in that town pained me so heavily, and I could feel myself fading away from my closely-knit family.

Driving those same roads hit me with an aching nostalgia about Lewis and a stabbing recollection of my assault. Everything that was familiar was unwanted. This was a part of my coping and my journey to healing. I avoided the people that took me back to that place, and the city that it happened in, which became entirely bad to me, even if it was the city that my parents were living in at the time.

I wanted to wipe away the slate clean and pray that no one would ever have to know.

Living in a city alone gives you a newfound discovery of self. It also makes you think that the city might save you, the thought of everything being totally and completely new will redeem you.

I was still running, but I knew I could not run forever. Eventually everything that we run from chases us down and wrangles us to the ground. Eventually, running just becomes so damn exhausting.

The first week alone in my new home, I slept every night on the couch in the living room situated between a tiny corner kitchen and a bedroom with two twin beds. I would watch the buildings glitter and light up in purples and pinks at night. The bank building across the courtyard used to flash every hue of the rainbow starting at 8pm…I loved keeping the blinds open, because then I was not trapped in total darkness, then I was not entirely alone. So, I stayed there until my roommates moved in, avoiding the loneliness of my strange new bed for an entire week.

I have realized that while I prefer city living any day, and while it has made me bold and feel a little less alone in this world, I also recognize that home can manifest itself anywhere I make it.

The city can be a lovely place, a harsh place too. Much like life itself, it is chalk full of opposites. It taught me what to see, and when. It raises a heightened awareness of surroundings and senses.

Living in a city for me meant I quickly grew used to some of the alarms and red flags. The cat calling was inevitable every couple of blocks that I passed, but coincidentally not so much nowadays that I have noticed.

At this point, it becomes a matter of personal safety, not of fear. Perhaps there is still a healthy amount of realism that lives on within me, but I do not live with the crippling idea that something may happen to me again. My mother lives with a sense of this, I think. She is fearful that I will be hurt at the hands of men again but that does not mean we stop living.

Living in downtown is a beast of its own.

Outside of my apartment alone, there are dozens of homeless men that have nowhere else to sleep but under the covered entry points of my building. As in my nature, I make friends with many of the homeless people in my city. I have grown used to sharing our morning cup of coffee together.

But at night, the city can be an unpredictable place, and being a woman is hard.

So many of us have been followed, stalked, yelled after, and threatened.

We never walk more than a block alone, and I am always asking my friends, "do you have pepper spray or a knife?"

Text me when you get home is our constant and ever present language after leaving each other's company.

"I grip my car keys in my knuckles so the punch will hit harder," my friend tells me as she facetimes me during her walk home from work, alone.

I remember yelling at a man who had completed pivoted around to watch me and Bethesda walk all the. way. down. the. entire. street.

"What the hell are you looking at?" I remember screaming.

"You're going to get us shot," an eighteen year old Beth admonished, practically dragging me away.

"I don't care," I nearly yelled back at her.

Thank God she managed to put up with me.

My tone has since quieted for my own mental well-being. And although I still remain the same fiery and defensive individual I always have been, I have also found a way to reel in my anger, instead of seething with it. There is still so much that makes me mad about the world, a hunger for change and justice that rages on inside of me. I am still fighting the fight, but I must harness the patience to pick my battles.

It is true that some men looked as if they had never seen a woman before in their entire life. Naturally I wanted to ask them with my usual sarcasm, three unanswerable words: can I help you? Is there something that staring at me, is going to fill in the emptiness of you?

My therapist has since told me to see mirrors when I walk down the street. Mirrors reflect what is being looked back at them. So, if I surrounded myself with the company and safety of mirrors, then I would deflect all the cat calls coming my way.

For safety, I say nothing. If I am alone, I keep walking. I do not let the baseless, senseless words of strangers take and take and take from me.

The more I give them, the more they take. I have spent plenty of years yelling, fighting back. Now I just walk past, and onwards, listening to their mumbled insults because I chose not to respond. I choose instead to put up my mirrors, to deflect their energy. I have plenty to say, perhaps just not to them.

And oh, how quickly their compliments turn to insults. This is just one way I reflect my own energy while walking down the street. Instead of feeding into my own anger and lashing out with it, instead of giving these catcallers the response they crave, they walk away infuriated that they have been ignored. And I walk on.

My anger provides me with nothing but takes away more and more from me the more I give to it. I am so sick and tired of being angry because so many have done me so wrong. It is time for me, to do me right. It is time for me to do right by me and to feel okay with what I clothe this body in, and to feel safe with who I am accompanied by. It is time for me to not let fear inhibit me from the places that I want to go, and to not let any phase of life hold me down.

Chapter Ten

Living In Black & White

When she looks at me and explains that I live my life on an either/or, starkly divisive, and bitterly divided shading of black and white, I blink more than once, stumbling on whatever words may or may not come next. I swallow hard and scrunch up my nose.

"I'm not sure I do that."

My therapist looks back at me with a half-smile, as she senses my revelations brewing. I lean back, contemplating this for a moment, considering if perhaps she is…right?

Is it not almost our responsibility to deny our therapists when they so abruptly counter our long held beliefs? Is that not why we are in therapy in the first place? When our therapist first points out our problems, we deny it, further proving why we are sitting on this very couch. Right now, she asks questions of me that I have never managed to ask myself. She is etching color into a black and white world like mine. In fact, this world has been black and white ever since I can remember.

As a child, we are taught the clearly defined difference between right and wrong, what should or should not be done, and what is acceptable or not acceptable. No grey, only white and black, two opposite ends of the spectrum. Lies versus truth, good versus bad, kindness versus cruelty. There is nothing to be blurred or questioned.

Let me clarify that there is nothing wrong with living life in a clarified state of honesty and truth. The grey areas can be messy, even shady, littered with "what if's" and "little white lies." That is not the kind of in between that I am referring to. I am speaking on the way in which we view the world, and how we choose to exist inside of it.

I admit, it really is all 1920's-silent-film and every bit lacking in rainbows in this little big world of mine. Where color belongs, I see black. I exist in the dark. I love the night. I sink into the night. I have a crescent moon tattoo and all of my grand ideas come to me at night.

And yet, the night can be a scary place.

We all need a splash of color. Light that seeps in. A reminder that out of the ugliest sea of black, there can still be illumination. We all need luminosity, and we all need daylight.

While it is true that we often live in a realm of crystallized opposites, or rather inverses (darkness is the absence of light and valleys are introverted mountains as someone important once reminded me) not every opposite is a counter.

Contrary to my long-held beliefs, grey CAN exist. There can be a blur. There can be, in fact, color. And shade. And texture and depth. Life is not one of two opposite ends of the spectrum.

I can love people and still disagree with them.
I can love my family and never speak to them again.
I can love you even when you hurt me.
I can leave you even when you love me.
I can date my best friend.
I can love myself and still be a work in progress.
I can wish to marry someone like the man that my dad is now at fifty-five years of age, but not the father he was for me growing up.
The world can be both a perfidious and beautiful place.
People are not entirely bad.

Am I allowed to make the distinction? The answer is yes, start now.

However, my obsessions and compulsions have held me in a white knuckled grip my entire livelihood, instructing me to divide my life up into compartmentalized sectors.

One for white, one for black.

One for truth, one for lies.

One for the lowliest of lows, and one for my greatest "Ne Plus Ultra's" (Latin for the highest place).

Either I have succeeded greatly and far before my time, or I have failed miserably at what my life was "supposed" to form itself into.

Either I am exceptional, or empty handed.

Light and dark, but never dusk.

Divided, filed away, scribbled down, charted. How dull that everything else ceases to exist. I have never accepted anything unless it was not extreme, never accepted that which is pale, opaque, and grey.

As therapy is teaching me ever so slowly, opposing objects can stand up against each other and exist simultaneously. Me, in my black and white realism and my most negative persuasions, have fought this coexistence my whole life.

Either I love you or I hate you.

Either we talk every day or not at all.

If you cause me pain, I cut you off.

Or worse, I cut you off before you have the opportunity to sting.

These characteristics are classic survival and fight-or-flight defense mechanisms that so many of us cling to, in order to protect our scars and our hearts. There is no "in-between", no "if", no "maybe". There is only what we latch on to in order to protect ourselves from enduring the kind of hurt that we have long known and never wish to know again. Changing the narrative involves doing the work and stepping into the grey equates to rerouting my brain. It is difficult, but necessary. It is the work I must do to protect and to sustain my future self.

None of this any longer needs to be true, at least not for this life.

I do not have to merely exist in black and white. It does not have to be either I love you so entirely that it all consumes me, or I love you not at all.

The black and white says that if I do not open myself up to you, you cannot hurt me. The shading which etches itself so thoughtfully in between says that I am allowed to be safe in my honesty and vulnerability, I can share who I am with who you are.

The black and white says that my failed relationships were wasted time not lessons learned. When the color creeps in, I begin to see all that I have become and where I have come from, and that it has been a worth while journey to become this.

The patterns of extreme ups and downs that were so ever-present in my life, are clearly defined as black and white. My obsessive compulsive disorder-black and white. The way that I was less than accepting of each phase of a relationship if it did not align with my exact expectations-black and white.

Going with the natural ebbs and flows of love and life are color. Choosing to accept that my previous dead relationships still provided me with an opportunity to grow more into the woman that I am today, is grey. Lots and lots of color and grey and a lot less black and white. A painting to get used to.

Black, white, and grey. And color. And light. Each exists because of the other.

There are many times in my life where I will myself to label that which is black, white, and grey. You, black. Me, light. The world, grey. Yet sometimes I have found that life does not require color blocking. Even the darkest bits of life are still capable of being the purest and brightest. I lend myself over to the unknowns of perspective, interpretation, and perception, searching for color where there once were simply cut-outs.

Balance-and color-can and will exist. One does not belong without the other. So, knowing full well that It WILL exist in my reality means that I am now finally free to fill in whatever blank outlines my past has left me with. Whatever darkness exists then is no longer preying on me now.

And whatever darkness will be, I am wholly willing to accept, because life is naturally all variations of EVERYTHING.

So, maybe we can finally start now…coloring the void.
Spending time trying to find and define color again.

Chapter Eleven

I Am a Dancer

"Dance is the hidden language of the soul." -unknown

Even now labeling myself as a "dancer" out loud makes me want to break out into Cassie's song from A Chorus Line. And if you aren't familiar with the Broadway Hit, "Let Me Dance for You," ends with this:

> I am a dancer.
> I have come home!
> Let me in.
> Give me somebody
> to dance with.
> Give me somebody
> to be!
> Let me wake up
> and feel entirely proud
> that the girl
> in the mirror,
> is me!

Well let me just say that the girl in the mirror certainly was not me, could not be me, didn't even faintly resemble me. And I cowered away from her reflection, disdainfully and with disgust. Post-assault, looking at myself all day long in a dance studio mirror became very difficult for me, I felt caged in and studied all hours of the day. I was forced to look at every inch of myself in these expanses of reflected glass, and I looked nothing like the bold, bad ass nine-year-old dancing in the very front and center of the stage, to the Black-Eyed Peas.

And I wanted so badly to be her again, to be what I thought I had lost.

I consider myself incredibly lucky to be in a creative field so far ahead of its time. We are completely and utterly (for the most part, and in my experience, particularly in these recent generations) accepting of all people, all genders and sexualities, all identities.

Artists are humans, simply that, and we have the unique ability to just. Be. Human. No façade. No fraud. We are lucky enough to work out of an authentic, raw place, to collaborate with others, to experience physical connections with other human bodies, to touch and to see and to sense. We dress however we want; we express however we feel the need to express…we're "artsy." Hell, we're fun.

We don't have to sit at a desk from 9-5 or wear a button-up. We get to roll around on the floor and climb on to each other and brainstorm strange and wonderful ideas, and then watch those ideas grow from conception to the stage.

There is nothing wrong with any other profession in the world, because we need the 9-5ers. But we get to experience everything that they miss out on day to day: a chance to connect, to touch and to feel, to be inside of and outside of and within and without and around and beside and below. To see and be seen. To be vulnerable, to look people in the eyes and register that. To feel comfort in being pulled and grabbed and lifted by one another.

I remember when the New York City Ballet sexual harassment claims surfaced. I realized that times were shifting, and light was infiltrating through the cracks of flawed systems and secrets. I was devastated. During the time when I struggled with my body post-assault, dance saved me. It provided me with the chance to move when I was left wordless. I didn't have to speak. I could just dance it all out and feel everything without having to tell anyone anything.

Dance gave me the platform to make baby steps into coming back into my own body again.

One of my most favorite poems by Ocean Vuong is called "Almost Human" and my favorite excerpt from it is this: "it has been a long time since my body, unbearable I put it down on the earth the way my old man rolled dice. It has been a long time since time. But I had weight back there, had substance and sinew, damage you could see by looking between your hands and hearing blood."

It has been a long time since my body...it has been a long time since time.

I felt separated from my body.

When I heard about the events transpiring in New York, I took it personally. Movement was our bubble to express, and now that safe space had been infiltrated. I was more than bothered.

Dance has long been a largely female realm, so we have an advantage on breaking gender barriers in the workplace. However, we aren't immune to abuse of power. What happens when a room full of female dancers are headed by a man-the wrong man-at the front? That man thinks that he has "plenty to choose from" is what happens. He seeks out the vulnerable, and perhaps young. He chooses the easy target, the one who is eager to please, it blurs the lines. What happens when a boyfriend in a dance company, passes around photos of his fellow dancer girlfriend to male colleagues? She gets degraded and slut-shamed and defamed and must fight tooth and nail to get those men fired.

One of those men who participated in the sharing of Alexandra Waterbury's photos was the brother of an old friend of mine. He was also a star principal dancer.

Oh, how it all so quickly turns gray.

Once again, I felt my hope dwindle as I watched Waterbury battle not just in the world as a female, but in a world her and I both shared as being dancers. She was victimized similarly to me, but this time in the one realm that I thought kept us safe and sane.

Even in the dance world, I have noticed that we often have no one to advocate for us. We are unaware of who to report to when these problems arise. (And what happens when our assailant is the one that we report to? There have been plenty of instances in the dance world itself that remind me we are never safe, not even safe within our art).

Oh, how it seems that the washing machine cycle will spin on to no end. The laundry stays dirty. I am airing it all out.

I was so sick and sickened by the zones of judgment I had endured, and the one place where I wanted to feel embraced, was inside my profession, inside those dance studios and mirrors. I just happen to think that the arts are full of some very open people, open-minded and open-hearted, and open people are exactly what I needed at that time in my life, and we must preserve and protect that. Artists have the responsibility not to ruin a good thing.

My junior year of college, one of my professors of dance, Jason, told me that when he looked at me, he saw that something or someone had taken my confidence. He read my eyes without me even saying a word and could sense I was on the journey of rebuilding.

I will never forget when he told me this, "your light never got taken away from you, only dimmed. It never burned out completely because it was always burning within you. You have a fire inside of you just need to find a way to ignite it again."

Dimmed, yes. Extinguished, never.

The wonderful thing about having something that you love and hold dear to your heart, is that it has the healing properties to save you. It could be a person, it could be a hobby, it could be one's faith…for me it was the art of movement. I loved dance for everything it was and for everything it had done for me.

Therefore, I dance. This is why:

"Let me write to you about my lover, the one I would give anything for. Let me talk to you. You leave me breathless; you leave me reaching for all the right words, you make my spirit whole and my soul complete. This is the letter I write for my first love: dance. To you, I am undeniably grateful. Forever in awe. Forever in debt. My love affair, a war with body and spirit, but fresh water for my cracking skin and warmth for my aching bones. You envelope me in your healing powers. You bring tears to my eyes that I let no one see. You have taught me to find pleasure in pain and comfort in the discomfort. You ask these tasks of me daily, and I have learned to find rest in the anxieties. You push and pull like a lever; you chip away at me day by day like an exhausted old wood smith while building me up ten stories tall. You give and you take. You take and you take but the end reward tastes so sweet. To whom much is given, much will be required. With my gifts, I lend myself to the world, and the return is much and great and plentiful. It is far beyond all that I could ask for. Dear art, you make me whole. You etch color into my world. You drive purpose into my entity. Everyone needs you. Everyone needs something they love, so bittersweet you are. Dear dance, before I chose anything else, I chose you. My indecisive nature fought back when it came to you. I was so certain. You are the thing I love most, next to the ones who birthed me into life and the God who breathed life into me. If I love the way I love you, I will live worry free and never bored, for the rest of my days. Even when my feet need rest, my heart is still dancing.

That is enough for me."

-October 2019

The fall semester of my senior year I danced in a work titled "A Decline from A Sound and Prosperous Condition" which is the dictionary definition of decay. Our choreographer compared it to a reverse baptism, where we were being pulled out of something good, and our souls were fighting against it. The last night on stage, I fell apart.

My love for dance is magic. It is an irreplaceable feeling, a moment. There is no greater experience in my being that combines body and soul equally, then when I hear a room erupt into applause, stomping feet, cheering voices, my name being yelled from the back balcony. Tears course down my face as the spotlights expose me to the world and then fade into darkness, and I give into it all.

I collapse, my heart. And I weep because I would give anything to sink into a moment like that forever. It is overwhelming and perfect. It is both infinite and finite, because although it seems to last forever, it is fleeting.

Dear dance, what you bring out of me is so heart wrenching, but so filling. I cannot possibly hold it in.

I look around and I hear the fellow sobs. Tears stream down chins and flutter away like dust.

When it is over, it is really over.

When the curtain falls, we retreat to life. But you, my lover so otherworldly, you bring me back to that special place time and time again.

I can't thank you for humbling me enough, and yet lifting me up out of a pit and teaching me all the self-worth that I needed in the world. I hope I fall in love and fall in love well, because I have already been loving this, and it may not make sense to most, but it means the most to me.

I will never forget moments like these. Moments as these can change your entire life. It did. I will never be the same, and how glorious is that? Everyone changes as necessity, even when it is change born from discomfort and hesitation. Everyone shifts, not one soul remains unchanged, untouched, unaffected. We were all born into one life, for however long, and then we return to dust, or maybe to the stars, to that warm light that I have gotten used to my entire life.

Dance was a saving grace for me. Inside of it, I was utterly free. Outside, I was every bit the opposite.

Chapter Twelve

She Drowned in The Ocean, I Heard

Ironically, the kid who said I was crying rape had a mom who was the first adult I told. My confidence in her was assured and full but my disgust for her sons was overwhelming.

Harris lived in a big mansion which hosted every homecoming and prom after-party. During senior year of high school, he bonded very close with Bethesda. That was what made his actions even more depraved and disappointing because I had let him in, and he shunned me.

Harris called me a liar; said he didn't want to hear it. He blocked my number, "wished me well" …as if to ignorantly paint over the years of hurt and healing that were paved out ahead for me. As if wishing me well could wash his hands of the entire situation that he wanted no part of. He also happened to be the family friend of my rapist, so I suppose my assault would be titled "acquaintance rape."

He is what I refer to as a "predator protector."

As long as people (and particularly defensive men and boys) like him stand up for abusive, violent, and/or criminal behavior, assaults will continue to plague our nation and worst of all they will be JUSTIFIED. Furthermore, many will suffer on in silence, for fear of being judged, shamed, ostracized, and made to feel an inconvenience or a burden. Because the topic is heavy, it makes us feel heavy, as if we are too much to handle. Our story is one of unwanted information, the "I didn't ask for your sob story" story. I am sorry I inconvenienced you.

Well Harris had a mom, the first adult I told what had happened to me. For the sake of respect and privacy, we will simply call his mom Elle.

Looking back now, I wish I had been able to tell my mom. I wish I had not waited a full year to explain to her what had happened to her baby. Because the adult I really needed was the one who had given me life. But I will always love and appreciate Elle for the way she offered me a hand in one of the darkest hours of my entire existence, for encouraging me to discuss those unutterable words.

It always seemed, though, like I was the one educating her on how this whole thing worked. While forgiveness was the message she preached for our assaulters, it was one she had not accepted for herself. She had hardly forgiven herself or given herself a voice. Her reassurances to me were ones laced with guilt, like the way she told me to, "never let a man take advantage of you." But I had not let him, I explained to her. This was not how any of this worked.

Decade-long-best-friend Bethesda was always good at helping me to say what I knew I wanted to say but somehow could not manage. Sometimes the words could not come, or they came all at once and I could not decode them. Either way, B helped me make sense of it, all of it. Grateful is the word that comes to mind when I think of her immovable strength.

Here are a few words I texted to Elle during one of our many conversations, words that Bethesda helped me frame:

May 2017:

Messages between me and "Elle"

One message from her: "you are strong! I pray you can find forgiveness through this; it is the only way you will survive."

Me: "It's sad when you believe that people are inherently good. Consent is an easy concept to grasp but apparently people do not understand.

However, moving forward takes more than forgiveness. Rape doesn't just strip your innocence away, but your sanity in calamity when you wonder if you'll even manage to make it through tomorrow. It's not something you get over and move on from. It haunts me at night even."

She called me one-night, slurred words, the clock nearing 1 am. I figured she was drunk, it was a Saturday night, but she was sitting home alone I was sure.

Elle told me she was sorry that her sons (both of them) had "disappointed me" (her other son Harvard, one who I had "talked to" when I was seventeen, had begged me to tell him what was going on when he sensed something was strongly amiss. Harvard and Harris were only a couple years apart and hung in the same crowd. When I sought him out in confidence and safety, he held on to me. But then he told Harris, and before I knew, he had gone from comforting me to blaming me, his tone shifting cold. Younger brother Harvard told me that I could be very flirtatious when I was drunk "you know how you can be." Oh yes, so I had asked for this! Of course!

On the phone that night, Elle's somber tone was one of pain, reminiscent of the memories that plagued her, the memories that were now mine to carry. Elle told me that she believed me. It was edifying, to hear a mother say she was sorry for how shitty her sons were acting instead of excusing their behavior, she was saddened by it. She admitted that I probably looked at her as a "failed parent" but she had done her best and if she could do it over, she told me her life would not look like this.

My heart sunk for the middle-aged mother of five.

Her words slowly thawed away at my heart, for all the hate I had for her two sons that I had once called friends. We had grown up together, and spent so many late nights hanging out, sitting by the bonfire, running around their house after prom and homecomings.

It was no secret that Elle had a drinking problem. And Elle didn't care that we were young and drinking in her basement back in the day, either. So, to me, growing up, Elle was a pretty cool mom. But truthfully, she was broken in two, never having received a fraction of the help she so deserved.

And that night on the phone, as night faded into early morning, I buried myself under the covers and whispered to her in the dark of my bedroom, "no I am not pregnant." I got away from him there was no chance I was pregnant. "It was in the bathroom of a house." I think I remembered the name of the street. "I met him through your son." I hate your family. "Yes, I am okay." No, I am not.

Her tone of voice betrayed that there was no way she truly believed I was doing okay.

I never could have prepared for the story she was about to tell me that night. Her story isn't mine to tell, but I was pained by the recollection she had of childhood abuse at the hands of her father. A spring break trip gone wrong. A gang rape where she was held down with a knife. An assault at a party in the upstairs room. She told me of three instances in addition to her cheated childhood.

Suddenly the puzzle pieces of her life seemed to clarify for me, and I knew why she hid bottles all over the house, creviced between the washing machine, hidden in backyard bushes in the summertime, even. We used to laugh about it, but I was not laughing now.

In fact, while I felt nothing but love for her, I was determined not to end up like her. She was an alcoholic, a loving mother but more of a best friend to her kids. She was giving her daughter drinks by thirteen. She was hiding her drinking from her husband. Her husband was cheating on her, even more reason for her to keep turning back to the bottle. She never received the proper help or professional therapy that she deserved.

Her sons failed to understand the definition of respect or consent, their mockery of the "me too" movement in the coming years would have strongly disappointed her to her bones. I could not be like her. I would have her heart, but not her life. I could not do that to myself, especially for her.

She told me that she loved me, that she would always be there for me, even when her sons had failed me. She told me that once again, she knew I was not lying, because it had happened to her. Elle was my first encounter with a "me too" woman. Someone else who could nod their head in the silence and say yes it happened to me. And in that solemn solidarity, there was something forged: it was hope. The knowing that you are not alone.

Years before the "Me Too" movement was birthed into the spotlight (and thank god for it, because it made me brave) I was exposed to Elle, a woman over two times my age who offered me a light at the end of the tunnel even when she could not offer that for herself. I think now about how she deserved more, so much more.

And how I was away at college and could not make it back in time for her funeral, but even then, I knew it was best to avoid my hometown.

I got the call from my dear friend Jacob, who heard it through the grapevine and could not be sure. It was late night and I was alone. My body shivered; my eyes blurred. But I could not manage to cry. I felt so numb that I fell asleep that night not having shed a tear.

"We were supposed to get coffee," I just kept whispering to myself, thinking of the words left unsaid. "I was supposed to go over and see her." My heart was in my stomach and my bones ached. I felt it all, but I never let myself cry during those days.

The next day it was confirmed that she had drowned in the ocean just fifteen days short of the two-year mark of my assault. One chilly day in March down in Florida, the waves just swept her away and we heard nothing more of it. Her daughter from my knowledge, had been standing on the shores of the beach when it happened. Her youngest son had dragged her body to shore.

Was she intoxicated, was it on purpose? I would never know the answers. There are so many things I wish I had the answer for.

Her last haunting words were something along the lines of: "I'm getting too tired. You go ahead without me." So, her son swam on without her, and when he turned back, she was lifeless floating limbs.

I write this for her. For the ones who didn't get help. For the ones who deserved something much more than this, for you I write this Elle. I will go on ahead without you on this earth, but your spirit will fight with me every step of the way.

It took me a few days before the funeral until I could finally find the courage and the right words to message her son on social media, the son who had "wished me well" and blocked my number 730 days prior:

"It's taken me almost two years

but I forgive you.

Your mother helped me when I needed someone to tell me I wasn't alone

he was the first adult I told-I only recently told my mom and dad.

he spoke with me often in the early morning hours

bout personal sexual assaults she had survived, haunting childhood abuse...

She shared with me the same kind of pain I experienced when my body was violated. And over and over all

she kept saying was one day you'll forgive them. And she told me that was what saved her, was letting go of

all the bitterness.

I never lied, not once. I remember everything.

and I remember you telling me I was crying rape

And I remember your mother's words too.

And I forgive you *Harris*. And I am so sorry *Elle* is gone. I am so very sorry.

I'll never know what it feels like to lose a mother before her time. You never deserved that. You only

deserved good things.

And you'll never know what it feels like to get pinned up against a wall & raped and to be told you're a

liar or a flirtatious drunk like somehow you deserved to have your virginity taken away from you.

I pray God holds you. I pray God provides peace. I pray God heals the wounds you have from the loss of

your mom. I wish you nothing but love."

His response? "Thank you for your forgiveness."

That was all.

It was more than I thought I would get from the boy who had cut off all communication with me, and perhaps would lead me to a closing of one book in order to go on writing another.

I put my hate for him to rest as he laid his mother to rest for the last time.

With the realization that life was short, and my one adult confidant was now passed away, I knew the time was nearing for my story to spill out to the ones I loved.

Three months later I came home, sat my parents down and told them everything, realizing that their words of total love and assurance would be the only ones that mattered.

Chapter Thirteen

His Name Is...

Telling your parents something horrific happened to the child that they raised in a bubble of protection and love, is earth-shattering to say the least.

The domino effect of pain and shock is enough to rumble an earthquake. The worst part of being assaulted and telling people about it, is seeing what it does to them. It is no longer about us, when we see how it is affecting the ones we love. When the person we should be most concerned about is ourselves, we worry the most about them.

Telling my parents that summer left me without air.

I call him the one that got away. I hid in the shadows of pain for one year too many, uncomprehending of what had truly been done to me, and fearful of the damage it would do to my parents. In the three-hundred-and-sixty-five days that had passed, there would be no evidence, let alone the "unprovable crime" that had been committed. Still, I went to the police station and to this day it is public record, filed as a "complaint". I complained about my assault. That phrasing will never make sense to me.

The dictionary definition of a "complaint" is a "statement that a situation is unsatisfactory or unacceptable. Second, it can mean an illness or medical condition, especially a relatively minor one." To me that reads as, "it kind of bothers me but I'll live."

A complaint sounds like an inconvenience, a protest that gets shrugged off. The response to an assault doesn't equate to a "complaint", but rather an uproar. It doesn't call for a filed piece of paper, but rather a repaired justice system that stands up and says "No. Not again. Not this time." If there is on file a report that someone is being accused of rape-especially on a university campus-red flags should go up everywhere. This should not just be information tucked away in a folder, collecting dust in the back of the city archives building.

My hope was that if there were ever a complaint made about him again, they would have me as back up, as ammo. But then I would slow down and assess my reasoning: "if he does it again…"

I had been diminished down to a "if it happens to someone else, they'll have my story as some kind of secondary proof." A prayer that the "next" girl would be believed. So, would there be a next girl? Oh God, no, I thought to myself. What I really wanted was for the kid to get what was coming to him.

In my sophomore year of college, I swallowed a rather hard pill and wrote an essay for my composition class on college sexual assault statistics. This was the first time I would stand up and speak my story, or rather elude to it, and this made the floor shake from beneath my feet. But it also made me stand ten times taller.

I rattled off a harrowing list of statistics, felt my heart beat in my ears while I tried not to make eye contact with all my classmates, and finished the words "this happens to more people than you think, someone even sitting next to you. It happened to me." I divulged no more details, but this was my first public nod of a head: "me too."

Fast forward and there I was, sitting at the edge of my parent's bed, swallowing hard, palms sticky.

I decided to sit down with my parents thanks to my older sister who made me ever so bold. She was with me every step. She encouraged me to seek their support, but I worried it might break them.

"Our parents are stronger than you think," she told me. That statement made all the difference.

"Mom. Dad. I need to talk to you about something…"

That was the beginning of everything for me.

"You had sex didn't you…" was the first thing my mother said.

I can still feel this day, bright in my memory. This is one day that never fades to me. I don't remember what time of day it was or what we did after. I don't remember how or when we ate dinner, or when we went to sleep. All I remember is that I came home for a week over the summer to visit, and my guts were brewing with confessions. Confessions of someone else's wrongdoings on my behalf.

This is where I say thank you to my sister Lauren. Older by four years, I can still envision the photograph of her holding on to my fresh baby skin on our forest green plaid couch in Orlando. She was so excited to have a little baby. Growing up, she was my second mama. Not always to my excitement, the girl was always keeping a close eye. She was my fiercely protective defender.

As we grew up, I took it upon myself to stand up for the both of us, against the outside world. While Lo had no problem speaking her piece to me, she found it difficult to confront our foes. I would step up and defend us in a split-second moment, never one to watch my sister drown. I was only around seven or eight when I recall such an instance. It set the track for our lives. I was here to slash all the bullies and the bad boys for both of us.

I was the big, little sister.

As the years progressed, my sister's spine grew stronger, firmer, and it surprised and impressed both of us. She has always been my biggest advocate, but finally she could voice it. She would stand up to anyone if it meant standing in front of me, protecting me, confronting them anywhere if it meant defending her little sister.

When I revealed this topic to her, she treaded with caution. Later she would tell me that the full effects had not sunken in on her yet.

It is hard to really grasp your mind around what this single word can mean for a human life, and the ricocheting effect it has on loved one's. Like grieving in death, the process is slow and rigorous, but yields light at the finish line, although the question of why forever remains unanswered.

There is no right way or right time to do this.

We were sitting at Joe's Crab Shack by the river, she was visiting me over the summer before my junior year of college. I had chosen to work a job and stay that summer, even more reason for me to not have to go home and face what awaited me there.

"The pin in your bedroom," she said to me, "is that in you supporting the movement or did you have an experience with that?"

Her eyes were wide, and I knew she was referring to my giant "ME TOO" pin that I had on my makeup table.

"In support of the movement," I smiled lightly, sipping my sweet tea with lemons. "And also an experience…"

I trailed off, averting her gaze. An experience, I had said it so mundane.

"It's okay," she said, instantly reading me. Her tone grew even more soft, her eyes wide and deep, "you don't have to talk about it. Maybe another time, not here."

She motioned around at our surroundings, as I nodded. But I secretly, I didn't mind. While my stomach twisted in knots, my tongue was screaming to form words.

"I'll tell you about it," I remember saying, "I will tell you."

My tone made it seem like this was going to be an eventual steppingstone for us, but later that evening, she would come to find most of it out. I avoided the graphics and kept it as short and simple as I could. All the details would come out later (I would spare her as much ugliness as I could), but for now I just needed someone to lean on. I needed the support only a big sister could give, and the encouragement that I needed to come forward to our parents. The only person that knew them as good as I knew them was her, and I needed her for this.

Lo, you are a champion, the purest human I know. Clever, witty, patient, and mature…the perfect combination of stability and softness. The strength I needed in this aching time. Thank you for being the safest middle ground in our family: You manage to make us laugh when we are fighting, you manage to curb the tears with embraces instead, you relieve us of the heaviness when it is so desperately needed with comic relief, or with hugs, or just with your steady, quiet words and wisdom. Thank you, my love.

As we sat there at the edge of my parent's bed, I shook my head. No, this wasn't to let them know, "by the way I had sex even though I said I would wait but I never really thought it through, and I was young and…" this was not that.

It was uglier than a funeral for me.

I broke my foot in the tenth grade while I was dancing, in the last two minutes of class. I just had to go across the floor one more time. I remember hearing the crack of bone, the split as I landed full force on my metatarsal. It felt like someone had just sliced off my foot.

It was intense, then dull. It was sharp as a knife, then steady like a bee sting.

This feeling is exactly how it felt to tell my parent's that their daughter was sexually attacked. It felt like my whole body was caving in on me all at once, like I was dreaming in some nightmarish reality that would surely fade by morning. It cut sharp, then evened out to a hollow pain that never went away. It was a thousand broken foots.

My mom was wailing now.

"My baby," she was screaming. It was agonizing, the way she sobbed so hysterically. "My baby was raped!"

It was ugly.

My dad was yelling at her to calm down now, telling her to get it together for my sake.

I began to sob as my sister-the middle ground-held me.

"I will fall apart later," my dad said, "but right now I need to know exactly what happened."

My father, our rock, warrior, and leader, but also teddy bear, guardian, and biggest cheerleader...had just looked me in the eyes and told me he would fall apart.

I wondered when and if a tomorrow would ever even come.

My mother went into the bathroom.

My father grabbed my hands.

"When?"

Next, came the "who."

Also: "where" "how"

"did he penetrate?"

I grimaced.

Discomfort, pain, more discomfort...a moment I wanted to crawl outside of and be right on my way.

No script for this.

"Do you know his name?"

Yes.

His name is...

Chapter Fourteen

So, Now You Know...

It was ugly. There was no good way to do it. It was the hardest thing I have ever had to do. I think. It drained the life out of me.

Whitman writes in his poem "To You", "None has understood you, but I understand you. None has done justice to you; you have not done justice to yourself..."

None had done justice to me. How could they when they were calling me a liar? Do you think I wanted this? Do you think my mother planned this for her daughter when she was just born?

I didn't ask for this, justice sought but never reached, my story never fully heard nor fully told. None had done justice to me, but I had not done justice to myself. I have the power, now.

And when I told my parent's, I realized that no one could understand me like them.

The more we talk, the more we listen.

The more we see each other, the more I really see you, and I really see me.

"None has understood you, but I understand you."

Salma Hayek wrote a New York Times article about Harvey Weinstein's abuse titled "Harvey is my Monster Too." One of her lines reads, "I had brainwashed myself into thinking, that it was over and that I had survived; I hid from the responsibility to speak out... in reality, I was trying to save myself the challenge of explaining several things to my loved ones."

If a famous actress like Hayek felt this way, imagine how my nineteen-year-old self really felt when it came to facing my family?

My mother told me later that it all seemed to make sense now. The days I spent sleeping in so late, oversleeping for classes, the mood changes. She said she should have known, but I feared she would blame herself. How could you have known mama? We held on to each other for so long...

That day broke me.

I always thought maybe this was an event I would tell my parents about ten years from now, when I had children. A memory I would reveal to my big sister over coffee when we were both near thirty. But the time had come sooner than I thought, even though deep in my core it was long overdue.

I had wanted my parents to see that I was okay now that time had passed, and I was doing "great." I thought that by waiting it out, I could figure life out on my own, handle it myself. That was my mistake so many times in life, the idea that I could take care of it. "I got it handled," I used to say, "I got this." But I didn't have this.

So now you know. I wish I could shout his name from the rooftops, but for this book I must emit it. He was a friend of a friend, I know his first name, last name, and nickname.

I want you to know. But he might sue me...my rapist would have grounds to sue, how backwards. All I know is that I figured his right to privacy is as important as mine. And since he disturbed and disvalued and dismembered my right that night, then shouldn't I be able to forgo his?

Fast forward a year and a half later and I am sitting here finishing Chanel Miller's "Know My Name" memoir over Christmas break, and the themes of redemption but also agony have pulsated through my Holiday with complete reality. Our stories a line eerily, but I am sure so do many other stories of survivors.

And yet, one vastly gaping difference: everyone knows Brock Turner's name and associates it with a horrific crime, but nobody knows ****** ****** is a rapist.

All I know of his past is that his father died, and he posts a lot of pictures with girls and beer. He is a college drop out. So perhaps I am the one that should feel sorry for him, because he is nobody. He is nothing. And I am everything that my future promises me. I don't empathize with my rapist. Instead I choose to see the bigger picture, so that I may remain strong. I can see the bigger picture long enough to see that he doesn't have a fraction of the life I was blessed with, or the life I strive towards. He will die one day, having lived his life out holding on to that beer can that he is posing in photos with.

Right now, this is how I feel:

"To my rapist.

Go die.

Thanks to you I will always be the one that "had it happen to her too."

Fuck you."

That is how I am feeling tonight.

It is hard to take my memory way back. I have spent so much time and effort taking myself back to that place just so I can conquer it. It is hardly fair for those that survive, because we do so by going back to that place. We must, or else we will bury it, and it will come clawing back at us when we least expect, resurfacing in the light at all the wrong times.

It is true that even through facing our biggest enemy, it will still haunt us, but how we handle it is what saves lives. I was determined to be healed not haunted.

Looking back now, I see my direct reasoning for waiting to tell my parents, and dear readers, if you have found yourself where I was, please know you did the best you could.

People don't speak up for a slew of reasons, the most primary one being "they will not believe me."

"It cannot be proved."

"Nothing will happen to him."

"People will call me a liar or a slut."

"My parents will be devastated."

"I will be looked at as damaged goods."

"Guys will see me as the girl who got raped."

Mine was two-fold:

First, my parents will never look at me the same way. I will no longer be their precious, innocent daughter. Will they see me as damaged or ruined? Will they fear for me all the time now? They will see me differently from here on out.

Second, it is horrible timing. My parents will want me to report it and press charges and go to court. I don't have time for this. I'm moving away to Pittsburgh. And what if they are so paranoid for my safety, that they make me move back in with them and stay here? Irrational and unfounded but completely valid, and just a small part of our daily world as victims and survivors.

But those were my two fears. I didn't want to devastate my parents, I wanted to protect them. I wanted to take this on myself. I could handle it.

I was moving away in August, transferring colleges in a plan that had been set in motion since the previous year. What if they called it off and made me stay?

I wrote in my journal the next month in May:

"I am afraid. Afraid of my past coming to light, afraid of people viewing me differently, afraid of what will come of my future. I am afraid of finding myself in dangerously familiar circumstances again, I am afraid of people, I am afraid of being alone. I am fearful of the hurt, fearful for my safety and my sanity. I am afraid that I do not fully understand what I deserve and scared that if or when I experience a normal sort of love, I will have the burden of telling him what happened to me."

This is just a small glimpse into my mind, my brain reeling. My first instinct was to draw back, to hide from others, to take it on myself.

I underestimated my parents. Many storms have weathered them, but never prevailed. They are the most beautiful, rare and real humans I have ever encountered, overflowing in love, abounding in grace, much like the God I have come to believe more and more in. There was no way for me to guess their reaction and that is the hardest part.

How hard will this be, how bad will this go? How long will the bad last? Withholding my truth came from fear and shame, two ugly identifications that I never should have claimed as mine. It was not my fault, but I carried the weight of it as if it was.

There are many unspoken things in this world that call for this sort of secret shame, and most have absolutely nothing to do with the person feeling these emotions.

Shame from unwanted touch.

Shame of a young pregnancy.

Guilt from verbal and physical abuse.

Fear of coming out to family and friends.

The facts are this:

The person who yells in your face holds a loose-tempered anger that isn't your fault.

The family who is so quick to turn their back on you harbors judgments of their own.

The ones that are quick to shut you out, are the most unstable themselves.

The person who takes from you what you never gave them… they are sick in the head, and they are at fault not you.

The pathetic person who uses their words to batter you has a mountain of their own insecurities that they project onto you.

The person who uses intimidation and abuse of power, is inwardly the weakest.

The family member that ripped away your sense of safety and security and left you powerless, does not hold that power over you now.

These unspokens are from faults of others not ours. Yet they warrant shame and guilt as if we are the ones who got away with murder and still have a conscious.

Well, guess what? I didn't wake up and decide I wanted to kill a part of someone today. So why am I walking around, head down, as if I have done it? I didn't ask for this. I didn't choose this. I didn't plan this out on a calendar. I didn't lie about this as some sort of sick ploy for attention.

I didn't say "I can handle this world!" because no one is naturally built to withstand such an ugly thing as this, but we do it anyways.

I have known plenty of human superheroes. Two of them are mom and dad.

I had not realized that for all the healing I had tried to do in the past year for myself, for my parents, it was as if the assault had just occurred. The news was brand new and fresh and raw and rearing its ugly head. They would have their own journey to go on.

This was a Wednesday, and on that Saturday, I stood with my mother at the end of the driveway, car loaded, preparing to get in. I had collected the rest of my things and boxed them up in the jeep trunk to head back to my apartment.

I do not want to leave them, I kept thinking. I cannot leave them now.

My mom and I held on to each other for as long as we could, just standing there, clinging to each other. The safest space I have known is in the arms of the one who was the first in the world to hold me.

"I'm okay mommy," I remember telling her as we peeled away from each other. "Please don't cry. Everything is going to be okay."

It took my mother a few months to come back to life. She told me later that it was hard for her to get out of bed sometimes. Her and my dad started seeing a therapist who specialized in sexual assaults or family's dealing with it. She told them to take their cues from me. I wondered why they stopped asking questions, and I realized it was because their therapist had told them to tread lightly, to leave it up to me.

I remember a month had gone by and it was around my birthday in September. I realized that my parents had not really checked in on me in the ways I thought they might. I had not received many questions lately. I worried...had I done something wrong?

They were taking careful, precautious steps, waiting for me to light the way. They were doing the right thing any good parent would: being patient with me, being patient with time. But I wanted them to know, I wanted them to ask. I wanted them to see how far I had come. It was almost like I was trying to reassure them so much that it reassured my own aching heart in the process. I figured...if it was all out in the open now, could we not talk about it? I craved someone to see me and hear me and validate me. I was so used to having to explain myself over someone else's crime. But with my parents, there was no explaining necessary, just comfort, much needed, much overdue comfort.

I must admit even now it is very hard to bring it up to my parents and we have not talked about it in a little while.

I remember the feeling of pulling my white Jeep liberty out of the driveway and watching my mother disappear in my rearview mirror, the driveway diminishing into a speck.

I felt every burden had just been released off my shoulders. The night of my nightmares was out in the open, and I now had an army of support within my most treasured humans: my mommy, my daddy, and my sissy Lo. The secrets had gone to die, this was who I was, this was their daughter. And they held me and soothed me and told me they would always be there.

But deep down I knew there would be pain, because in telling the truth there is always some pain that snakes its way along into life. And the months ahead would be long and tumultuous and gray. But we would come out on the other side.

Once the crying had stopped, I told my parents I wanted to read them what I could manage to choke out from the notes section on my phone. As I drove the four hours back to my job and back to school which would be starting in a few weeks, those words filled my lungs with life and made me strong.

In my notes section on my phone, I had put the title "glory came from nothing."

Dear mom and dad:

Now over a year later, I can speak these things out loud because I no longer feel the sort of stigmatized shame that comes with sexual assault. The embarrassment is not mine to have.

my friend's sister was raped. By more than one guy.

my roommate was raped. And molested as a kid.

Elle's dad sexually abused her, and her mom passed away without ever knowing.

This crime happens to Guys and girls alike, and yes, I am one of them but that does not make me a victim or a statistic.

I am not a percentage or another number. I am proof of an epidemic of rape culture in our society, I am a survivor of assault, I am strong, I am brave, and I am not limited to my past and the things that have happened to me.

God has graced me with forgiveness, the impossible forgiveness he showed us, the kind of forgiveness I am trying even to this day to still feel for that drunk kid at the University of Dayton that I wish I had never met. I also know that he will forever remember that girl Sophia.

I read in Ecclesiastes the other day
On a good day enjoy yourself
On a bad day examine your conscience
God arranges for both kinds of days
So that we won't take anything for granted
Whatever happens, happens.
It's destiny is fixed
You cannot argue with fate

I also read this in Jeremiah:
'I was ashamed of my past, my wild unruly past
Will I ever live this down?
God says I'll refresh tired bodies
I'll restore tired souls.

I am telling you this because it is a part of me whether I want it to be or not, it is now a part of me. And I will fight for others and for myself.

I learned a hard lesson on safety, it will forever be with, what happened. But through seeking safety and comfort and wisdom in my closest friends, my therapist, and most recently, Lauren, I realized I am not alone nor could I ever carry around an unnecessary shame that is not mine to carry. That is his.

And I will continue to speak up and fight for women, and to have faith that God intends to prosper me if I keep my eyes on him.

Lastly I read this in Psalms:

'God's love is meteoric
His loyalty astronomic
His purpose titanic
His verdicts Oceanic
Yet in his largeness
Nothing gets lost

Not a man not a mouse
Slips through the cracks.'

So I know I haven't I slipped through the cracks. And I don't know why fathers die from cancer or college students get assaulted I don't know why terrible things happen but I know that I've survived everything I've seen and done, only by God's hand and I know the bad is not by His doing but by the worlds. Because nothing in the world is good but everything is good in God. I have learned to look past my pain, to look past a mortal world where everyone will let you down and we will always fall short. But I know that God promises us something far more beautiful, and I hold on to that and that is what continues to help me heal.

So now you know…

Chapter Fifteen

Even If You Were Dancing Naked on A Table

My therapist used a phrase quite often and familiarly, it is called "taking your power back." Thoughts of "taking my power back" produced actions that became my saving grace.In therapy, I met my match: a lesson in relinquishing the blame.

My therapist used to tell me, "even if you were naked and dancing on top of a table, that still gave him no right…" I think she repeated it every session, but each time it felt like I was hearing it for the first time.

You mean I wasn't asking for it even if I had been drinking tequila?

I never drank tequila again. The salty ocean water smell made me gag, to me it smelled like that night.

You mean I had not been asking for it even if…

This knowledge, though so obvious one might think, came to me with total disbelief. Because as classic victim blaming goes, we somehow always find something wrong with US. I must have done something wrong; I should not have gone out that night, I should not have been drinking, I should not have kissed him. I was asking for it, asking for it, asking for it. I say bullshit. Nobody asks to be raped. What kind of sickening culture have we been born into? To think that somehow, this could even be an ounce of our fault.

Rapists are rapists. Whatever made them this way: an f-ed up childhood or an f-ed-up society where the odds are automatically against us women, I don't know, and I don't care. Because no normal, respectable person wakes up in the morning saying, "today I am going to assault someone."

And no girl or boy or young woman or young man wakes up thinking, tonight is the night something horrific will happen to me, because someone will prey on me because they think I am vulnerable.

It isn't my fault; it isn't your fault. It is no one's fault but his. The blame is his, not mine to carry. The shame is his, not mine, to carry.

I saw him again after that night. Two more times in fact and then never again. I showed up to a Cinco de Mayo party unknowingly coming face to face with my very own nightmare. Since he was a friend of friends, he was at the house that night.

It instantly revived within me all feelings of panic and anger. Bethesda does not cry. She cried that night. She held me as I cried in the driveway. Seething, we latched on to one another and she whispered to me through gritted teeth, "I want to kill him."

What do you do when the one who hardly ever cries, is crying for you? My heart was breaking into little tiny pieces of shattered glass. I kept thinking about how I wanted to erase all of this and 'unlive' it.

"Come on let's go," she grabbed onto me, nudging me towards where our car was parked down the road.

"Okay," I stumbled through my words as she ushered me down the sloped driveway.

"Sophia, Sophia!" someone was calling after me.

It was Harris' younger brother Harvard.

"No, no, no," I whispered to B, shaking my head. "I don't wanna talk to him…"

He couldn't see me like this.

"Get in the car," Bethesda instructed me, unlocking it.

"I'll handle it," she reassured me, as I sat in the driver's seat of her Toyota. "you just stay here."

I nodded like a lost puppy, nose red and eyes puffy.

Harvard was jogging now.

"Bethesda what's going on?" he looked at her with concerned, wide eyes.

"It's not my story to tell," she shook her head with defiance, biting back the tears.

"Is she okay?" I could hear him asking on the outside of the car. I refused to make eye contact.

One look at my face said I was not. I was nowhere near okay.

"Sophia talk to me," he was imploring as I hung my head.

I don't remember saying anything. I just remember opening the car door and the next thing I knew he was holding on to me as I cried, telling me it was going to be alright although he had no idea why I was crying or who or what had even made me cry. He didn't realize that he was offering me false reassurances. That my attacker was in fact his older sister's fiancé's family friend from way back (did you follow that one? basically a cousin of a cousin's step-cousin's cousin…and he was still protecting him).

Those deeply rooted ties would cause Harvard to turn his back on me, to raise a finger, and ask "well what did you do wrong?"

Classic. Blaming. At. Its. Best: "maybe it was you."

"I'll take care of it," Harvard told me once I explained to him in brief detail what had happened to me, two months prior.

My curiosity got the best of me and I remember following him to see what he was going to do.

I crouched in the pitch-black darkness behind some bushes as he pulled the guy out of the back door onto the driveway.

"Do you know a girl named Sophia?" he prefaced the conversation. "Who? No…"

Strike one thousand.

Harvard came back to me. "He says he doesn't know you."

"Really?" I had proof. "Show him this."

I handed H my phone, where I had pulled up a picture of the two of us together that I had taken with him at the bar. We were not SERIOUSLY debating whether he knew me or not. He not only knew me, but he had done this to me.

Harvard came back.

"He said you guys just kissed and that's it. He remembers girls he had sex with."

That's good, I thought, because it was not sex, it was rape. And I was a virgin. That was not what I wanted. I didn't want him. No way.

"It wasn't sex. That's not what that was."

Meanwhile Bethesda returned to the car with her older sister Menna, who she had retrieved from inside the house.

"Sophia you know how you can get," he was saying now, his tone flat lined and growing condescending.

"I know what?" I seethed.

Any bit of his empathy-if there ever was some in the first place-had been erased by a society that would never side with me.

"Whoa, Harvard!" Bethesda glared at him, shocked. "What is wrong with you?"

"I'm just saying you know how flirtatious you can be when you're drunk," he shrugged, shaking his head.

B led me away. "Okay, we're leaving. We're not going to sit here and reason with crazy."

I was crying more now.

"Look, I kicked him out," Harvard told me, as if that made it any better.

Except for what Lewis would later tell me. As soon as I left, Harvard told my attacker that he could come back. I believe firmly that you are the company that you keep, you are the people whom you choose to protect.

This was the night that Lewis found out as well. He said he pieced it all together himself, overheard Harvard talking, saw me slip out of the house crying. But what did he ever do?

This was a night that I fell apart.

One by one, I watched the numbers dwindle, as friends let me down and humanity disgusted and disappointed me. My group of supporters I could count on one hand. You really get to learn a person in the dark hours.

This was a night that my best friend saved me. She saved me. Got me out of there and took me home, let me lay on her chest because I could not sleep. Her older sister Menna reassured me the whole ride home, "you did nothing wrong Sophia." I knew this in my heart, but my mind was reeling, never quite ingesting this critical bit of information, always repelling away from it.

These two women were two of my sisters not bound by blood but by choice.

Bethesda brought me back every time to the place that no guy ever could: to safety, to trust, to patience, to ease.

I saw him again. I sought him out.

I saw him at the bar one summer night in June.

I approached him with a small smile, to get him to acknowledge who I was. I wanted him to think I was just another girl, interested in him. I wanted him to notice, to see me.

He looked up from his group of friends and eyed me curiously.

"Hi," I said politely.

He recognized me; I could see it in his eyes. "Hey," he said.

The only way I can describe the expression on his face was in his eyes.

It was smug. It was invasive. It was hungry. His gaze was silently saying, "so you remember me huh? I remember you."

And then I reared my fist back and I punched him square in the nose.

"What the hell!" he was screaming as I made a quick get away into the crowd.

Bethesda was behind me the whole time.

"Get me out of here," I told her after, "I want to go home."

"I'm so proud of you Sophia," she continuously reassured me, "how did it feel?"

"Like everything I've been wanting to do these past few months," I was shaking, "my hand doesn't even hurt." I felt nothing but chest, pounding. Really, I wanted to do more, so much more.

And I did. I figured out where he would be, and with two cars full of my guy friends, I drove to that place.

Looking back now, this was either incredibly dumb or incredibly brave, or a good amount of both, but either way I did the one thing many girls/women/men/boys will never have their day for: Coming to face to face with their attackers.

If that is the case, or if you are like me and you never got the public justice you so deserved, then take heart in knowing this: Judgment befalls us all, whether in life or in death, and a day will come.

Well, I followed him back to the house that Harris and a few of his roommates were renting. I knew I would find him there, but I didn't know what I would find there.

The night proceeds me as a blur. Blacked out in anger, heart pounding in pain. A lot of yelling.

I don't like to talk about this part.

The part where I found myself in the same room as my rapist, but this time because I had chosen to be in the room. He would listen, I would make him admit it, I kept telling myself.

We went with the intentions of having my slough of guy friends beat him up. When they heard that he was there in the club that night, they immediately asked me where he was, they would talk to him on my behalf. They would make the difference; they would throw a swing or two, put him in his place. But I knew that he had already left the bar before I could even spread the word that he was in the same vicinity as us. My gut told me that he had to be at the one place everybody went to on a Saturday night in the summer: Harris's house. It was instinctual and unfounded but turned out to be true. My rapist was indeed in the company of my very own "friends."

My male friends told me to wait in the car. I didn't. Maybe I should have.

There were so many of us, I felt like maybe for once I had a shot in the dark at justice. It was as if my male friends were an army, marching up to that front door with defiance. I kept thinking: Thank God, someone has my back. Maybe the world is not entirely bad as I have been led to believe. Maybe there really still are people in my corner.

I feel so bad for her, that girl sitting in the backseat wondering what is going on inside the house. I can't believe sometimes that she is me. I want to pick her up, I want to scoop her away. I want to tell her not to get out of the car, or perhaps not to find herself in that car to begin with. But everything in the story has unfolded the way it was meant to, whether or not I can truly understand.

Well, she did it. That girl got out of the car, because she was brave, because she was stubborn, and because she would never be told to sit on the sidelines, to hang back. Because she wasn't afraid of what was waiting behind that door.

I remember it like it was yesterday, quietly letting myself into the house, tiptoeing through the entryway and hiding in the shadows. I had been inside of this house so many times, except this time felt achingly unfamiliar. I was standing around the corner from the kitchen, listening to the conversation happening on the other side of the wall.

My friend Tony kept asking him. He kept denying. He said, "why does this girl keep saying this about me? I don't even know her."

That was when I came out from behind the wall.

I should have stayed in the car.

They had to hold me back; nobody has ever had to hold me back like that before. I wish they didn't touch me; I wish that they had let me go, unleashed the wrath. I wish they had let me swing again and again, fist contacting his nose, or maybe an area much lower.

I wish that they didn't yank me away like I was some unhinged, incapable psychopath.

"You don't know me?" I kept screaming. "I know what your dick looks like. I know what it looks like, you motherfucker!"

You might begin to see why I wanted to forget all of this for so long. I was looking at him in the eyes, telling him to confess to a room full of people, my army of support standing beside me but so stunned that they didn't know what to do.

Everything was black, everything was blurred. I don't remember who was standing where or what the looks on everyone's faces were besides shock. Bethesda might have been crying, but I can't remember. Mouths hung agape but everyone's faces are a shadow to me now. Some people excused themselves from the room, I think someone suggested that we take it outside.

I don't need to remember; I don't think it's important. I think the important part is that I got in the car to begin with, and then I got out of the car, and who in the hell does that? Who faces their gutless, lying abuser with not a damn given? I am not sure that I can even truthfully say that I would do it again, because I do not know what I would do nowadays. It was as if something had completely possessed me and taken over, like a fire ignited. Sometimes, I surprise even myself.

Somewhere between the cops being called because of a neighborly noise complaint, and me screaming at the top of my lungs and throwing glass beer bottles, I remember saying the last thing I will ever say to my rapist: "I hope one day you have a daughter, and that you pray to god she never meets someone like you. And that when you go to sleep at night, you see my face. And I hope you fucking live with that."

The cops showed up. I should have said something. Only two months had gone by, maybe they would have done something? Maybe they would have done nothing...

A friend walked down to the edge of the drive where two cop cars sat: Everything was okay. Just some heightened boyfriend girlfriend fighting. All settled now. I watched at the window. He wasn't a friend after all.

The cops drove away. There goes my chance. Maybe I never had a chance.

One of Harris's roommates, Gordon, chased everyone out with a knife, told everyone to get the hell out. It was chaos at its finest. Me yelling and the girls that were there sitting around the table, confused and trying to figure out what had happened here.

Trust me, I am still trying to figure that out.

We have never spoken of that night again, not one of us, not even the people I am still friends that told me to wait in the car. Did we forget or did we just pretend?

I never told my therapist those stories in their entirety. I did tell her I saw him at a club and punched him and she said, "I'm proud of you. That's a prime example of you taking back your power." A world where boys rape girls and girls punch boys is a world I would much rather not live in.

I am left sitting here, thinking about what changed.

Two cups of decaf tea and my hands are still shaking. I went drinking last night. Not because I needed to, maybe I just wanted to have fun. Maybe my anxiety is back, and I wanted to escape it, to laugh. Either way, it was not worth it. I didn't need to fall back again.

And so, I am sitting here now,

Thinking about what changed.

What has not changed

What never should have changed

What still needs changed.

Change…as certain as death and taxes.

I am sitting here thinking about change and why I can't seem to forget although I want to. I want to forget, I want to erase those months of turmoil, the choices that I can't seem to make sense of. Because no one can ever make sense of anything traumatic. What happens after trauma is collateral damage of the actual thing, and I suppose for that reason I can't blame myself one bit.

Perhaps I find strength in reminding myself that I don't have the luxury of lying to myself, of forgetting. Because like it or not-and I hate it-this is apart of my story. It does not define me, but instead has sculpted and molded and cracked me and bent me. I can't forget.

There is an unrelenting strength that comes in sharing your story, and Tracy my therapist did me a world of good. On most days, I realized I was doing all the talking, and she was just sitting there looking at me. I would call my mother, frustrated, "why isn't she doing her job?" But she was.

"Why isn't she giving me advice?"

"She just looks at me and asks me "how does that make you feel?" or "I don't know Sophia, what do you think about that?"

I didn't realize that she was giving me the most important skill and job in the entire world: Having a voice and using it. She was making me answer my own questions, she was making me validate my own self, my own opinions, my own spoken words. The point was not for her to give me all the answers, I already had those deep down inside of myself. But I was not asking the right questions to myself. In fact, not only was I lacking in questions, but I was not even having a conversation with myself.

I had shut down and shut off, and she gave me power in being able to speak and share. She assisted me in releasing the inhibiting shame that comes with assault, the shame that prevents so many of us from talking about it. Just like childhood abuse, there is shame in this, the "maybe I have done something wrong."

It silences us into never saying a word, burying the thing that is quite possibly too heavy for any one single human to bear on their own.

Before therapy, I could not even utter the "R" word or say it happened to me, too.

Therapy gave me a safe space to speak, but then suddenly it was not enough. There was a need to speak that brewed up from inside of me, and when I felt that need to speak up, it never went away.

As the days pass, people have come to know more. It is no longer something I hide, but rather a scar that I present to the public and say "Look: This is what makes me, me."

When I acknowledge my own Goliath, it is my way of stating: "The girl that you are friends with, is dealing with this. The girl that you exist with, also exists with this."

If the humans that I choose to surround myself with, can't handle the truth of my past, then they can't handle me. If I can't entrust this information to them, then what can I trust them with?

If I find myself around people that make tasteless rape jokes without a second thought, then why am I even with them in the first place?

I notice more. I listen more. I see more and I discern more.

Speaking up has furthered my support system even more than I could have ever dreamed. Friendships died but then better friendships were birthed, trees were planted, flowers bloomed despite frost. Fellow classmates have me sought me out and said, "let's get coffee. I had the same thing happen to me."

The same thing happened to me in high school.

The same thing happened to me when I was in eighth grade.

The same thing happened to me when I was a little girl.

The same thing happened to me with my boyfriend.

And suddenly, puzzle pieces began to fall into place, and my story coincided with so many other females, and we felt safe with each other. We found solace in the sharing of stories, in the validating of truth, in the vulnerability of saying, "your story is so different than mine, but so alike. I believe you and I will protect what you have to say.

It then became our job to turn a society upside down that raised boys and men that were capable of this. There is strength in numbers, but also a great sadness.Grieving is easier to handle with company, but why must we grieve at all? Why did this have to happen at all?

It is a most melancholy feeling to be understood. Thankfully, it has made me feel accepted and assured. But I wish that rather, no one would have to understand. I wish none of it existed in the first place. I wish you didn't have to relate to me in the way that you do.

Sometimes, I wish it had only happened to me, I tell myself I can take it, I am strong, I can be the martyr. But her too? And her, and her, and him too? I am so grateful for people that understand out of experience, but I wish they didn't. I wish they had never had to go through it at all. The world is a sad place, a fallen place, but there is hope.

As the years have gone on, I have grown insurmountably. I have formed relationships in which I am able to say, "can you look at me for who I am, can you handle this?"

It has birthed more authentic, deeper, soulful relationships. We connect on a deeper level, sometimes from a place not many can go to with us. We have the ability to cut through the b.s. and really see each other.

Most recently, my best friend Jordan and I have decided to start our brand new 2020 off with this singular phrase, "and I'm okay with that." We got it from a tv show jokingly, but now we often postface our thoughts with "…and I'm okay with that."

But what do you do when you are not okay with what has gone down, not at peace with your own very pertinent thoughts? Maybe this is quite possibly the only part of my life where I can look evenly at myself, and say, "I am not okay with this."

This challenges my willpower, turns me towards my very own strength, and forces me to say, "so what will you do now?"

Chapter Sixteen

Our Eyes Were Closed

Walt Whitman once said: "my voice goes after what my eyes cannot reach."

In the years that followed from my assault, I could feel myself stumbling through life with eyes closed. That is, until, I found ray of light after ray of light that forced me, for the first time, to really see.

I wrote in my journal on April 12, 2017:

"Pain has the potential to ruin lives. It is pain that turns morning into night, brightness into black. Pain sucks you in and spits you out. It forces you to close your eyes, it covers your mouth, and throws you into deeply uncharted waters. It teaches you in this bottomless existence, how to either swim or how to drown. I do not want to sink. I do not want to lay here in darkness, grasping for a light that never comes, or a dawn that never rises, or a hope that I set out to find but never do. The good thing about pain is what it teaches you. It may take all the air out of your lungs, but it does not last forever. You will not stay stuck down there forever."

In my junior year of college, I was awarded something I thought to be so intangible, untouchable, mythical almost…it was this: complete, unending, limitless acceptance.

I was understudying for a show during our Fall semester and every night Tuesday through Friday we spent rehearsing the fifteen minutes of J*A*Z*Z* dance. Our professor of dance//rehearsal director, Mark, had a social experiment he was known for: The infamous "character study." Those who wanted to participate could and those who didn't want to, could abstain. We were sent a list of questions and had to answer them from a place that was either completely vulnerable or totally unlike ourselves. The upsides of playing a "character" were that you could still be yourself or every bit the opposite, just give it a fake name.

Mine was Mercedes, and the slogan I lived by was "the best or nothing" which is Mercedes Benz famous line. Some characters were completely unlike themselves, and others were playing the character of their most pure, vulnerable self. Many tears were shed, and I had never experienced an "experiment" like this.

Well, I got up, with a planned script in mind.

We had to answer a select set of questions, here are a few:

I am the one who…survived.

My greatest strength is…compassion.

My greatest weakness is…compassion.

Slowly, I veered off script, as life tends to do to us.

Before I knew it, I was sitting crisscross legged in front of my peers, swiping away at the tears that started to fall.

"On the outside I appear confident but really…" is all I remember saying. The rest was totally improvisational, and probably the rawest any of my classmates and colleagues had ever seen me.

Sometimes, you just sort of black out and start saying the first thing that comes to mind, and there I was, saying every first thing as it came.

We were a room of tears and choking back sobs, coughing on the mucus, our hands found others. I was emboldened and made brave by classmates who had no idea about who I truly was. They made me strong, their quiet acceptance, their nodding me on while I stumbled through my words. I felt, for once, safety in my truth and in numbers.

There is power here, I kept thinking. There is much power here in the ones who speak and the ones who are willing enough to listen.

Artists have power, I thought to myself.

In silence, lies much ignorance. Ignorance that our country runs rampant with and that we need to fight with guns blazing, to combat daily and desperately.

But in that safe guarded room that night, I felt completely whole, welcomed into a group of people who knew little about my innermost parts. We were observant and open-minded, and I couldn't help but think how the world needs a lot more of that.

Again, I insert another Hayek quote from her NYT article: "But why do so many of us, as female artists, have to go to war to tell our stories when we have so much to offer? Why do we have to fight tooth and nail to maintain our dignity?"

Our eyes were closed as we sat in the circle that night, tears silently streaming down our cheeks. We were closing out our character studies with a reflection back on each character we had "met" that night.

My teacher yelled out "next we meet Mercedes character, a sassy life force with a story of her own" and asked everyone, with eyes remaining closed, to yell out words that they felt about "Mercedes". Words they felt about me. Me.

So brave.

Beautiful.

Me too.

Alive.

Real.

Honest.

I'm in awe

So incredibly amazing

A force

A powerful woman

Stunning

Strong

I could feel the silent stream of tears coursing down my cheeks. It was the first time someone in the same room as I had said "me too" and without sharing a single word, we had shared everything. It was the first time that I heard the voice of men telling me I was strong and powerful and brave. I didn't need validation anymore. I had grown too much and come too far. But it was all the words I had never heard before, from friends that had let me down and boys that had walked away.

These words had the sanctifying power to wash over all the words I had agonized over hearing after that night, the words calling me a liar or a flirt. The fingers pointing at me, never at him. These words were like a lone traveler's first meal in a long time. My spirit was completely and utterly fed and full, brimming, overflowing.

And I cried.

Our eyes were closed, and our hearts were open.

Chapter Seventeen

Not Even a Safety Pin Could Have Saved Me

It is true, perhaps, if you were to ask me what I was wearing on that night that I might be able to pin it down to the exact detail, literally.

I had safety pinned my top together in the middle because it cut too low. My efforts at shielding any cleavage that might have been "too much" in photographs, didn't shield me for a night ingrained so deeply in my memory. It punctured a wound so deep in my consciousness, that I am writing about it on Christmas Eve.

Why was I, that next morning, in my brand-new floral blouse, the one that felt she was wearing damp clothes covered in mud clinging to her bones? Why was I the one that gave that entire outfit away to Goodwill as fast as I could run? I can peg down to the last detail the jeans I wore, the black boots, the shirt, the way my long hair was curled. I remembered which matte lipstick I was wearing. I had fake eyelashes on. But to this day, and trust me I remember every damned thing, I can only remember his jeans. His pants appear to me quite clearly, his face I make fade with time, but other than that I only remember what he did and what I was thinking. These words remain fresh in my mind, words scrambling and racing, plotting my escape, calculating how could I get out. If someone were to ask me how I remember my answer would be quite elementary. I remember because it is the one thing I can't forget. And I forget mostly everything else earlier in that night, the events that came before...but I do remember how happy choosing that outfit had made me, and how pretty I had felt. I remember how ugly I felt just a few hours later, and the rebuilding that has taken years. The one thing I didn't pick out of my closet and chose for that night, is the one thing that hangs on. Like an ugly sweater you can't manage to get rid of, my ugly sweater is one I didn't buy, but it hangs in the guest closet still. It remains untouched in the back, moths nibbling away at it, puncturing holes in the sleeves. But still, the shredded fabric remains.

When victims of sexual assault take a seat in court, they often get asked what they were wearing. But how many times have people pointed at a rapist and asked them "can you please explain your outfit from the night in questioning, in detail? Don't leave out a sock." That would be the day.

I remembered how I had safety pinned that top because it was just a little "too much" for me, but that didn't save me. The pictures that I would have to quickly delete off my phone because they were too painful to look at because they were separated on my "before and after" timeline.

I realize that there was nothing I could have really done except for what I managed to do: escape. I told my rapist to go get a condom mid-way through, because I knew it was my way out of the bathroom.

His bedroom was up in the attic, and we were cornered in the black and white tiled bathroom off the kitchen. I thought that if he went upstairs to "get a condom" that would give me enough time to scramble out and through the back door and that was exactly what I did.

I understand that flight or fight instincts have been studied, but to this day, I don't know what my reactions would be considered as.

When he took the bait and let me go, I ran, never looking back.

For a while I just kept running, refusing to turn around. Now I can finally say I have faced these demons because I want the best possible life for myself. And I can't have that if I am still running to this day.

Don't you get it? I finally told myself after one therapy session chalk full of light bulb moments.

You could have been wearing anything, doing anything, nobody had PERMISSION to rape you. People walk around in their swimsuits all the time, that doesn't mean they're asking for it! Nobody had PERMISSION to invite themselves into your sacred space, to touch you or minimize you. You are a human, damn it!

I learn a little more and more every day. Sometimes the past is just a hard pill to swallow. But I am ever-changing, always evolving into the woman I know I am and see myself to be. I wrote in my journal one warm August day by the river, just seventeen days before my junior year of college:

SELF-FORGIVENESS.

My therapist had another common phrase that would forever stick to me: "secrets keep you sick." But I always thought they kept you safe.

I wrote on August 10, 2018:

"My greatest weakness was what I thought was my biggest strength: "I can handle anything alone." I am so hard on myself. Judgmental of my own mistakes. Ashamed of the ways I have coped- the mistakes I have made as a result of the wrongs done to me. I am my worst critic and have put countless expectations on myself. One year later, and I am okay, but I am still a work in progress. I am not perfect, I am working.

A horrible thing was done to me and there is no script on how to navigate through these things. I am proud of myself for the things I have been able to do of late-talk to a therapist, tell my parents, be open and honest and honest with myself. I am giving myself a chance.

Secrets do keep you sick. They fester, they grow like limitless vines, crawling through every crack in your body, until one day, you start to remember. They do not ever go away: the words we hide within ourselves, the memories we think we can bury. They always come back. But now I know better. A lot of the time, peace comes with conversation-the more I talk about it, the more I face it, the more I conquer it, the less it holds over me, the less it closes in on me. The less it keeps me sick. This week I heard a gentle whisper, 'forgive yourself.'"

I scrawled that down in my journal over a year and a half ago, and I think that very entry was the catalyst for another life. It was my start to a new beginning, to a life of shamelessness, a life where I would claim my story as mine and take my life back as mine and mine alone.

I have so much I want to do, places I want to go…these things he won't stop me from doing. I don't want to be stopped from the ability to chase after anything and everything I want.

To my rapist:
You took a part of me that night
but I built myself back tenfold.
You will steal from me no longer,
You will take nothing from me, with you.
I am wholly me, apart from you.

I visited the house. I didn't mention this prior to the completion of my book, so instead I went back and have inserted in it here because I feel it is important for you to know.

I don't know what I was looking for, what answers I hoped to find. I forgot about this part until I had already sent out copies of these pages to a few select friends, and finally my parents. But I am placing these words here, because they should not be forgotten, although they temporarily escaped my mind. I most importantly wanted to take down the address in case I would need it later, although I was not sure what for. I really wanted to know if he was still there, still here in this house…if he could still be tracked down and killed (okay, not killed, but you get the point.)

It was a place somewhere between hell and earth, and Medford and E Stewart Street. The little dingy white house on the corner glared back at me, mocking me with how unassuming it looked in broad daylight.

I pulled up and parked on the same side of the street, carefully studying the dingy front porch, the rickety screen door…peering in on a life so far past me. A kid I didn't recognize was smoking a cigarette on the front steps, thin white paper dangling from his lips.

He didn't see me watching him, but I knew that we didn't know each other.

Slowly, I got out of the car.

It was bright mid-day outside, right off campus. I clutched my pepper-spray at my side.

"Hey!" I called out from the street, maintaining the sidewalk and front lawn as distance between us. "You live here?"

I motioned behind him to the home I hoped might get struck by lightning or rendered condemned and torn down by a bulldozer.

"Yeah. You lookin' for someone?"

"Sort of."

I scrunched up my eyes, studying the stranger, summing him up, realizing that he had no idea where he lived, or what had been done here.

"Those guys moved out," he nodded, answering my question for me before I had even been able to open my mouth.

"Do you know when?"

"Just a few months ago actually, maybe sometime in May or June. My landlord had to kick them out."

"Kick em out?"

"Yeah, for the drugs, I think."

I remembered the coke in the attic, his bedroom with the squat ceilings and the Kanye poster. I remembered everything.

"Doesn't surprise me," I shook my head, attempting to appear nonchalant. "They were pretty wild."

"Yeah, you're telling me," he half-chuckled. "They really trashed the place before I got here."

He looked at me closely, "you havin' trouble getting ahold of them?"

"Yeah. They owe me money."

"Oh damn," his eyes widened. "I can give you my landlord's number?"

"Sure, that would be good, thanks," I smiled, still standing out in the street.

His bulldog was sleeping peacefully near the open front door. "Your dog is beautiful," I said.

"Thanks. Yeah, she's an old girl," he smiled kindly at me as I attempted to return the favor. He really didn't know.

Imagine that.

Imagine the things we unknowingly surround ourselves with, the homes and various places that we move into having no prior knowledge as to what acts occurred here. The unspeakable acts that happened in his bathroom off the kitchen. The attic that once housed my very own monster.

Imagine all the shadows we leave behind, and all the shadows we walk into, never knowing, never seeing or finding.

He read me the number out loud off his phone as I nodded with a thank you.

"I'll tell him to expect your call."

"Thanks again for the trouble."

"No problem," he shrugged it off, extinguishing his cigarette at his feet.

Inwardly, I thought the number sounded fake. It started with 333. I never called. I simply filed the digits away in the notes section of my phone next to all the other bits of information I had collected about that night—names, first and last, and addresses. Details I thought might help, but I was not sure what I was trying to help, since my cause seemed to be two years too late.

Regardless, I collected every piece I could. Maybe I was collecting for this very page you are reading now, but I never would have guessed it.

"Hey, listen, whatever these guys were into, they were pretty pathetic. Lame college drop-outs. I'm sorry they owe you money."

"Yeah, me too."

I let my eyes wander over the house one last time, mentally taking close notes of the house number and the layout, which was just as I remembered. Somewhere between the line of hell and earth lies house number 807.

As I climbed into the jeep, new memories dawned on me, reminders of the other boy who had lived there-the tall, brunette with a good smile, big brother All-American looking sort. His name was Maury.

I wish I never saw this house, ever.

I wish someone would repaint the dirty white that looked like chimney dust in the glaring sun.

I wanted to remember. I couldn't forget.

People would ask—or maybe no one would ever ask again—but my story would always be wholly the same.

I never lied. I didn't have to. In my few years on earth, I have learned that the truth has no versions. I had managed to fill in all the blanks over time, thinking that it might be of some shred of importance. The picture that I had formed was quite clear.

But, no safety pin to protect me, nothing to obscure me from this tiny crumbling white house on the corner.

I got in my jeep and drove away.

To whoever is reading this: Have you been where I have been?

Have you walked these lonely shores, have you felt at a loss for where to go next?

Have you found yourself at the front lawn of the house you never thought you would return to, or perhaps have never gone back at all?

I drove away. I left and I never went back.

So just remember, every step is a step forward.

You are moving, your wheels are grinding ahead, you are never stagnant, you have made it this far.

I know now that the fault is not mine; it is his and admitting that is a milestone in itself.

Every small insignificant roadblock we surpass as survivors is in fact a milestone that is larger than life.

Chapter Eighteen

I Can Wear What I Want

I like what I wear, when I wear it, and how I wear it.

I find myself growing incredibly defensive when my appearance gets called into question…mostly from my dad, who-even to this day-my mom says will never stop looking out for his daughter. "He doesn't mean it like that," she tells me reassuringly, "he's just your dad."

It is really very difficult to be a woman who was sexually assaulted and have a father who is your best friend. You don't tell your best friend everything, but you are typically transparent with them. It hurts me when I think about the knowledge that my father has of what happened to me, and what that must look like for a man who only has two daughters. He asks me, "when can I read it?" and I brush it off and say, "when it's in hard cover." Inwardly, I hurt.

My dad has always been so curious to read what I have written, sometimes he would even sneak peeks at my journals when I left them half open on the couch. I was so embarrassed when my parent's read my words, because each page scribbled in markings and edits were so deeply personal. But my mother and father loved everything I had to say. I am so thankful that they wanted to read and to hear.

I suppose I am just so very sorry that they must read this. Dad I know you are strong, because that is how you raised me to be.

It was Christmas eve 2019 when I felt especially triggered. I usually know that this is coming when the anger washes over me like a crashing wave, and I attribute it to being catapulted back to that place. Three years. 365 days times three and this still happens, and I presume it will for the rest of my life, which I have not particularly come to terms with yet. In my quiet anger, I am steady outwardly, but there is nothing steady about this storm. And this Christmas Eve, I was angry as hell.

I stood in the evening church service, feeling claustrophobic and caving in on myself.

My mom saw me. My mother is one of the few who truly sees me, and I consider her my angel on earth, my protector, my rock. She emboldens me. She whispered to me, "what's wrong?"

Everyone was singing and I was mentally gone. When she saw that absent look in my eyes, she took me outside to get air.

"Why did dad have to come for my outfit like that?" I muttered, as her and I stood outside in the cool breeze. "I am a grown adult."

I started to think of what men saw when they looked at me, and what my dad saw when he saw his precious daughter get sent out into a world that slammed her to the ground.

Something so insignificant as a protective dad looking at his *adult* daughter and saying "your skirt…" bothered the life out of me.

And while other people might look at their dads and just chuckle and say "Mike, I'm grown," I was annoyed.

My dad is a bit more traditional, and I thrive on the ever-changing aesthetics and trends of art and fashion, which combined have defined who I am.

So, I tell myself he doesn't get it; I think to myself, "I'm not fifteen anymore." I shrug it away.

But then I question if maybe I should draw some boundaries with him. Boundaries like "stop commenting on what I wear, I like what I wear" or maybe being transparently honest and saying, "these kinds of conversations take me back to a place I don't like."

I am an adult, and we are still doing this, my father and me.

160

I think him knowing what happened to me makes him worry more. I count my parents to be my angels on earth. But sometimes, comments like these can be triggering to those of us who are reeling inside, boiling over to the brim with the words "It's Not My Fault!"

Now please don't hear what I am not saying. Never once have my parents eluded to the fact that I am "asking for it." Instead, they fear for their beautiful daughter living in a world that has done her so wrong. And if they could bubble wrap me forever, they would, and I would probably love it. But my parents have been the number one people to let me fly through it all, and I thank them for their ability to grow with me.

While my father means well, he also makes me start asking questions to myself, like where do I draw the line now that I am not a child anymore?

If I dig a little deeper, I ask myself why do I do the things I do? What is it that I really want? What way do I want to be perceived? What makes me feel most confident?

A lot of life is about perception: the way you view what you see, and the way that you are seen. I figure, if what I wear and how you twist it is your fault, then how could it ever be mine?

I am twenty-one years old, and sometimes I still feel like I am having an identity crisis with my clothes. But at some point, I must put my foot down and tell myself not even the safety pin that night could have made a difference.

I still go through it, even tonight, even on Christmas Eve, the clothing identity crisis parallel to my entire middle school experience heaves back in on me. That is when, as I am zipping myself into my Christmas Eve outfit all I want to do is cry. I forgo acknowledging the fact that I am here, functioning, legs still standing, getting dressed to begin with. I don't think of this simple fact that I survived.

I dress to impress me, not you. I do the things I don't for you, but for me.

I am proud of who I am, I am proud of these long arms and long legs, and torso where all my weight falls, and my butt where more weight goes to. I appreciate my body and what it does daily for me. I must nourish this body, water this body, feed this body, take gentle care of this body, and protect this body as best I can. I am thankful that I can look in the mirror and smile, because after I was assaulted, I found trouble ever looking in the mirror. Ever looking at my naked body in the shower, or ever feeling safe in a swimsuit.

I anxiously await the day when the world changes: when people stop sexualizing certain races and identities, and the paradigm shifts. I wonder if this day is ever coming when women won't be objectified-in the media, in advertisements, in the clothing industry. I anxiously await the day when people will stop sexualizing members of the LGBTQ community, as my best friend Jordan has made me so aware of. I anxiously await the day when masculinity complexes become a Neanderthal ideal from the past, where men don't get angry to be more of a man. I can't wait till generations that proceed me, realize that power does not a man make. That it is okay to be sensitive and to cry.

I await the day when my country stands up and says that sexual assault is unacceptable, that rapists won't be protected, let alone tolerated. I wonder when women will be met with open arms and solemn acceptance, when judges will give rapists as long of a sentence as a killer instead of releasing these murderers of souls out into the public to reacclimate or perhaps never to be imprisoned in the first place.

I wonder if these days will ever come, how soon, or when? Will I be alive to see it? Will it happen for my daughter? For now, I hope that one day down the line, society has changed so much, that we will defend victims of rape instead of asking them all the wrong questions.

I wonder if the day will ever come when I feel totally comfortable in my environment, when I will feel completely left alone and unbothered by the world because the cat callers have been silenced and the naysayers have died off.

My sophomore year of college, I noticed an exhibition that had been placed in the far corner of the lobby in one of our main buildings. It was called "What I was Wearing" and there was a little plaque that read "potentially triggering." I walked into the pop-up exhibit anyway.

Suddenly, it was as if I was being closed in by a dozen mirrors. Around the room, mannequins were displayed in various outfits, with place cards next to each.

I bent down and squinted my eyes at the words. One read: "It was an all-black halter dress that I wore to prom. I was so excited to wear it. I remember scooping it off the floor, after. I put it back on and I never hated that dress more."

I swallowed hard, feeling my throat tightening closed. I rotated around, and to every part of the room that I looked at, I was being stared back at by my past, embodied in every possible outfit imaginable.

I realized then that rape does not discriminate.

None of these outfits screamed anything close to "come get me, come take me without permission." One girl was wearing an all-white tennis outfit and sneakers, another girl was wearing sweatpants.

There was a stack of pens and cards and a box with a slot in the top. We could anonymously submit our own personal "what I was wearing" story. I waited for some of the straying observers to leave until I was left alone, just the exhibit and myself. I quickly scribbled out a few words before anyone could see and dropped the card into the box:

Forever 21 long sleeve blouse in teal with flowers that covered it, it wrapped around and tied at the waist. A safety pin to close the top. Jeans in light wash and black booties. I really loved that shirt. Pale pink underwear. I gave everything away to Goodwill.

There was a poem by Mary Simmerling that I picked up and took back with me, slipping it inside the folds of an old journal. This poem hangs in bathroom to this day:

"If only it were so simple, if only we could end rape by simply changing clothes. I remember also what he was wearing, although it is true that no one has ever asked."

I don't have all the answers for everything, but this much I can tell you for a fact: claim your life as yours and do what makes you the happiest. You can't please all, so instead please one: yourself.

Also, go easy on your parents. Give your dad credit if he is still in your life, and if he knows the bad things that have happened to you, and fights for you every day even long after you've left the umbrella of his parenting.

Most importantly, when the whole room closes in and I just want to keep screaming "I CAN WEAR WHAT I WANT!" I choose to look myself back in the mirror and say instead,

"You look beautiful. It's not your FAULT."

Chapter Nineteen

I Wish I Never Had Sex

When you grow up in a family that promotes saving sex till marriage, or a private middle school that makes you sign your literal V card in the seventh grade, having sex can feel shameful to say the least.

I wrote these words in my journal on December 6, 2018:

"Rape. Virginity. Punishment. Waiting. Forgiveness."

"Rape—the more I hear it, the more-harsh it sounds. It is so heavy. I have noticed my parents do not use it either, they say "sexually attacked." Virginity—I wish I never had sex. I have said that to myself and to others so many times. Something I always wanted to be so special became such a lifeless act. When I stop to think about it, it resonates with me more. The faster I go in life, the longer I can forget, and when I slow down or take a step back, only then can I see it all clearly. I avoid and I hide. I regret, even though I am always saying I want to live with none. My experiences are ones I cannot take back, and it really sucks, because years later I feel as if there is nothing I can do. Punishment— I want him to be punished. He screwed with my life and now everyone knows it. It is no longer my secret to bear, but now my mothers to cope and my fathers to face. What is he doing tonight? Where has he been? Will he do it again? Where did I go wrong? I wish this never happened. If everything happens for a reason, then why this? why? Waiting— I am waiting for the right person, I waited to go to my parents and to tell the police, is it too late? What was I waiting for? Waiting… Forgiveness—I struggle with forgiving myself after that night, for even being there that night in the first place. I often say, "I put my parents through this." But I didn't. It was not me; it was him. I still have a long way to go in forgiving myself before I can even forgive him, if ever."

There have been many men, not always physical, but always life draining. And I can't say I am proud. For all the time I held out on sex, waiting to be in love, I felt the universe had spat in my face by throwing the night of my nightmares my way. I kept thinking, I was hanging on and waiting, for THIS?

I have lived 1000 lives and I am only twenty-one years old. The names I admit, are many…men who I dated, who I hurt, or who I was hurt by. Never anything serious and never anything offering the promise of longevity. Mentally I make a list, compartmentalizing some names, forgetting others. These letters mean nothing to me anymore; simply lessons learned. Sometimes I wish I never had to learn those lessons at all, but then I would not be here, would I?

Growing up I bounced around from school to school as we moved back and forth from the South to the Midwest, but in the sixth grade I landed at a private school. Thankfully, this was the place where I met my best friend B, and together we can share many a good laugh about our defining years.

Purity culture was rammed down our throats, and unfortunately, it was at an age where we did not understand what we were being told…or even why. I understand the well-intentioned message of trying to protect our youth, but at that point in time-crammed into an auditorium with the entire junior high-I did not feel protected. Instead, with the handing out of cards and pens row by row, I felt bizarrely guilted to sign a little black card that would sit, forgotten and tucked away, in my bedside table for years.

I did not understand the mechanisms of having sex, or the reasonings behind why one has sex. Therefore, I believe myself to have been totally incapable of knowing what I did or did not want. It was too early, I was too young; this decision was one which I could not fully understand at the time.

Signing a virginity pledge at the age of twelve is not a proper go about to encourage abstinence. Safe sex, consent? We never had to speak of those things, because it was under the guise that we would not be having sex until we were married.

Some things they didn't account for? Some people never get married. Some people get raped.

And if you were a virgin when you were raped, are you still a virgin? Is virginity physical or is it a social construct? Because the first time I had sex wasn't actually sex. But how was I to decipher that? To me, it was a crystal clear act and a physicality. No matter how it happened, it happened, and so you aren't a virgin anymore right?

It is frustrating that when I think back to so many girls' health classes that I partook in during my late middle school years, there were missed opportunities and an almost shamefulness tied to the human body. Many things we did not understand, and it stayed that way. Knowledge is supposed to be power, but we had no knowledge, therefore we had no power. We could not be (and were not taught to be) empowered as girls growing into women. We never really harnessed a true sense of bodily autonomy, control, or pride.

Mostly, we assumed that our worth was equated to what we could give a man (of course

A crystal clear memory of a rose hangs in my mind. I laugh about it now, yet it is still alarming.

Mrs. Cochran was at the front of the room with her name scrawled on the big whiteboard. She was today's "guest speaker", but we all knew who she was: the drama department director. And let me tell you, Mrs. C put on quite a skit.

She stood stoically at the front of the room and pulled a frail object out of her bag. B and I scrunched up our nose, leaning forward to see what this bizarre puppet show would be. And... it was a rose.

A single, long-stemmed, blood red rose. She held it up and twirled it around between her thumb and forefinger, like it was on display. In a whirlwind of cinematic tension, she began her speech:

"This. Is. You."

The rose is me, okay, sure. Inwardly I'm rolling my eyes at the not-so-subtle symbolize of a rose for a woman.

"You are this rose, fully intact." She held it up higher, as we all hunched further down in our seats with agony. Our bodies sighed, pleading for Mrs. C to round up her demonstration and leave.

Still, she drawled on.

"With all of your petals, you are this rose. Beautiful, vibrant, blooming. But then…"

Here we go.

"You lose a petal."

She dramatically rips one off and lets the deep red fall to the tile floor.

"Not so noticeable at first. But then…"

One by one, she starts yanking off each petal, letting them twirl through gravity to meet their fate.

Yikes. I am this rose, I thought sarcastically. A stem.

"Each time you give your body away, you lose a petal. You lose a piece of yourself that you will never get back. Until…"

The floor surrounding Mrs. Cochran's feet was thick with rose petals, and there in her bony fingers stood a bare brown stem of nothingness.

"This is you. When you give away your body and your heart. You must protect both."

She then launched into a final anecdote about how all we will have left to give our husbands is a petal-less stem (so, we need to save ourselves for our husband).

The end.

Am I a rose after I've been raped? A rose-beautiful, full, richly-colored-or a bare stem, disregarded and left with nothing?

I am still a Christian, and although this book is not directly speaking to my beliefs, I think that you can probably tell. Underneath the surface, it has set the tone for this entire book-that I believe in a higher power, in everything in life having meaning, hope, and purpose. Therefore, it is with the full knowing of God and His grace, that I can still critique the Christian school which I was brought up in, and to make mental notes of what I will or will not be teaching my children.

I don't care what you define yourself as, what your gender identity is, where you fall on the vast spectrum of sexuality, how many people you have slept with…your life is your life. It is a part of your story like this is mine. I worship you for being authentic and real and admitting who you are in all facets of life. I understand that I am only one small piece of the puzzle, and that I do not represent all sexual assault victims in our entirety. If I know one thing to be true, it is that rape does not discriminate. Evil does not discriminate. Violence has many faces, and so do we.

So, I beg of you, please do not misconstrue this chapter and read it for what it is not. My lived experiences may be strikingly similar or vastly different than yours. But I share my story with you simply in the hopes that one day you will share yours with me, knowing that my story is not universal, but it is familiar.

So. Let this be known. I don't judge you; I don't shame you; I hug you; I embrace you.

I was there with you and I still am.

And no. matter. what. Whoever you are, and whatever you have done, you never deserved anything but the best. You never deserved to be hurt in this way. You never deserved to be made to feel less than full, to be limited or belittled into nothing. You never deserved to be violated. You never deserved to be stripped of your power and your voice. You never deserved the humiliation; it isn't yours to carry. You never deserved the burdens of this, too heavy for one human soul to bear.

No choice of ours ever warranted this.

But my choices that followed the event I did not choose, I can't say I am incredibly happy with.

I just really, really wanted to be in love first.

There is such thing as taking your power back, and another thing called "trying to erase what I didn't choose by piling on top of it, what I did choose."

I didn't choose to be assaulted, so instead I would choose the guys I wanted, when and how. But this was not fulfilling to say the least, and I never ended up getting exactly what I had wanted.

I wrote this in the notes section of my phone March 4, 2018, 1:43 pm:

"It was then that I realized

What I was running away from

What I was hiding from

And why I was doing this.

I used to hold sex in such a high regard

It wasn't just physical it was emotional for me.

But when that ideal gets shattered

You lose your vision of that perfect idea of what your life is supposed to look like and how it's supposed to

go.

I no longer held it with such high importance.

Because it wasn't to me anymore.

It was physical and I felt nothing emotionally.

I was numb with the sort of denial I had used to cope all those months ago last March.

It has almost been one whole year later and I am still suffering through the aftereffects.

One of those is trying to forget by doing whatever I want... trying to replace the memory of an unwanted

sexual encounter with one that I did want.

If I never would've been raped

I don't think I would be having sex today.

It just wasn't like me.

But once I got so many things ripped away from me

I tried to take it all back and regain the control I had lost.

But I wasn't going about it the right way

I was burying and denying

Because that was how I survived.

I don't want to ignore it anymore

I don't want to be numb.

In fact, I would like to think that sharing a connection with someone is still important

That feeling safe and secure is still important.

And that what I uphold still does matter

Because I refuse to let what happened to me 365 days ago define what happens to me every year that follows."

The first boy I ever slept with was six months after the assault, and I was more than eager to erase my horrible sexual experience by replacing it with this one. He was my boyfriend, but after only a month he was saying he loved me, so I should have known something was up. Regardless, I dove in headfirst.

Still, no rainbows or butterflies, no fireworks or fourth of July extravaganza. It was a few days after my nineteenth birthday, and I mostly just liked that a hot guy was taking me out to nice dinners and holding my hand.

What I realize now, is that I was simply craving acceptance, touch, affection, comfort. To feel safe and valued. To be dotted on and showered in gifts.

What I really needed was someone to say, "I believe you" and "I hate him just as much as you do." I wanted someone to fight for me, to stick through this battle with me. I wanted him to say, "I'm proud of you" and "I know you can do it alone but from now on you won't have to."

Besides my dearest male friends, I am yet to find someone like this. When I do, I am sure he'll be it.

It is not asking much of a man, for me to want to tell my story in all of its actuality and painful authenticity, without fear of judgment or shame. Many times, I have been made to feel like my story was too much of a burden to the male mind. That my romantic interests were too "saddened" or too "angered" or otherwise too uncomfortable to hear the rest of the story. Or even to read this book.

But I lived it. The least you could do is listen.

Well, my very first and only boyfriend of all time, had only one thing to say about the matter: "Maybe you should talk to your parents about it."

And while he was right at the core, it was not what I wanted or needed to hear. He was emotionally inapt to handle that information, but I was the one who had to handle LIVING with it. Experiencing it. Being INSIDE of it, immersed in it. It had become my world for so long. And here he was, unsure of what to say, just because I offered him a part of my life. Instead of comforting me, he was pointing me back in the direction of my parents to deflect from him.

It was almost as if he was saying, "maybe your parents should help you out with this one, not me," instead of him giving me advice like, "I think maybe your parents need to know, but I will be here every step"

Seeing how men respond to this occurrence in my life has always been a key indicator as to what type of man they really are, and if they are worth a second date or a second more of my time.

Marguerite Duras once said, "my memory of men is never lit up and illuminated like my memory of women." Unfortunate, but true.

Putting aside a handful of male friends and dear old dad, I realize that my memory really does light up with a mirage of strong, powerful females, as if we belong in some unspoken sisterhood: my mother, my sister, all of my dear friends, my professors. And it is seemingly the men, that have let me down.

Well, ex-boyfriend Peter never said anything else about the matter. He never brought it up again, asked questions, or took the time to wonder if I was even alright. The assault was so fresh in my mind, that he was my perfect escape. I welcomed this frivolous, short-lived, fake love, because with Pete I could be young and fun and giddy. He didn't care that just five months prior to meeting, I was an ugly mess left on the side of the road. Good, I thought, maybe this means what happened to me doesn't actually matter!

I was part relieved, part disappointed. Relieved because he didn't see me as the "girl who had been raped", but disappointed because he didn't care. It was clear that neither of us wanted to think about it or speak about it, and we never did again. Perhaps this is a key indicator that he was never-not once-concerned for my mental wellbeing, peace of mind, or healing.

I expected Peter to waltz into my life and pick me up and fix everything. That was the biggest issue in the entire relationship, or the fact that we even had a relationship in the first place: I thought he could change things for me. I thought he could slap a bandage on my infected wound and poof, life would be dandy.

Until it was not.

It was only two months in that I found out that my first boyfriend, had another girlfriend. Peter was living a double life: one at college and one in his hometown just a near thirty minutes away. He was "in love with me", but also in love with his girlfriend since eighth grade. Things didn't exactly fizzle out, but instead ignited into a forest fire. It was messy, and I was smart enough to know that when a guy tells you that it's just "not that simple" and "I love both you and her" (oh and he just needs "time to figure it out", whatever "it" is) then it is best to run, run, run. You cannot sprint away fast enough from someone so disastrously problematic.

After Peter came "the baseball player". He hailed from Miami and was a gorgeous Cuban with a man bun. He danced with me around his bedroom, had a slick way for words, and possessed the darkest eyes that could catch me from halfway across the room. He was fascinating because I could not have him.

After that came a restaurant coworker-"the pizza boy"-and then I returned back to "baseball boy" like I was dodging some kind of obstacle course made up of brunette man buns.

Somehow, we always came back. And not just baseball boy, but every boy. We always circled towards each other one last time before it faded away...but not after it had drawn out far too long.

After baseball boy graduated, moved back to Miami, and fell in love, I fell in line. I realized what I had been doing had wasted so much time. But as human nature tends to inflict upon us, we continue to keep doing the things we wish to stop, and we don't know why.

After that came another baseball player. I met him at the first birthday party I ever had enough courage to throw for myself. Next came Airforce boy. Recently, he lives in London; we talk every now and then. I have found that often, they come back. They always come back until one day they just don't...

There was a nineteen-year-old who told me that he loved me, but I knew he could not possibly know that after only a month. There was a DJ that was too old for me. In the end, I was bored. I was alone. I needed entertainment, I wanted attention...wrong, wrong, wrong. I have been broken by my past, tied down and held down back there in that place I don't belong in anymore.

There have been many more: summer encounters, flings through the fall that ended right before Christmas, Valentine's Days spent alone. The funny thing about this part of the story is that none are worth mentioning.

They are all nameless, faceless humans of my past, ones that I scooped up at one point in life and then left behind when I realized my feet were moving too quickly ahead. My life didn't fit with theirs quite like I had hoped, our journeys did not align but rather collided.

"We bumped into each other in the courtyard-you look exactly my type.
We met at the red light
We spoke for the first time at the beach that day.
We met in the dimly lit party at your apartment.
I invited you over for breakfast,
You took me out for champagne,
You never took me out…
I have lost track of your names.
I have lost count of the number,
Too many times I have met the like of you,
Every time you disappear.
Each instance always a little different than the last,
the longer it goes on, the number I become.
I am so tired of first times
And wanting to know your name…
And then having to forget it so quickly after."
-October 12, 2019.

Today, I am alone, and I like it. Alone, but not alone.

Too many good people in my life to call this "alone." Lonely sometimes, yes, but also in good company, and good with being on my own, okay with being by myself. I am okay with listening to my mind speak. I am okay with nighttime, okay with the silence.

These are things I have never known before.

To be okay with my own company, to sit idly with my thoughts and sift through them without panic, to spend a day with myself, to take ME out for a day.

I am writing this just two days away from 2020, and I have come to realize that in the past years, I have had an overwhelming capacity for chasing after what I can't attain.

Time and time again I see the red flags, I get the memos, I hear the guy tell me he isn't ready to be in a relationship or he is still getting over his ex, and I dive in headfirst anyways. Here, pick me, let me be your emotional punching bag!

I love a good chase. It is never to my benefit, but the human in me screams "do it anyways," right before I fall. I go right on in, manipulating my mind into thinking that it might just work out for my benefit.

"You're not ready to be with me? You don't want a relationship? Your ex screwed you up?" Sure, no problem, I'm still here for you, I'll be here, right here like a damn doormat. I am too nice, too forgiving, too quick to give a second chance or an undeserved chance to begin with. You should not trust until it gets broken, you should have the trust earned before it ever comes.

I have previously enjoyed the cat and mouse chase, the games, the rollercoaster ride with the ones who should have given me all, or nothing at all.

It was all on wasted time. These mere boys have been a complete and total waste to the timeline of my life, because they didn't feed my body or soul, they didn't grow me emotionally and mentally.

It was romantic, we had chemistry, it was really going somewhere…

There are a million lies that I could make up in my mind, but the main thing I realized was that when a guy tells you he doesn't want a relationship, what he is really saying is "I don't want a relationship with you."

I realized somewhere down the road, that I had been living in a false reality where I thought my life might look like my parents. I have since concluded that my story does not and will not (and should not) look like my parents. I am young. I am me and my story belongs to no one else. In this day and age, I am not falling in love in college. Besides, I have too much I must do first.

All I have ever had is a handful of meaningless connections-fires that fizzled out fast and hearts that repelled like two opposing magnetic forces.

I didn't have love, I had lust.

I didn't have affection, I had attraction and attention.

Now, I needed the real thing.

But first, I had to love me.

I had reached my breaking point. I could not go back to that self-destructive, defeated place. It was time to love me more, and to love me the most.

I wrote this in September, to all the ones who have done me wrong. To the ones I miss and don't miss. But particularly for the very first one, my puppy dog prom love. This is for all the ones who have gone away:

"The daytime looks like you

But nighttime sounds like you...

Or maybe the absence of you.

Still, silent, dark.

Thinking...thinking you over in my mind.

Closing my eyes,

Listening,

Listening to the pounding thrum of my heart beating inside my ears.

I. Forgive. You.

Three words and three years,

I choke them down,

I hold them back.

I bury my fists at my side,

I pull at my hair.

Sometimes all I can hear is your voice,

Now the only one that fills my mind is my own.

I. Forgive. You.
We have known these three words since we were children-
Since we were the careless youth dancing through the grass-
But these three words have taken me what feels like forever
To grasp.
I have stopped looking past forgiveness
And chosen to say it aloud.
You could not hear my words,
But they were meant for you.
What matters is that I have said them,
That they have been breathed into reality
The way air fills lungs with life.
I know that you would never apologize
I did not need your acceptance
Of my forgiveness.
I had come to accept,
What you had done to me."

- "3 Years."

Months later I sat alone by the point in the city where three rivers merge. I opened up an old fifty cent book that I had rummaged out of the dusty but beloved record store on Liberty Avenue. Two words: Oscar Wilde. In an effort to perhaps encompass this entire chapter, I leave you with this:

"For three long years they will not sow or root or seedling there: for three years the unblessed spot will sterile be and bare. And look upon the wondering sky with unreproachful stare. They think a murderer's heart should taint each simple seed they sow. It is not true, God's kindly earth is kindlier than men know. And the red rose would but blow more red, the white rose whiter blow. For who can say by what strange way Christ brings His will to light."

Chapter Twenty

S-E-X Is a Bad Word

The S-E-X word.

Third grade. A memory that makes me smile every time. When I was near the age of seven and living in Florida, my friend Camryn told me about a music video called "Sexy Back." She showed me some dance moves at the lunch table, and we doubled over laughing. When I went home that day, I started asking my sister about some of the worst words she had ever heard. When I told her that mine started with "S-E-X," her eyes went wide.

"Where did you hear that Soph?" Immediately, she went to get dad.

"Tell dad the word you learned," said tell-o-Lauren.

I was too shy, looking up with big wide eyes at my father. "Sexy."

"Do you know what that means honey?"

"It means someone is hot."

No amount of sex education could have prepared me for this.

Frankly, we don't talk about it enough, and when we do, I think it is never handled properly. Why is consent not taught but a teacher will gladly-and ever so awkwardly-wrap a condom around a banana? Why is the R word scarier than the S.E.X word, when truthfully the two go hand in hand, separated by a "yes" and "no"? Where did it all go wrong?

There I go again, back to my timeline. A single black dot in the middle, the "before" on one side, the "after" on another.

Right next to my timeline I decidedly draw another imaginary line. This is my "what if" timeline.It is no longer before, middle, and after, it is just before and now. No grandiose event to mess me up, no stark comparison between who I used to be and who I am now, no massive traumatic experience to shatter my notions of the world.

What if that never happened to me? What if I was never assaulted when I was a virgin? What if the idea of sex had still been protected and intact for me? What if my trust in men had not been damaged so drastically? What if these past three years had not been spent tripping up and falling and getting back up with bloody knees and then walking again and then running and then tripping again...? Would I be wiser, more selective, more discerning with men instead of distracted by them? My life has become a strained series of what-ifs, mirrored by the "what is."

What if these past three years had been just living life, not rebuilding it?

I wanted to go back to "before" and change what had happened so that I could reappear in an alternate "now". But I can't do that. Middle school health class never warned me against this, only told me where babies came from, not that sometimes they showed up unexpectedly, or not by choice at all.

Nothing broke me down like this.

Nothing took me so far off the path as this.

I woke up in unfamiliar territory, so far from home, so far from the top of my mountain. But I could see it through the clouds. I could see the warm illuminations of home, no matter how desolate the space I was in, or how far from me that those orange glowing lights really were.

I could see it, I could see where I wanted to be, but how could I ever get there?

Sex is supposed to be so powerful & incredible, but we have been desensitized to it until it means nothing to us. The act is just an act, sometimes painted over and covered up, encrypted with the pathetic excuses of "I don't remember" or "never again." We were exposed to all the wrong things too young or robbed of what we were supposed to choose. When our choices looked us in the face with promise, we looked away for but a moment, and had been stolen from right under our noses.

Maybe a lot of people go off to college and experience that "thing" for the first time in their lives, or maybe they learn what it is in fourth grade but don't actually know it until prom night. And even then, they know nothing of it.

My one male friend told me, "Yeah I was thirteen, she was seventeen, it was whatever I guess…kinda thought it made me cool."

No, it wasn't "whatever", I practically scream. Do you truly not see everything wrong with that sentence? That was a crime, I yell inwardly. Your first time wasn't a first time at all, it was rape.

The desensitization is astonishing, but culturally we have dismissed bodies to be nothing but objects, and intimacy to be mythical. What happened to sex being good, what happened to knowing someone for their body, soul, and mind?

After I was assaulted, I found myself having a conversation within my mind that always started and stopped with one sentence: "I never thought I would be here."

I thought sex was a power play, and I could use it to manipulate my circumstances and attain the power that had been stolen from me and claim it back. But sex didn't make me gain anything. If anything, it required a dependency that I could not afford. It leaves us wondering, "will he text back?" or "what did I just do?" or "I wonder what it is like to really love someone?" It leaves us lonely and wanting more, but more will never be enough, so the cycle continues.

I don't care if you disagree, because that is your story, not mine. And whatever makes you happy, makes you happy, and own it. But my story and my truth are this: I have been taken from for far too long and I can't fool myself into thinking it was all for something, because it wasn't. And that doesn't make me happy.

As the days fade onwards, and we age with each dying month, we find ourselves saying something like this, "I can do what I want." And it is true, you can. That is your power in choosing, but perhaps not your freedom.

I am grown. I can do what I want...

But not everything is going to be good for me. I can't keep living this life anymore.

Something needed to change. Taking my power back didn't mean throwing myself away, because in the end that was what I ended up doing: throwing it all away and chucking it so far downhill, that I was ten steps backwards on my mountain every time.

Change. What a frightening idea, especially when your patterns of thinking and living have become so engrained into your being that you can't see a tomorrow without them.

As I change and grow and shift and move into my better tomorrow, I can't help but feel downtrodden. My spirit is new, but my body is old. While I am promised something new for myself, my body is still the same. My mind is revitalized while my bones dangle on. I can tell myself that everything will be different, but when I look down, I see the same thing staring back at me in the mirror.

Thank God for restoration.

I am not the same person from that night, or any night after. I don't want to ever go back to that dark and dreary hole that I was in, so consciously I make a choice not to dive deeper. I am trying to get free, not to be enslaved by my past or my body or the things that have been done to me.

Now this isn't a "save sex for marriage" talk because to each his own. We all make our own choices in life. That is, until one day when someone decides to take that autonomy away and to choose for us. Instead, while I leave this conversation with an open end, I also leave you with this question to ponder on: "What are you enslaved to?" I don't want to be bound by sex, bound by the physical, bound by what lets me down, blocked by my blessings.

A glass of wine might feel nice, but then 10 drinks later and you have catapulted yourself into another universe of self-destruction. Pretty soon, every weekend you have turned to the bottle, your coping mechanisms weakened down with every drop.

We tell ourselves that money makes the world go round. And while building up our wallets and saving up our income brings us a sense of accomplishment and pride, when does it all change? When do we become a slave to the coin? At what point do we find ourselves completely ensnared in the money-making trap, the work till you die mentality that I have touched on in this book?

I can do anything I want, but not everything is going to feed my soul. It might fill me up temporarily, but it will starve my body in the end. And I may have the best intentions at the beginning, but my humanness will in the end betray me.

What ties you down, what holds you back? Is it sex, is it money, is it a substance, is it the idea that if you have not made a name for yourself you have failed? Is it the thirst for revenge that fuels your daily decisions? Is it the need to get back, to get even?

Without it would you die?

The one who attacked me took away my feelings of safety, of trust, and of protection, and left me instead with shame, pain, and aggression. My energy was all misplaced, but there is really no right way to 'do' healing but live each day the best you can. I choose instead to feel secure again, to hold myself up on a pedestal, to speak encouraging words to myself every morning when I wake up, and to be okay with going to sleep alone the previous night.

I look at a sexually charged generation that we are all drowning in, and think to myself, why does a rape culture perpetuate and prevail?

Everywhere you look, it is shoved in your face. Human nature tells us to go after what we see when we want it and men think they can have it and take it. Humans are used to satisfying their appetites. We are living in a world where "we have to have it now" and this leaves us eating not because we need the food to live or even like it, but just because we can. People fantasize like any normal human being, but then they begin to glamorize "rape fantasies" unbeknownst to them of how traumatizing a real assault is, and how far it shuts down one's body.

Every basic consumer product sexualizes and objectifies women, catering to every desire and need and slamming it in the face of every passerby. There are essentially nine female strippers for every male stripper, a whooping ninety percent female and eight percent male. Equality where? Does the porn industry perpetuate rape culture? Is it freeing or is it constraining, when you begin to think of the ways in which it is hungrily viewed?

The tale as old as time is this: Women are their bodies, they are objects.

And the porn industry has emphasized this objectification by taking away the humanity from women: they are not mothers, friends, and daughters with real names, but instead sexually charged, sex-hungry characters who will do anything for a camera. This isn't real life, this is entertainment. This is a job that both male and females hopefully chose for themselves and were not forced into. So, supposing that this field of work viewed by the millions is both consensual and for payment, what makes men think they can go out and find their very own porn actresses? Because that is what we are not.

And what about the basic topic of consent? Why is the word "no" not advertised for in the way that half naked women are? "Sexual appetite is natural," we tell ourselves, but what happens when it has been dumbed down into something cheap and manufactured? Real love, what is that?

Curious, I asked a few of my friends regardless of gender identification and aged twenty to twenty-five, what sex represents to them, regardless of how many people they had sex with or if they had ever had sex at all.

Here was the first answer of what sex means to them: "Sex to me, means a connection between two people that has a deeper meaning than just doing the actions. It is you combining with another person on an emotional and physical level that shows you care about each other. Ultimately, you are giving a part of yourself to the other person. So, however you handle that responsibility, I guess just be okay with the outcome."

A second answer was given as follows: "My view of sex continues to evolve. Real sex represents love that two people have for each other, but people have sex for selfish reasons now and try to trick themselves into thinking that it will satisfy them."

The third answer began with the words, "I think it is two becoming one" and continued with, "it is an experience in which you know someone in a way that no one else can know them how you know them. It can take your relationship to a deeper level, because it gives you the chance to have souls connect, if you give it that chance."

As I gained more and more answers to these sometimes awkward questions, I realized how alike we were. The next answer: "I think it is something that starts off physical, that you feel internally yet physically. For me, personally, I am desensitized to it because of the things that happened to me as a kid. I either want to have a lot of sex or I am completely disinterested. In its rawest form, sex is when two people genuinely feel a shared energy, aura, or love. And it is also a release. I think sex can be love in its purest form, but a lot of people are afraid to say it."

I then followed up by asking, "Do you have any regrets? Has sex made you feel liberated or guilty or both or neither?"

The first answer was this: "For me, sometimes I would do it for him because I would think it would make him want me more. But it has always been passionate between us, so I always felt liberated during, never guilty after. I have never sat back and thought "oh no,

I should not have done that…" So maybe not guilt, but instead this nagging feeling that I am stuck in this moment with him and nothing is getting better and nothing is getting worse. We are so stagnant."

My second survey led me to this response: "Regrets? Yes and no. Because it showed me a part of myself that I didn't know about, but at the same time I don't think the people that I shared it with were necessarily my best choices. I think I was too young to understand what I was doing to myself. Because I have never been in a relationship where I am committed to that one person and that one person is committed to me. Not really regrets maybe, but I look back and say, "what were you thinking in the moment?" Like why did I even do that? Why did I feel the need to? Not a regret, but just what the hell, why? I wasted myself away to those people more than I regret doing it, I gave a part of myself away to these people. It was a waste of a night."

The third answer sang the same tune, just slightly different: "I don't have any regrets on who I had had sex with. Personally, sex makes me feel unsatisfied. It seems like fake love and fake affection when it is with someone I don't really like. I don't necessarily feel liberated or guilty. I feel wanted. I would take back the relationships that made me more insecure as a person. I would take back the times I ignored the red flags and my brain telling me to run."

Perhaps the answer that hurt the most was the one least expected: "Sometimes sex is something you regret, but you were not the one that chose to engage in it. Along the lines of how we raise our children, sometimes you regret sex before you know it is sex. Most of our psych is based off childhood experiences and our first encounters with it. So, if you were touched or raped as a kid, you might be a closeted person your whole life because you were not given the chance to deal with your sexuality. My brother dealt with this. I have dealt with this. Sometimes, it isn't even being a closeted gay but rather closeting your feelings about sex as they spill out into all other aspects of your life. Sex being normalized can degrade your view on it…meaning you could find yourself so obsessed with it, or at times find yourself completely uninterested even when you know the opportunity is there."

Next, I wondered to both my male and female friends, if they thought that females were sexualized more than males? And then, if they thought this influenced rape culture?

"Yes, and I think everyone is at fault for this. So, when men look at women as just sex, then that leads into a culture feeding into that, whether it be in clothing, advertisement, entertainment, etc. It makes it seem more normal. Then because it is normal, younger women and girls see that and get the wrong idea. They think that sex is getting attention and receiving love. In turn, this makes men think that an instance where they hooked up with one girl will be the same scenario for every girl. So, when a girl says no, they aren't used to it. They think that women are always going to be compliant. It all starts from sexualizing women, like a chain reaction."

"A hundred percent. The fact that women are so, "you are your body" gives men a point of owning it…when we cannot be owned. We are not our bodies, and culture makes it all about what your body looks like. Men are very visual, and our culture adapts to those visual aspects that men have, oversaturating their brains."

"A thousand percent. I can't remember the last time I saw a half-naked man in an ad, but I can tell you how many times I've seen a half-naked woman in commercials just today alone."

"That question is a hard one. I believe women are sexualized, so does this give men the permission in their brains that rape is okay? Perhaps. But also, each case is so unique that I have trouble generalizing why these men are doing what they are doing overall. This is a good one for me to think about."

"It really depends. Some people like being sexualized. But as far as culture is concerned, absolutely females are over-sexualized. It makes a lot of men think they deserve more female attention. I think men have a lot of resentment against women. They are bombarded with seeing women all the time that maybe they cannot have."

I asked a followup question: "Why do you think that men have so much resentment against women?"

"Social awkwardness, getting turned down, embarrassment, issues with mothers, good woman role models and male role models who showed them how to teach a woman, society's standards of what a man should be that as a man, you might not add up to trauma. The list could go on."

"Females are absolutely more sexualized than males. Even the perks we get like easily finessing men at bars for the free drinks or getting in the door for free, the "you always get what you want because you're a female" are ultimately because we are so sexualized. I think it perpetuates rape culture because girls are constantly looked at as a prop to have sex with. We are dumbed down to just our bodies when sex is just as mental as it is physical."

My next question was an inquiry: "What should change with the way that our culture raises boys?" Here were the collective answers:

"I think that we should raise men to change their perspective about women, instead of women having to change themselves for men. I also think it is so important to raise men to show their emotions, instead of being stigmatized for being sensitive...if they cry, it automatically means they are girly or gay. That is a super unhealthy way to cope. I also think that every parent should talk to the boys that they raise about the perspective of girls in the world, like how unsafe women feel and how hard it is to walk in our shoes...and no matter what a woman is wearing, it does not give you permission, and it should not distract you.

Change your mind set about why it is distracting you, rather than us changing our clothes. Teach men to look at women with respect, instead of sexually objectifying us."

"Not shame them for watching girl shows or wearing colors that are not necessarily boyish like pink. Even possibly buying gender neutral colors for a baby, not just the stereotypical blue for boy and pink for girl. If you look at advertisements, I think that should change as well. Commercials portray these competitive, hyper-maniac boys playing aggressively, like killing bugs or shooting people and girls are more collaborative, decorating barbie's house and playing softly, baking a cake in their play kitchen."

"I think that we should raise our sons to feel more connected and accepting of their emotions and expressing those emotions in healthy ways, as well as raising boys to be men that know how to treat women with love and respect."

"Um, I feel like in the past 10-15 years as lot has changed and for the good, but I still think letting younger boys express emotions should be emphasized. Sad, happy, excited. And we need to stop telling them that they are being a girl because they are crying. I do still think that they need to be raised in a way that will show them how to be a respectful man and a strong man that can help others when they are in need."

"I would teach my son to have patience to deal with the stuff that others don't understand yet, and push into him to think for himself. To treat everyone like his brother."

"I think that we should get rid of the saying "boys will be boys". Boys are responsible for their actions and their feelings. And boys should be vulnerable because as humans, we were all created to be."

I asked: "What age will you teach your kids about sex? Will it be the same time you tell them about consent? Would you tell your daughter the same thing you tell your son?"

"I think when it comes to raising boys and girls the same, I was raised into sports but now I am an artist, so maybe I am a little biased that you have to learn both roles before you can choose which one completely suits you. I think you should fully experiment with both. In addition, as far as talking to my kids about sex, I don't think there is ever going to be a sit-down situation until closer to fifteen or sixteen. Before that, like if a scene comes on in a movie and they walk into the living room, I am going to explain to them what they just saw. I am not going to break it down completely, just yet."

"I want it to be an open conversation with them, I always want them to be comfortable and able to have an ongoing dialogue with me.

So, I guess whenever they're ready to talk about it, I am here… but not when they're five and asking how babies are made. Not then. I am going to say, "god gives a blessing in mommy's tummy."

"I am going to teach my children about sex when they are old enough to talk. It won't be exactly penis and vagina, but simply telling your daughter what her vagina is called and showing her the spots that no one can touch unless you allow them to. And I will teach her consent at the same time and that is with everything. People should consent to anything that involves their personal space coming into contact. That could be a simple hug…that needs consent!"

I then asked: "Why do you think we have been so desensitized to sex, and yet it is still not normalized into conversation (not talked about enough, still taboo)?"

My first response was a male friend, who said that, "it is a super vulnerable topic, and some people feel that they aren't ready to talk about it or they may get shamed for it." His friend sitting beside him chimed in, "I think the question answers itself. No one talks about sex because they are already desensitized, they already see it all the time so why talk about it?"

Next came a chorus of the same song:

"So, I think that we are desensitized to sex because the media tells us oh it doesn't matter, you can have sex with whoever you want, having sex is so freeing…it glorifies sex so much. Movies, tv shows, everywhere you look…we think that is how we are supposed to live. And we think that is what we like, but, we know that sex holds a lot of weight. I think that is why it is so taboo to say out loud because even though we act like sex holds no power, sex has all the power.

Realistically, if a girl has sex with a guy and also at a later date, with his friend, all the sudden she's a hoe.

And now her whole character is called into question, and she gets labelled and now you might not like her because she's a "hoe" even though two friends just slept with the same girl. But nobody cares about the guys…only the girl.

All because of a simple act that is supposedly meant to be liberating and freeing…ends up doing the opposite."

"I think that us trying to be desensitized is really just this mask that we have put on, because we don't want to think through why we are having sex or what that person means to us or the hold it can have over us."

"I think it is because sex comes with appearance first. Sex is based off lust.

A lot of people can imagine sex with a person just off appearance. They can get that quick gratification of looking at someone that they wish they could be with, having it at the palm of their hand easily accessible like pornography."

"Desensitized and deadened to the real thing, because I think deep down that everybody knows that sex is supposed to be something special, and they try and make it the opposite of that. It is almost like people are afraid of a good thing, so they rob themselves of having it before they even got the chance. Yes, it is normal to want to have sex, those inclinations are part of being a human being. But it is something that I believe is supposed to be shared with somebody very important in your life. Now I know that might be an unpopular opinion, or it might not be the case every time, as it has certainly not been the case for me. I think what I struggle with most about our culture today is how we sort of get into a hook up culture and then girls get labelled as sluts, but guys get labelled as the "cool guy".Guys get all the girls which is a status thing for them, but if girls like to have different guys, they get shamed. I just wonder if the ongoing hookups are rooted in something deeper. I myself found because I had lost that connection with myself, and that sense of self love, that I looked for it in other people. That is just me personally."

"I think sex is both overtly in our faces, and yet covert in conversation, probably due to the riffs between generations. I feel like in my grandparent's generation they would wait till marriage, but they would get married super young, maybe by the time they were nineteen. Now, women are working, and we are professionals and we are fighting to be equals. Marriage is getting pushed back later and later because we are all chasing our careers and our education's and our generations are taking longer and longer to "grow up". So, instead of women getting with men and having sex and having kids young, we get to choose these other options.

I think perhaps there is still shame that goes along with sex, because the older generation doesn't approve of our new choices. We get married at 27 now not 17. We are our own professionals and we don't need men to stabilize our lives and provide our income for us, so we stay single longer, we date, we talk to different people.

I do think that our culture has also lost a sense of what their morals are or if they have or need them, and yet judgment is at an all-time high. So, morals are fading away, but judgment is running rampant. So, people are quiet about it and don't tell anybody, because they don't want to be judged even though the person next to them is doing the same thing."

My answers to these questions are simple and summed up, dated back to a short poem I wrote while I walked home one evening:
"I forget what it is like to have a first date
To have my meal paid for
To know you in the daytime.
I forget what it is like to be known for my mind
Not wanted for my body.
I cannot recall the last time
That you asked me twenty questions
Or did not try to kiss me

Within the first five minutes of the movie.
I do not recall what it is to feel safe, really safe
In your strange presence.
I do not recall what it is to be seen, really seen…
For what I am
Not what I have to offer you.
It is sad really
All that we have lost
All that we lose within ourselves
And all that gets taken
All that never was.
My body is worth infinitely more
Then the consumerist price tag you slap onto it.
When did we begin selecting and taking bodies
In the way that we pick produce from the supermarket?
Who said I am yours to have anyways?
My body is worth infinitely more than what you deemed
Me to be
When you saw me
And sized me up in one look."

"You say, "I am allowed to do anything" —but not everything
is good for you. And even though "I am allowed to do anything,"
I must not become a slave to anything."
-1 Corinthians 6:9-12

"I do not understand what I do. For what I want to do I do not
do, but what I hate, I do."
-Romans 7:15
Sex isn't a bad word, but we made it bad. Lucky us.

Chapter Twenty-One

MY. BODY.

"Human Bodies Are Words, Myriads of Words…" -Walt Whitman

Why? I ask myself
Are we so immersed,
So inconsolably caught inside of,
So greatly measured,
By our bodies?
But not by the things that make them strong
But rather by what we see as weaknesses.

-excerpt by me

My body provides for me every day. MY Body. She nourishes, waters, grows, develops, and restores.

She is kicked, broken, and healed. She is resilient and courageous; she is soft yet hardened. My body has taken me here, my body has brought me this far. My limbs have refused to give in, my arms have bent with the wind but upheld, my knees have buckled yet pushed me onwards.

And yet I offer her the unkindness of a stranger, a narrowed brow of criticism and cynicism that she neither asked for nor deserves, an unfriendliness that supposes she does not belong here.

To be at home in one's own body.

What a simple yet complex thought. In upholding this ideal, there is much pain to be battled, yet there is a fruitfulness and fullness that is offered to one's spirit when one can accept that their body is theirs and theirs alone.

While this memory is still painful to talk about, I have not thought about it in a while. Sometimes when I need inspiration, a reminder of where I have come from, or simply a flash back into the past, I crack open one of my many old journals. Pages are scattered in bedside tables, bookshelves, and boxes tucked away in storage. When I read over an entry from 2018, I closed my eyes and put the linen bound journal away.

The first shower.

I don't like to talk about this, particularly because this is the part that still feels the most real-and the most confusing. The first shower was even more palpable than the night proceeding it, simply because it was the first moment when I had a full realization of what I was now stuck with forever. And although the gravity of the situation still had not hit me as hard as it soon would, I was beginning to get a taste of the heavy burden I would shoulder.

The next morning, after we woke up and left the campus of nightmares, we drove back to Olivia's house where she had grown up. That day was the day that she tried on her bridesmaid dress for her sister's wedding, the day that I called B on the phone and she spelled everything out for me. But first, I wanted to take a shower. Sometimes I wish I hadn't. I wish I had ended up right on the doorstep of the hospital first thing that morning, with all DNA intact. I wish I had told them to get the police, to listen to my story and to write it down. But instead, I just stood there under the rushing water; it was all I could do.

Oh, dear god, I thought to myself, this is a nightmare. This isn't real. It didn't happen. It didn't happen Sophia, God please take me back to the day before it happened, please let me go back in time.

The wind was knocked out of me, the walls were closing in, and my chest felt like it was going to burst. I couldn't take it.

I remember the way that the warm water felt pouring over me, rushing over my body like redemption. I was dirty. I wanted to scrub the dirt away. It wasn't coming off. Panic.

I wanted to get rid of all traces of him. I scrubbed and scrubbed, tried to wash out all any remains of blood from my underwear. I remember that the soap had a distinct smell, like a sickly sweet rose perfume, and the sun was extra bright.

I do remember how golden my body looked in the light that was streaming through the bathroom window. It was as if my skin glowed. It was a bitter irony, how bright and pure that sunlight made my bruised bones look.

As the minutes ticked on, I remembered more and more details, piecing together all of the fragmented bits of the night before, and deciding on how exactly I would be able to pretend it never happened. The picture became clearer and clearer the more I analyzed each detail of the previous night, and I think that was the first time that I ever felt a pain which made not just my heart, but my body hurt.

I remember everything even though they said it never happened. I still remember, although in the present I no longer have to go back to that place or find a need in thinking about it much anymore. Certain senses still remain in my memory, like the feeling of water or the way that the cold black-and-white tile felt when we slammed to the floor. Although I can admit that with time, the rest has blurred or evaded me. As the years pass, I don't need to remember anymore. I don't need to keep reminding myself that I'm not crazy and that it did happen. Because I know full well that it happened, and I don't need to convince anyone that it did.

I kept those underwear for years tucked in the far back drawer in the closet of my old house. Why did I keep them anyways? I half-hoped that I hadn't washed them out well enough, secretly calculating that maybe there was some DNA left. I always made mental notes of what happened to me, as if I was filing away the names, dates, and addresses like some detective. Meticulously, I gathered up the details that I would've given the police the next morning. I don't know why that was so automatic for me mentally, but I was always scribbling small bits of reality down so that I would never forget-the name of his roommate, the house number, the color of the walls. Secretly I hoped that one day I could press charges, with my legal pad of notes on hand. Or maybe I was just charting it all down in some feeble effort to remind myself that the truth was on my side. That I had all of the information right at hand even when I had forced myself to forget...to prove it had happened. I think that was what I was doing all along-trying to prove that it happened, trying to grasp at the facts which proved I was not crazy, no matter how painful.

In the stillness is when I become less of a shadow and the most like myself. Just as I was in the shower that day, alone with my reckonings.

It is the quiet which causes me to turn and face my reflection, it is in this very quietness of taking time to see who I am, that I can begin to accept what I am. To sift through my thoughts and to simply sit and be with myself, myself in all of its entirety.

A terrifying concept. To be alone with oneself. This can be a comforting yet unknown reality. It means that I must grapple with what I am and acknowledge what I wish to become...and am becoming.

I do not mind being alone. So many people evade their own selves, in this struggle of aloneness. And while sitting with ourselves is so often the hardest part of the day, being surrounded by a room full of mirrors can be almost crippling.

Growing up as a dancer meant that I was not only accustomed to scrutinizing myself in the reflective glass, but that it was also innately built into me to fix every small imperfection. The lines began to blur in my pre-professional training. As I either self-corrected or fixed my placement via teacher's instruction ("drop your hip down, straighten your knee, lift from the ribs, point from the ankle) I began to sink into the despair that perhaps there was something wrong with my body, and not just with my technique.

With each small adjustment, each head tilt and bent knee, I was unknowingly damaging my self-image. I was not simply fixing my exterior errors within the umbrella of my training, but rather faltering into the belief that my body-in its entirety-needed fixed.

When a teacher told me to lift up in my lower abs, I began to wonder if maybe my stomach was poking out of my leotard. And each time I lifted my leg in the air, and my instructor told me that I was gripping in my thigh, I thought maybe my quads are too big.

I recall various instances of dysfunction in my early years within those four dance studio walls (but that is its own chapter).

"Don't wear your tights like that," my ballet teacher chided an older student when she walked in the room. "It makes your butt look big."

But I was just wearing my ballet tights like that yesterday, I thought.

My other teacher passed on a lesson that her most recently graduated senior, Tia, had learned. Tia, who I used to admire so greatly, went to dance in New York City and had no issues getting booked for a job, even though she was stereotypically "short for a dancer" and athletically built.

"Don't use the elliptical machine, ever!" my teacher warned our class. I might have only been about thirteen at the time. "I told Tia to stop using the elliptical, because it was building up her leg muscles and making her look big. We don't want to bulk those up, we want to lean them out."

No one ever tells you that sometimes your body is merely a product of genetic makeup, and that you cannot change your actual bone structure and placement, your hip size, your rib cage, or your height.

The body that I was born into is not a mistake simply because it does not fix into the box that you created. In fact, your body does not even fit into that box.

We so often overcompensate and underestimate our bodies. We underwrite our flaws and overexaggerate our societally deemed "good" qualities. We mismanage feelings of inferiority, insecurity, and scrutiny. Our scrambled brains jumble mixed signals of both self-doubt and self-assuredness. We play the role of confidence well, but inwardly we are void.

Why are we so dissatisfied with what is ours?

Within my body, with just the gentle graze of a fingertip, there is electricity, there is warmth. There is a place I can call home, a safe space, and a temple. There is nothing dirty about that which I was born into.

As babies, we were all born into the universe purely and perfectly, unashamed in our bodies, welcomed into a world that would not welcome us back. Like Adam and Eve in the Garden, once upon a time, we too were completely unashamed in our vessels.

As a child growing up, each day was a new milestone for me, a welcome mat for growth, learning, and autonomy.

I have broken bones that have mended in time, like my heart seems to mend itself with familiarity. I have run across sandy shores and chased clouds. I have been washed over by crashing waves when I lose my footing. At times I have felt like little, and then I have felt like much. Too much.

Constantly, I battle my body. Too big, too small, too short, too tall. Too everything. Not enough. Not like the Instagram models. Not like the dancers standing on stage beside me.

Society is constricting. And mirrors are a lie.

Our reflections should be our truest form and most accurate picture of self, but instead the mirrors glaring back at us warp and bend with our dysmorphic aptitudes. Our bodies tell our story. They tell it in a way that no one else can.

It has taken me many years to accept each stretch mark, each scar-from the one on my thumb that I burned on a glue gun in third grade, to the light blotch of skin on my elbow from my bicycle crash in fifth grade. The amount of times that I have loathed this skin that I am in, breaks my heart. You break my heart because you have been there too or are there now. The number of journeys and adventures that she has taken me on leave me forever indebted. Why isn't it enough?

The human body is simply miraculous. A woman's body, that which can create life itself, is something of God. Why do we hate what houses us? Why do we batter our very own bones? The body is regenerative, we hold the power to restore skin cells and fractured limbs, regain consciousness and restore memory, master multiple languages, sprint marathons. Lips that breathe fire but hold the power to calm raging storms, the smallest etchings like that of a tree in just one palm, hands that can warm yet reject, a heart that can both welcome those we love, or shut them out.

We hold a lot of power…and certainly a lot of enigmas tied with a bow.

Our bodies lean into that which is familiar, foundational, routine, and certain. After all, we are naturally creatures of habit, and we can only operate based on what we can confirm is true.

What I know to be real is that the body remembers even when the mind has managed to deflect and repress. And although I am considered insane because I am suspicious, mistrusting, or not so trusting at all, I have learned that my body can identify a threat from a million miles away. Memory is not just a vague, intangible remnant; it is also very much an embodiment and a physicality. Memories are held as much in the body as in the brain.

After the survival of trauma, the body can feel like a nagging betrayal. Every time we look down at our own flesh, we see an unwelcome reminder of what we have been left with. Trauma is uniquely and unconsciously stored in our bodies, meaning that our very bones are the ones that bear the brunt of pain just as much as our souls.

Physical reactions become a palpable reminder of an invisible wound. A wound that so many are unaware of because on the outside, us trauma survivors hold it all together like our life depends on it. As we scrap up the pieces bit by bit and try to make it look easy, inwardly, our body rages and yanks us back with reminders that cannot be ignored nor repressed.

Our bodies have already deemed what people and spaces hold red flags and triggers from the moment we step into the room. It took me many years, but I now know when my body is secure with another-I have managed to decipher who is safe to surround myself with. I have decided who is safe enough, even to hug. Any physical touch, no matter how elementary or innocent, becomes a battleground for trauma survivors.

Don't touch me, don't look at me.

We are convinced that our fight or flight mode keeps us safe, even in our day to day activities that may not hold any harm at all. Even that which is harmless can pose a threat, as our body manages to decipher between the two. Constantly judging between what is safe and what is dangerous, is exhausting. Sizing up the room the minute we walk in to determine whether we should be on high alert, reading into each signal from our body's telltale radar. It is both mentally and physically draining

Post traumatic stress disorder manifests itself in many ways and presents itself with many faces. For a survivor of trauma, the taste of PTSD is bitter and constant. Our trauma, and whatever singular event or multiple events that our trauma pertains to, transforms itself into warped imaging. Clear memories are translated into fragments, then rebirthed as body signals. I force myself to forget, to encrypt my memories into a code I cannot break so that I do not ever have to see those images again. Scientifically speaking, different sectors of the brain offer varied responses based on the purpose which they serve to our bodies and the signals that they send. The three parts of the brain which function as stress processers, are the hippocampus, the amygdala, and the prefrontal/anterior cingulate (welcome back to high school biology class, right?)

The hippocampus is embedded into our temporal lobe located in the middle of the brain. It plays a determining role in our learning abilities, our social behaviors and cognition, our memory, and our emotion. Namely, feeling and reacting. Additionally, it is responsible for the retrieval of two kinds of memories: declarative memories and special relationships. Sadly, this is the part that I never learned about in science class; it seemed this discussion didn't make the cut when we dissected the brain functions. As we cross-analyze anatomy with behaviors, we see that nothing in the body happens by accident.

Not only is this a centralized part of the brain, but it is also incredibly receptive and malleable. Studies have shown that the hippocampus is a vulnerable structure that can become easily damaged through various and vast stimuli, such as psychiatric/mental health disorders. The hippocampus is eroded away by the more obvious Alzheimer's and dementia, but it can also be greatly affected by PTSD.

Declarative memories are factual events that are pocketed away: remembering song lyrics, reciting a speech, memorizing facts for an exam. Spatial relationship memories refer to the memorization of images, routes, directions, and mapping. Within the hippocampus, short term memories are transformed into long term. Our brain gets to decide what stays and what goes; what we remember and what we choose to bury.

Individuals with PTSD can experience fragmented memories, repressed images, and entire gaps of missing time. Within the diagnosis of Post-Traumatic Stress Disorder, there are four key emotional symptoms that take their toll: intrusion, avoidance, arousal and reactivity, and mood and thinking. Intrusion symptoms appear as nightmares, flashbacks, terror, or fearful thoughts. Avoidance manifested herself quite familiarly to me within my denial phase: refusing to speak about what has happened and avoiding all stimuli which acts as a reminder to the event (although I will pinpoint that avoiding our triggers is key to healing and knowing our limitations is OKAY). Reactivity means that we are apt to act in a manner that reflects what we have been through and what we are suppressing. This includes intense anger, random outbursts, hypersensitivity, anxiety, scanning a room for danger…all things I have discussed within these pages in length. I am now able to give a name to my traits, my dispositions, my emotional reactions, my feelings of "insanity" and "craziness." My responses were real; they are real now. I can now label what I am, and why I have acted in such a manner of utter and pure survival. Lastly, symptoms that affect our entire mood, such as depression, the inability to concentrate, a feeling of detachment or estrangement from loved ones, and a feeling I know all too well: guilt. It has been found that in individuals with depression the hippocampus loses its volume and potency. Additionally, people that have been exposed to high levels of stress are more likely to have a negatively impacted hippocampus. Trauma infiltrates all facets of life.

And while the amygdala-the center for creativity and rumination-sees an increase in function with the presence of trauma, the prefrontal and anterior function used for self-development, declines.

The amygdala experiences a striking disruption in connectivity. When one experiences either prolonged trauma or a particular traumatic event, adrenaline rushes through the body which then causes the memory to imprint itself in our amygdala's. But it is not just the picture itself that becomes stamped on our brains, but rather the very emotional significance which is tied to that event. The amygdala latches on to the exact intensity of emotion that we felt and the impulses that we feel now because of it. This is how our history of trauma comes to life, becoming more than just a vague etch-a-sketch of the past.

It has even been uncovered via early evidence of cellular memory that it is not just our brain, but also our body, which retains an impression of past traumatic events. Thus, the body really does remember, even when the brain forgets. Even when our minds deceive us, our body cannot lie.

I have found that it is our unprocessed memories which are in fact sticking points that prevent us from experiencing a full life and following the path of healing. It is in the very nature of trauma to infiltrate every bit of space that it can possibly infect, but the powers of true healing can cleanse even the deepest of wounds.

The term "trauma" is perhaps too complex to define. While the American Psychiatric Association defines it as "an event or events that involve actual or threatened death or serious injury, or a threat to the physical integrity of self or others" I have found it to be so much more. When growing up, we often hear the term PTSD thrown around in reference to retired veterans or people coming home from the military. What we do not realize is that people also develop PTSD without ever facing actual death.

We are the Murder victims who lived, remember?

We never died, but we came close to it. So, while this textbook definition via the APA might partially encompass the far reaches of trauma, trauma itself is also what I have found to be both undefinable and borderless. Trauma is not simply black and white-it is not just witnessing death or physical violence, although this is ugly and valid. It is vast and varied forms of pain, abuse, torture, grief, disaster, and threat.

Trauma presents itself with many faces, whether that is the presence of prolonged childhood abuse, sexual violence, molestation during adolescence, or even natural disaster. Research has even found that forms of secondary PTSD are suffered when one experiences the betrayal of being cheated on in a relationship. And although post-traumatic stress order is often trivialized as a stigmatized taboo, it is more real and more common than we even realize. These stressors tie directly back to our bodies, because while the brain is in a constant whirlwind of defense, the body also acts as a layer of protection.

However, I have found that the body is also where our survival mechanisms of rewiring the brain, seems to reroute and malfunction.

The painful memories have shapeshifted themselves into physical reactions and bodily sensations, such as shaking or shivering, stepping back from touch, and feeling skittish, avoidant, and dissociative. Sometimes it feels as if our body has betrayed us. That which we have tried so hard to bury and keep hidden has now been given a tangible physicality. Suddenly, we are standing in a room of strangers, and our hands are quivering. Additionally, many trauma survivors suffer from seizures and ticking, debilitating episodes which are the result of the body's own unprocessed and stored trauma.

Our bodies are constantly trying to decipher what is harm, what is good.

Run, my body tells me.

But if I listen closer, she is also saying "heal me".

Our body calls out for us to heal our minds. In doing so, we heal our bodies. One is helpless without the other.

This body is the only one I have got. And she is pretty damn willing…and bold and brave and resilient and dare I say it, beautiful. I realize now that I may finally give myself the permission I have been craving. When I look back at my own reflection, at my very own vessel, I can lend myself forgiveness, grace, self-love, and affirmative language. I can acknowledge my tattered scars, the places in my skin that tell a story, the bits of my heart that have been sewed back together. I can embrace what is sometimes deemed dirty. I can reclaim that which has been shamed into hiding. I can take back the power of what is mine, and what has always been mine. As Helen Keller once said, "although the world is full of suffering, it is also full of the overcoming of it."

Sometimes I imagine that life is like a picnic…this is something that my father often reminds me of. We have wine, fruit, bread, the sun is shining, the lake is sparkling, the little birds are singing. Then one by one, tiny black dots begin to barrage our perfect picnic. Ants ravage at our food, destroying our Instagram-able venture. Then suddenly, it is as if the very sky itself has split in half, and it begins to pour rain all over our blanket.

Life is a damn picnic. One minute it's sun, the next it's rain.

My body is like a picnic too: some days I look in the mirror and I love what I see. Some days it is the sunniest, brightest day to sit on the hill and lay in the grass. Other days, I manage to carve out every miniscule imperfection in my skin, as the ants make a home on my blanket.

I have learned to celebrate the good days while crawling my way out of the bad. Often it is my very own self-deprecation that brings ants to the picnic. It is my own self-talk that ruins a perfectly well-weathered day.

Each day is new and each day I am learning.

Once upon a time not long ago,
This body had become a barren land,
Vacant and destitute.
My skin was uncovered and unmasked.
Earth stripped of trees,
A garden divested of flowers.
denuded
uprooted
and rotted.
I want to go back,
I want to water this body,
To bloom.
I must begin in the morning.

I must remind myself daily of these affirmations which bring me gratitude and contentment with this body, I must whisper these words to the mirror itself, to the reflective glass itself which I had once loathed.

The words are few, but they are crucial: you hold value, you are deserving, your body is not a mistake, you are worthy, you are wanted.

This body has always been good, this body will do good, and this body has done so much good.

MY body is good.

What I did not find out until much later, was that my body itself and my autonomic nervous system were in fact sending messages to my brain based on my experiences and what I knew to be true, even if they were lies.

I am fascinated by my new found knowledge of this deeply interconnected mind, body, and spirit. The very things that I blamed myself for were in fact logical and physiological reactions from trauma in my very central systems.

When our ANS transports these signals to the brain, the brain then tries to interpret the information the best it knows how.

What happens next is that the brain formulates a story which becomes foundational to our core beliefs about the world and about ourself.

The body. How brilliant, how beautiful, how deceiving.

Our bodies can misinterpret signals of danger, even when we are completely safe, because this has become a core belief: that we must be on high alert. That we are always in danger, no matter the environment.

If we have been made to feel deeply unsafe in our past, then our future becomes a self-fulfilling prophetic reflection of this.

Upon further research, I began to come back into my own body and find my own power. I unearthed something which I had been grappling for perhaps even before I was eighteen years old and a victim of assault: control. It was the knowledge and understanding of the after-effects of trauma and of my own mental state of being, which brought me to a light bulb moment of feeling in control of who I was and what I saw myself to be. I was not defined by these trauma responses, even though I knew that they would prove to be stumbling blocks for many years.

A neuroceptive mismatch is where we see danger and become hypervigilant in situations where there is no danger. For example, someone's neutral facial expression might be interpreted as us thinking that the person is mad and that we are the cause of their anger. We might tell ourselves that their vague responses or silent treatment are semblances of hostility and agitation, or that perhaps they are hiding something from us. Not getting an immediate text back causes panic. We go to the worst case scenario in our brains and latch on to it, until it makes us sick. Maybe they are annoyed of us, maybe we did something wrong.

This habit of walking on eggshells and always trying to sniff out something that might not even be there, is a characteristic that I developed much further back into my youth. As a child, I often worried that my friends and family were secretly mad at me. That perhaps I had done something wrong, perhaps I wasn't good enough, perhaps I was to blame for someone's bad day. It was always my fault. I learned this early on as a child, attempting to people please and submitting to the need of over-explaining. I always saw danger where there was none, and in turn became suspicious, guarded, worried, and anxious, constantly feeling unsafe and never at ease. I ask myself: if I am already predisposed to being so hyper vigilant and so insecure of danger, why did I let this happen? If I have been this way since before I was assaulted, how could I let it get to this?

Maybe that was why I drank in those days: I was so exhausted of being hyper vigilant to other people's responses and emotions. Maybe I just wanted to have fun and stop feeling such crippling anxiety in my daily interactions. Whatever it was, I let my guard down, and it still wasn't my fault. Those are words I could have never said a few years back: "…and it still wasn't my fault." You can say them, too.

What once began as a need to make everyone happy in my youth, soon developed into full on anxiety, which then manifested itself into the deepest corners of my mind once I became a victim of rape. Victim blaming is cruel, evil, and ugly, true, but I have found that sometimes I am my worst critic. I have learned that to be a victim often means placing a blame on ourselves which we feel even worse than any outside voice could ever make us feel.

I realize now that this is not in fact me and my quirk, but that it is actually my trauma manifested into my body. This is what my trauma has done to me. And whatever neurological characteristics and trauma responses I might have already possessed from my childhood, certainly showed themselves even more apparently in the aftermath of my assault.

My anxiety got worse, my self-worth plummeted, my insecurities (that I was an annoyance, inconvenience, or agitation) were never far from my mind, my need for explaining myself was heightened, my fear was unparalleled, and my radar for danger was always screeching and blinking red.

I am healing, thank god. This body is learning through therapy, through new affirmations. Through finding the truth where I have only known untruths. Through accepting that I no longer need to over-explain myself…or even explain myself at all. That I do not need to crave acceptance or chase after it. That I do not have to talk people into taking my side, or into believing me. That it isn't my fault. That I didn't do anything wrong that night in April.

And it's my body. I don't have to explain a damn thing because I was there, and you weren't, and I remember everything. Because it happened to me… to my body.

The gaps in my memory
Bitterly infused with trauma
Are tiny black holes of nothingness.
Speckles of unwanted darkness
Like tiny ants on a picnic blanket.
Some moments are fuzzy, and others simply cease to exist.
Or rather, it feels like they never did to begin with.
These tiny dots of nothingness
Are like Splotches of white on blank canvases.
Nights I can't recall,
Days where I imagine it was someone else living this life.
How can the mind do that?
How can it erase that which has been so engrained into
my psyche?
My mind has forgotten much,
Deleted remnants,
buried them into nothingness.
How can it do that? I wonder?
How can it unlearn and unsee?
Yet my bitter reality
Has been in discovering
That my body can never unfeel.

-"Forgotten Mind, Remembered Body."

Chapter Twenty-Two

What Am I Doing? Where Am I Going?

Henri Matisse once said "don't try to be original. Be simple. Be good technically, and if there is something in you, it will come out."

I suppose this was Matisse's way of saying "don't force your genius, it will just sort of show up." I love that.

Well, this is my story, uncensored and unequivocally honest. In fact, I have never felt freer or more afraid than when I am furiously typing away at my computer screen.

This is my truth, my simplicities bundled up into a small gap of my life. This is my genius, my epiphanies coming out, and in it I pray there will be good. This is not me trying to be original, but instead be relatable. Our stories differ, but they still sound the same.

Whitman said in Song of Myself, "these are really the thoughts of all, in all ages and lands, they are not original with me, if they are not yours as much as mine, they are nothing, or next to nothing." So, I sing the Song of Myself, but I sing the song of you, too.

Our stories align unknowingly. If these stories can't be shared, then it is as if they never happened, buried in some far unknown corner never to be found. But the power of storytelling is that for as unlike our stories are, they are also much of the same song. Broken bits of each of us linger on in the wind, but when they connect with each other, they turn into a bigger picture. These little scraps of life manage to collect with one another and help return each to their rightful places.

We change, we grow, we heal, but our stories stray on, and people remember the things that one day-and for the last time-pass out of our minds. We impact with our words, and we cling to the testimonies of others. You tell me that someone tried to ruin you like they tried to ruin me, but both were fruitless in their efforts. And in this, together we share a small victory-we say the words "I am okay" and "I have heard that story before." Our pain can be healed by the sharing of pain, the sharing of good company. Sometimes, it is good to be alone, and other times it is well for the soul to hear that our commonalities lie in the wars that we have won against hurt and against self. For my words are nothing original, but merely a collection and reflection of all the things I have seen and felt and seen others feel. my words are as much yours as they are mine, our stories may be unalike, but they a line.

My story is one of redemption. My story glimpses how powerful of a bond a daughter and her parents can have. How the words of strangers can lift anyone out of the mire. How comforting it can be to hear you are not alone. My story is yet another in a long list of "me too's". I wish there were less of us. I wish the world was not so damn horrific. I wish that there was not power or safety in numbers, because the numbers are so alarming. I wish there was not so many of us. This crime is so rampant. I wish, I wish, I wish. When something as disgusting as this happens to one's body, one begins to question their very identity.

I used to write in my journal more often than I should have:

"What are you doing? Where are you going?"

This was my way of asking, "who are you?" and "where would you like to go, so why are you going this way instead?"

It was a gentle-or not so gentle reminder-to self, to constantly ask of my choices: "where is this taking you? Where are you going with this?" Dance legend Hanya Holm once said, "who are you? How can you encourage your vision? How can you enlarge your capacity of being capable?"

One can only hope that they are in fact heading somewhere and that their choices are leading to something that matters and makes sense.

What are you doing? So then why are you here not there? Are you happy? Did you mean to do this, is this what you want? Is this what you have always wanted? What are you doing?...

Where are you going? Where are you going with this? Where do you want to go? Where do you see yourself? What does your future hold? What would you like to see for your perfect tomorrow? Are you headed the right way? Where are you going? Is this going to be bad for you? This seems self-destructive, you should probably not go down that road...oh, you are anyways?

Late at night, when these realizations would hit me like a brick on the nose, I would begin to question if I really was proud of myself, if I had done the best thing for me, and who did I want to be even?

"Who are you?"

This became my desperate want-to-know back then. I was uncertain of who I was and what I exactly wanted for my life. Throughout my four years of college, I have been bombarded with the same theme of questions, slammed in the face with "what is your five, ten, fifteen-year plan?" In my final semester of college, the weight of the unknown has hit harder than a missed deadline.

I have been asking who I am and what I am doing for an incredibly lengthy amount of time. I mostly just wanted to get to a better place than here, a place where all the pain had gone to die, and everything was magically "all better". Did such a place exist, and would it ever shimmer into the horizon?

I did not want my parents to suffer. Naturally our instincts tell us that we must protect and preserve our parents at all costs, even though growing up, the shielding and sheltering was supposed to be our caregiver's job, not ours. Still, we take this defense on with anyone whom we love and wish to protect from the unconscionable bad.

I wanted to shoulder this alone because I knew I could. But I had been suffering in silence all along. I was glad to have them, I was glad not to agonize in the quiet, I was glad to have a voice. Having a voice meant feeling free for the first time in my life, it meant I could stop asking myself "what are you doing?" and instead ask myself "you're doing the best you can."

Still, I wondered to myself about what kind of woman I hoped to be. What sort of choices did I want to make from this day forward, never minding my past?

My past was always seeping its way into my future whether I liked it or not, so I had to deal with what was behind me before I could embrace what was before me.

My habits, my core beliefs, and my own confirmation biases have me in a vice grip.

I do not believe what is true about myself, because I have fallen into a sink hole of self-deprecating lies. I do not believe what I have been told, only because that is what I have learned to do-mentally bend and twist words. The men in my life come and go of their own accord, or because I let my cards show. I push people away. I am terrified of those who intrude upon my life. Their intentions certainly could not be pure, right?

"I am an imposter," my body tells me time and again. Where do I belong, if at all? Neither here nor there. Why am I always wandering aimlessly? Will I find my place?

If I was not "defined" by what had happened, then why did I look so different from the girl that I would have been if nothing had ever happened to her?

I really just wanted, above all else, to be happy. Don't all of us want that one thing? And what is happiness, anyways? An emotion, so subjective and based purely on one's own perspective. To be content with my decisions, which has possibly been the trickiest part of it all.

Rephrasing has become a big part of my healing process, as well. For me, that means I must reverse negative thinking. I must halt the thought before it infects me, before the input of the bad fills up my mind. I choose to reverse it into an outpouring of good.

Life has become all about these choices as they pile on top of each other. One misplaced block and the whole tower usually comes crumbling down.

I no longer choose to pose the question "who are you?" or "where are you going?" but instead, voice statements that put my feet back on firm ground, the edifications that start with "you are" because I know who I am. I don't have to keep fruitlessly wondering. When I tell myself, what is known for sure, I can breathe easier.

After all, it is in our human nature to do well with what is certain and firm.

We all thrive with the promise of what is set in stone.

So, I tell myself these "you are's":

You are incredibly brave to be here today.
You are a survivor.
You are a daughter.
You are human first, dancer second.
You are love and loved.
You are creativity embodied.
You are a symbol of forgiveness.
You are not limited to or defined by, yesterday.
You are fierce.
You are impossible to ignore.
You are worthy of love and loyalty.
You are light in a tunnel of black.
You are Sophia, damn it.

I can't say you will be the same because you will never be the same. You know this. But you will be strong, you will be mighty, you will be a force to be reckoned with in the days that follow. I can assertively tell you that you are brave beyond belief, that you don't reflect the hurt that has been inflicted upon you by a hollow person, that you are not alone in this. I can be certain when I say that you will be okay.

You will be okay.

If this has happened to you, if you are pained by the past, then I wish I was there with you tonight. I wish that I could hear all your stories, and all your ins and outs and how you have conquered them or are in that process. Thank you for picking up this book.

I am here with you.

These questions that I ask of myself-where am I going, what am I doing-also lend themselves to society itself-where are we going now, what will we do with this?

Perhaps we can trace this all the way back to kindergarten, perhaps our current issues can root themselves as far back as primary school. One of the largest, most formative possibilities that society should offer in education is the definition of rape and consent from an early age. If we are going to preach abstinence, advocate for condoms on bananas, and explain pregnancy through twenty-year-old documentaries, then we should make take rape out of this constructed "taboo" category.

Nothing should be off limits except for my body. Instead, the conversations we choose to have should strip rape down to its basis...to where it all begins. Consent should be inherent, but since it isn't, it should be CLARIFIED. This starts at a young age, and I was reminded of this when I surveyed colleagues and friends in the prior chapter, "S-E-X Is A Bad Word." We should distinguish between good and bad touch and reinforce the importance of children having their own voice. Both boys and girls can and should be taught this in the same room. By separating boys and girls, it creates a furthered mysterious taboo, and builds up a wall between genders. I think that putting boys in a room with a male teacher and girls in a room with a female teacher, further loses the importance of thinking from someone else's point of view. We automatically divide based off gender, when really we should be talking about it together. After all, the conversation is often directed toward the people in the other room-so why not discuss it together?

I was one of the few kids in the fourth grade that sat in the library during such sex ed talks. My parents signed the paper that stated they didn't want me in with the boys or the girls…instead I sat cross legged on the storytelling rug by the fiction section and read a book about a dollhouse. I felt left out then, I thought I was surrounded with a bunch of outcasts and nerds. But looking back now, I see that my parents could and did in fact, do a much better job than any pathetic public-school health class could. They wanted to be the one's to say the words some parents could not, and to open the floor up for me to define myself and ask questions. I learned about sex at the kitchen table after spaghetti night in our first-floor apartment. I remember shriveling up my nose and saying, "that's all?"

At least nothing was ever off limits, and perhaps from the fourth grade on and even before, I really began to see that my parents were really telling me, "we can be in it together, if you want. You can talk to mom and dad, even about these two strange body parts fitting together when you are older."

As we fade on into middle school and high school, the natural progression of sex should be discussed. I have never said, "yes, we may have sex now" to anyone. Often, it is a silent conversation between two people, not necessarily an audible, permission, although it can be. I have learned that a no, however, is always clear, a no always speaks louder. "Get off me" "stop" "not now" "I am not ready" or the shift in body language, the mere pulling back, pushing away, retreating, and protesting are all signs that say, "back off me now."

We should teach respect for other's bodies, which first comes from respecting our own bodies. You are responsible for your choices, not making someone else's choice for them.

Society obviously has a lengthy road to take, a long way to go. I am here pushing for the answers to, "where are we going? What are we doing?" and I encourage you to think about these things for yourself as you read my book.

Although subjects of rape and assault are predominantly female based, they are often dealt with by professionals, therapists, seminars, and support groups that key themselves exclusively towards women. Since my time in college, I have met an unfortunate number of males-both straight, gay, bisexual, and nonbinary-that were raped, molested as children, or assaulted by a trusted advisor.

This reminds me that often times rape does not pick by sex or by gender, but rather by vulnerability and opportunity.

I have noticed in life pain is divvyed out in ways I can never possibly understand, but the more I see, the more I recognize that we all have our own "thing". Everyone has a "thing". Every stranger you pass on the sidewalk has their own hidden secret of what makes them tick, what makes them hide, what keeps them up at night, what makes them a shiny-but dented-penny.

Mine is this. Therefore, I must do something with my pain so that it is all for not. In this I have realized I just want so much to help people. There is so much wrong in the world that it overwhelms me, for long it overwhelmed me into silence. An errored system that has done us so wrong, a society that has taught girls to hide rather than boys to behave. A world that asks us what we were wearing, but not what he was wearing, because apparently there is a dress code for getting raped but not being a rapist. Apparently, being a black male in a sweatshirt makes you guilty and being a woman in a skirt makes you compliant.

We can hardly thrive in a world that asks us what we did to deserve this, not if we are okay. A culture that says, "maybe you did something wrong" long after you are dead. A country that elects a man as president who likes to "grab em by the pussy." Well guess what? We grab the fuck back, sir.

On November 22, 2019, I wrote in my journal:

"I have plenty of beautiful people in my life that make me happy to be here today, to be doing what I am doing."

I am here today, doing what I am doing, writing this…that alone is enough for me.

So, I stop asking questions about when I will get there and why and instead, I don't stop. That is what matters most.

In a world like this, I chose not to drown, even when they tell me to. It seems simple enough but getting here has been a long time coming.

These are the steady facts of life I cling to.

Are you ok with where you are going?

Chapter Twenty-Three

Oh, That I May Have Wings Like a Dove, I Could Fly Away and Find Rest…

In July of 2019, a hometown friend overdosed and passed away. Bethesda's older sister was especially close to him, but she had already left for the Peace Corps when he passed. So, it was just Bethesda and I, in all black, in a church downtown, back in the town where it had all started. His birthday just passed in fact…January 18th.

Back when I was managing to keep afloat in some of the darkest hours of my life, I read through a book in the Bible about a man named Job.

I read the whole book just days after the night that it happened to me. I was house sitting that week, all alone in a big two story house meant for a husband, wife, and three kids. I just remember thinking how my jeans smelled like his cologne and there was a bruise on the back of my forearm. In the early blooms of spring, there were trees still bare and grass still bone dry; everything was dry.

I sat on the living room sofa in the beginning days of April, and pulled my knees into my chest as the day turned to night. I couldn't really sleep during those days and I kept thinking of that Robert Frost poem from high school, "the woods are lovely, dark, and deep, but I have promises to keep and miles to go before I sleep." It felt like a journey which may take forever to endure: being able to sleep again. I wondered how many years it might take to fall asleep without fear, without a lamp on, and with no thoughts of him in my mind. To be fully at peace with what the day had brought me. Eyes closed and shutting out everything in the world that could wait until tomorrow to face. That was how it felt as a little girl. I didn't think those days would ever come back.

As I sat there in the dead of silence, I glanced over at the coffee table Bible. I thought maybe it might give me something to cling to. I remember in those days I was so desperate, like someone searching for religion or meaning to life. I closed my eyes and flipped through it blindly. And I still remember to this day what I whispered out loud: "whatever it is You have for me to find, let me find it. Because I don't know what I'm looking for but I know I can't do this." I felt so sick and so isolated in this desolate loneliness and shame.

I opened my eyes and there it was.

The book of Job. The very first page.

I embarked on the story of a man who had it all and in a flash, had nothing. His health, his family, his wealth…he lost all that was held to his name. But he wasn't cursing God. So I kept reading.

After everything had been ripped away from him, he was returned to a life even better than he could have imagined. After he had survived his own personal hell but never stopped fighting, he was blessed a thousand times over and named his first-born daughter Dove. I think about dove's and olive branches, and I think of hope. I had a dove tattooed on my wrist the summer before we lost our friend. At his burial, we watched as a dozen pure white doves were released from their cages, swirling over the green lawns of a cemetery.

The day was bright and beautiful but oh so dark. And then the man who set all those beautifully pristine doves free, read these words from the book of Psalms:

"Oh that I had wings like a dove that I would fly away and be at rest."

A couple years later I set those words into stone, inking them onto my forearm with the purpose of reminding myself daily that the freedom which I always yearned for could and would be mine to claim. Every time I look down at that tattoo, I think of how it felt to stand there in the cemetery that day: arms hanging helplessly by my side, watching the doves released out of their cages and feeling like a caged bird myself.

I prayed that maybe for the first time in Jay's life, that he would be at rest. And maybe it was my turn to feel that too, just down here on earth before I joined him up there much later.

The summer that followed the spring of my assault, I decided to get this tattoo on my back: "You will lie down with no one to make you afraid." It was from the Book of Job. The book that changed my life. Words of suffering but hope. Words that brought forth new life. I love when people ask me what my tattoos mean, so I get to share a brief bit of my story. I tell them this:

"Life will be brighter than noonday.

And darkness will become like morning.

You will be secure because there is hope;

you will look about you and take your rest in safety. You will lie down with no one to make you afraid."

Job 11:17-19

And if I had room I would have covered my whole body in those words because they changed my life.

Rest. Safety. Peace. Doves. The dove signaling land in the great flood of Noah and the Ark. Hope. Job's daughter Dove. Beginnings. The dozen doves released in the cemetery that day we said goodbye. Our souls made free.

I've been to so many funerals. I've missed just as many. I've been to weddings, too. Sometimes in the same churches. Sometimes in the same places where we celebrate life we also celebrate death.

So, how then, might I fly away so free as a dove and find my place to rest?

In every society and every religion, doves have seemingly become universal symbols of pure spirit and peace. The dove symbolizes the soul's release from its time bound on earth. It reminds me that I am not bound to my pain, or to the things of human nature or the very things of this earth. I am promised more than that. In fact, I am promised a future…not just a long life, but a good one.

I wondered how I would make it, how would I fly away from all that pinned me down to dust and dirt? I realized that in order to be free, I might have to make a list of rules to abide by: a total juxtaposition. In order to be free, I would have to think constrictively.

In order to let go, I would have to look back. And looking back meant going back to that unwanted place in order to conquer it.

The first thing that I have found is to not apologize for who I am. A victim blaming society that perpetuates a culture of sexual violence turns towards the attacked, not the attacker, and begins to ask all the wrong questions.

I began to rack through my brain: what I had possibly done to carry this burden in life? Why did I to have to tell my daughters what happened to mommy when they were old enough? But would I be extra paranoid when they left the house? Would I try with fruitless efforts to shield them from the world and all its damages, and would they think I was suffocating them?

I am twenty-one years old and already thinking of the repercussions this will have on my unborn children, already hosting my personal concerns for the daughters and sons I may never have. I make no apologies for myself, because I know when I am wrong, and in this circumstance, I have done nothing. I am not at fault. I am me.

In my journal I scrawled these words:

"When you walk into a room, this is you. Demand to be heard. Do not be sorry. You are not too much."

I was so sick to my stomach of apologizing on his behalf. And for what?

So, I decided to live by leaving no stone unturned. I suppose I did this very thing when I punched my rapist in the face. I wrote in my journal:

"Speak up when what you have to say needs to be heard. Dig your heels in. Go on a fearless journey, no matter how daunting it appears at the foot of the mountain."

I began to understand that nothing good could come from keeping my mouth shut. I scribbled this down in my journal sometime in November 2019 at 11:50 p.m.:

"Your opinion matters. You matter. You are not a pawn."

No one ever made a worthwhile statement from being timid. Change isn't born of fear, but rather from having a voice. No one ever made history by doing nothing. Sometimes saying nothing speaks volumes and your greatest voice will be in your silence. And other times, you must act. You must speak up, because people will listen. They must.

My next thought process is a bit of a doozy. Not my favorite thing to do and yet I wrote it anyway. Learn to show someone your heart…key word being learn. Because being vulnerable and open is not something that blooms overnight. I wrote:

"Transparency can be painful. Vulnerability may be the greatest and most pure struggle of any single person's life. But find the right person, or people, and the safest environment, to show your heart to. Do not let the thought of love shut you down. Be open to feeling and being seen."

I have also come to realize that it will forever be my job to keep my very own best interest at heart. Most importantly, and above all, your actions should not be a direct reflection of simply trying to please someone else. If you think like that, you will never win.

Lastly, this one is inspired by Tennessee Williams: Ask yourself what it feels like to be wild at heart…or to be wild at heart again. I realize that I am still the same me, the same Sophia, but I have been on the fight of my life to regain my sanity.

"A prayer for the wild at heart, kept in cages…"

But that was not me, the one so desperately in need of prayer and escape. I was no longer a caged dove.

For me, being wild at heart meant being utterly free. I have been wild ever since I was a little girl, and then I went through my extra wild phase, and now I just want to simply be wild at heart. It reminds me of what it is like to be a child again, to have courage, to be bold. To look after the light, to chase after it.

I realize that now, all I ever wanted was to be the little bird who could be free and unbounding.

And if I can find that kind of wild freedom coupled with the peace that could still this beating heart, and ground me again, then that was how I may fly away like a dove and find rest.

Chapter Twenty-Four

Unbounding: ME

Sometime during mid-October, I was fascinated with the word UNBOUND.

An incredible mentor of mine told me that every day she opens her big coffee table dictionary and sifts through and learns a word. It is a foreign word to her, and she studies it, and ingests it fully. She does this every day.

I thought to myself...how brilliant. To be everything that our society is lacking in, to always be hungry to learn more, to expand. If only the world were more like her, then perhaps we would not have so much ignorance. Perhaps we would be an earth brimming with possibilities as opposed to foreclosures. If only words could cure us.

Sometimes, I have figured out, they indeed can.

The word unbound caught me like a fish ensnared, and I googled it not only because I loved the rich sound of it, but because I wanted to be unbounding (how great does that sound?). To be unending, limitless.

The Oxford dictionary defines the word "unbound" as "not bound or tied, not provided with a proper or permanent cover, not held by gravity or a physical force. To unbind is to release from bonds or restraints."

Synonymous for free, liberate, release, disentangle, emancipate, escaped, unchained, unfettered, unleashed, uncaged, unrestrained, unconfined, footloose...unbound. Boundless, endless, fathomless, horizonless, illimitable, infinite, unlimited, unfathomable, extensive, immense, vast, countless…unbound.

In my extensive research of this singular adjective, I unearthed a synonym that seemed ironic: abysmal. At first, I was bewildered, understanding the word perhaps only for its negative context.

However, I found that abysmal can also mean bottomless, deep, and profound, in addition to its more popular negative connotations. I have been familiar with the word abysmal only when it is used to describe lowly places: "an abysmally low performance." But if abysmal means bottomless, then it can also mean unending. I realized that every word that coincided with the word "unbound" was exactly what I was striving to be. And that thinking outside of the box meant that even the most unprofitable of words, such as abysmal, also held an alternative meaning that could be used to my advantage.

To be unbounding meant that I held the weight of my future in my very own hands and the knowing that no one else could take this from me. I wanted to choose for myself, the chance to look onwards and upwards, never back and never down. I wanted my life to be boundless, a place where I could visualize not one single boundary, no matter which direction my eyes took me.

During my junior year of college, my final project was to create a short dance film. I titled the film "Ne Plus Ultra" which translated from Latin, means that one cannot physically reach or go any higher than where they are at in the current state. To me, this was symbolic for more reasons than one. I wanted to make it to the most exceptionally highest point where I could not go any higher. I wanted to escape into a space of freedom, a mountaintop where I could bathe in the light forever. I wanted to be unbound, not bound by my past or by the horrific events which I had endured. Not bound to the person that had done this to me, or all the failed relationships in my life that had fallen short.

I wanted instead to be limitless, to be liberated, to be released from the past. I wanted to emancipate myself from his hold. I wanted my future to be horizonless, fathomless, and infinite. I wanted to climb out of the murky pit that I was caught within and stand high once again.

I wanted to live unbounding, me. Yes, me. But in order to do so, I would have to go back to that place that drained the life out of me, dwindled my spark down to nothing. One will never change if they don't have the awareness to do so. Einstein defined the term "insanity" as the act of doing the same thing over and over again while expecting the same results. In other words, an inability to change.

I knew that if I wanted to find my high place, I would have to first find myself yet again in the lowly past, in order to rid myself of it.

I wanted to be unconfined, but I was still held by pain.

How do you move on from something like this? remained the recurring question often at the forefront of my mind. I cannot accept this for myself, I never wanted this to be a part of my timeline. Where do I go from here? How do I get out of this dark place? I wanted my "Ne Plus Ultra", my highest point.

My therapist made me write a list of all the words that came to mind with my past. This giant word bank is in fact the very opposite of being unbound and free, and I knew that these were the words I had to pen down first before I could touch the latter:

Ashamed	Angry	Falling
Disappointed	Hurt	The R word I hate saying
Frustrated	Restrained	Bound by my past
Confused with Survival		Victimized
What this makes me		
Ignorance	"What now?"	Identity
Disregarded	"I will never let anyone in again"	Ignorance is bliss"
Annoyed	Defining	Damaged goods"

| Voiceless | Denying | Recklessness |
| Weakened | Am I done with this yet? | Holding it all together" |

I didn't want any of these things anymore. I had grown to claim each one of these words and phrases as chapters in my story, but I had grown so sick and tired of this burden. Each one of these words had shaken me to my core and changed the very way I looked at myself in the mirror every morning.

Assault strips away your identity, then places you in a bottomless ocean of denial. While you are wondering if this really did happen to you, you experience an intense lack of disregard for your trauma from people who don't understand and are not willing to listen. This in turn leaves you voiceless and weakened. You then grow frustrated and annoyed with all the people in your life who don't get it. I was angry at him for doing this to me, for giving me this backpack full of rocks to carry up the mountain. I was once skipping up my mountain called life, and now I was trudging. This made me ashamed. I was supposed to be the one who had it all together. So, then I became confused, questioning: "what does this make me?" I had been victimized and was now asking "what now? What next?" Next came survival. Next came defining what I wanted and needed for my life. What I would do with this.

I would be unbound. I have decided I will use all the willpower I can muster in this life and come out on the other side. Because I do believe in the elusive existence of the "other side". I believe that we can make it out of the depths into our ne plus ultra. I believe that I am not alone in this. I believe I am a conqueror, my very own personal hero. I believe that others have made me brave and I in turn have done the same for people I have met along the way. Not all will understand, but we will make them listen.

I wrote on my brainstorm list of words from my past: "falling."

But doves don't fall. The unbound don't fall. They float, they fly away, so why was I still here on the ground? I don't want to be in limbo anymore. I want to be infinite. I don't want to find myself falling, but instead climbing higher. I had fallen time and time again, and each time I managed to stand back up torn and battered, bruised knees, and not any better for it. I am not better for this. I didn't need this as a life lesson. I still don't know why it happened to me. It infuriates me to think it happens at all. Then I think about my highest point and that brings me back. I feel safe again, I feel hopeful. I remind myself that I am on my way, and I am accompanied by so many up the mountain, who have let their rocks fall one by one. I am on an unending journey like most, whether it is faith, God, happiness, peace, contentment, or love that you are searching for. Mine is a few wrapped inside of each other. In order to one day find love, I knew I would have to make peace with my demons, and in order to do that I knew I would have to forgive him and forgive my past, but that would take me a long way up the mountain.

Trauma doesn't ask you whether you are ready. In fact, it picks a time in your life when you are anything but. It doesn't come at a time of convenience or need, and certainly no necessity. It shows up whether you ask for it to do so, only leaves you asking, "why me?" Mine came at a time when I thought I had everything figured out, a life plotted out on a timeline that would soon grow sporadic and skewed. It jolted me into knowing nothing for certain, anymore. It rid me of my clarity, buried me nose deep in what I was so unsure of. I was drowning in my very own ocean night after night. I was scrambling to escape my pit of snakes. A psychology teacher once told the class that "killers steal away one's life, but rapists steal away a part of one's soul."

Trauma doesn't ask whether you are old enough. It randomly selects and I have no comfort in this. But it is often intercepted. I don't think I would have made it without the strength that I can call on from my loved one's and my God. I am constantly reminded that nothing truly good can ever be found on this earth…but if you find the good people that combat the bad, then never let them go.

I think of the girl in that black and white tiled bathroom, scrambling for an escape, pleading "go get a condom." I think of how it felt to rush out that door, slamming it open with my entire body. That is what I call an interception.

I think of Bethesda's father sleeping restlessly on the couch night after night, growing thinner day by day from the lung cancer as we snuck around, tiptoeing past his sleeping figure. I think of the day that we found out that the lung cancer had disappeared from his X-rays, he was inexplicably healed. I call that an interception.

But then I watch a world go by where a girl struggles to regain her identity even after she "got away" and where her rapist posts online, offering his "life coaching services" to men that need more confidence to "get that girl or get that job."

And I think of a daughter who is left fatherless because the cancer metastasized to a brain tumor.

And I think to myself, why oh why did we need this?

I think of everything I took for granted, the days that would surely never come back, and the people that were staying behind with them.

I am pinned down by their realities, the utter opposite of free.

Twyla Tharpe once wrote in her book, "Each day completes itself-the next day is new." That one is going to stick with me for an eternity. I cling to that idea that every morning is a new chance-a second chance-because yesterday has completed itself with finality. I can't change the past. But I can damn well change my today, and preserve my today as MINE, and make tomorrow meaningful and unbounding and new.

Until tomorrow…until the next time I see you, or never have to see you…

"I ascend from the moon; I ascend from the night…" Walt Whitman.

Chapter Twenty-Five

The Grieving of You

*Trigger Warning: Male Suicide

Every now and then we dip into the pool of grief. Life hands us our cards and it becomes our turn. But grief isn't just death. Many I have mourned who are still well and alive. A bitter irony to life's many moving parts, wouldn't you say?

It scares me how people expect one to so quickly get over the traumatic events that they have been dealt. If you were abused or bullied, existed within a terrible childhood, were raped at a party, or even found yourself caught in a relationship with a gaslighting narcissist…you have been exposed firsthand to trauma and to all of its effects. Trauma comes in many forms and often plays on our weaknesses so that we are affected long after the actual act which caused the trauma itself. This is why we are a society chalk-full of unhealed children parading as adults. We were never taught nor given the breathing space or tools to heal. And so we, unequipped, live on with our trauma many years to come, having never conquered it let alone addressed it.

Society says "take all the time you need" without ever actually offering any time at all for us to do so: to heal. American White Supremacy culture says you work yourself to death until the day you die.

This does not consider that while you are in the middle of living, life happens. And trust me, it ALWAYS does.

Society equates our worth to our work. Making a mistake is often associated with being the mistake, and overworking is glorified and gratified as having a bold work ethic or "chasing the bag". We can maybe, but not always, take a day off for the flu, but we can never take a mental health day. A fever constitutes as a passable excused absence, but not a debilitating day of panic attacks. It is truly a swim or drown way of life, and it seems that where people have the opportunity to offer us life jackets, they merely push our head under.

I am still expected to be a productive member of society. I am still expected to give and to produce-in my career and in my relationships. I am dubbed "crazy" for faltering into a moment that is considered "weakness" not "humanness." I am offered no grace. I am labeled as "unhinged", the girl who could not hold it all together. No one gives me a hall pass, only raises their brows.

What a nutcase they must think I am.

Time off? No way. Unpaid leave for personal issues? You're joking.

"Put your mental health first," they tell me, followed up with a deadline at midnight.

"I am so sorry," they say with a nod of forced understanding. I can hear that their words are laced with hidden judgments.

I plead back with a subtle but fraught, "be patient with me."

My words are met only with furrowed foreheads and a world that is moving so quickly onwards without me. I am unrelentingly chasing after the city bus, but it has already trudged so unforgivingly past the stop.

I am in my entirety merely a sum of what I can produce, provide, and perform. I am more than my work, than my overwork, and more than my traumas. But often we are deprived of the tools needed to heal, unequipped for true and authentic success.

I knew a man once who exhibited each of these characteristics. I do not think we were in love. But now that he is dead, I can look back on him with love. I have love for him; I had it then and I have it now. We were not meant to be together, but I wish he was still here. I now hold the full knowing that he was not my person, and I can accept that fate played its role in loosening our ties to one another. So much so, that by the time he passed away, I was not the girlfriend left behind in mourning, but rather the woman who had already moved onwards and would have to dive deep into the past to find him again, and to grieve him.

Do you remember the night we met? I do. Meeting you was grieving you.

September. I wasn't looking for you because I had someone else. But that's just the thing, isn't it? That's how these events tend to unfold, don't they?

One day you're going about your business, semi-satisfied, blinders on, path paved out...and then, when you're least expecting it...something or someone shifts your direction. And it was the smallest shift, that meeting of two minds. But it was undeniable. And regrettable. Because now when I think of you, I regret so much that I cannot possibly spill it all out into the right words.

We were totally enthralled with each other. Not me and you, but me and him. Your old friend from college, a mutual friend that accidentally brought us together. I thought that he was the one for me, not you. And I was completely blindsided when we sat beside each other that night, and I realized that the British blonde who hardly matched up in my taste in men was indeed not the one for me. But it was you, rather, this quiet yet hilarious, tanned brunette who had taken in an interest in the real Sophia.

Your friend invited me out that night for his birthday, and while the British Blonde and I sat in the VIP section together sipping champagne and laughing, you looked over at me and later you told me that you thought I was so beautiful you couldn't look away. You were looking at me and you saw me, but I never noticed, never registered you as anything other than a face. You never made my radar, never opened my eyes until later.

And because as all college students know, when the night is over it is never really over, there was still a chance for us. After the club closed, we all wandered over to a friend's row house down the street. I ended up making my rounds, meeting friends of friends six degrees separated and aimlessly chattering about life, school, and where we went out to that night.

And then I found you again, or perhaps it was you who found me. And while I am unsure of the smallest details pertaining to how we spoke to each other for the first time or in what order, I do remember standing on the back deck of the second floor and telling you my name.

We talked for a while about nothing magical and there were no fireworks, simply because I was not looking for you. I wasn't looking for you, so I wasn't really seeing you either. Remember what I said about "before"? When we are going about our lives, blinders on, we are not actually ever paying attention for anything other than what we already have or what we think we want.

So, since I showed up with him, I wasn't looking for you. But you saw me anyways, and you saw me from the first moment we said hello. Although it wasn't immediate, soon I saw you too…and that was a scary thing.

I recall a few evenings later being at home by myself, mindlessly scrolling through social media as one usually does before bed, and there you were.

I thought to myself, who is this kid? Oh yes, from the back porch that night.

Suddenly and all at once, I found myself completely stalking you. I was scrolling between photos of you in Miami and you coaching kid's soccer, and a smile spread across my face as I began to see what I had missed.

What if I had met him first? I pondered to myself. Shame.

Because I was now in that accidental and ever so sticky in-between. I was "kind of sort of" barely involved with your friend, but I was "kind of sort of" actually interested in you. And that didn't hit me until later that it took meeting him, to meet and to know you.

Sure enough, British Blonde and I didn't make it more than a quarter of a mile down the way. He was sleezy, shady, and predictable. Same old ladies man, same old waste. It was amicable; I didn't care and neither did he. I was too busy living a good life to care that a match made in the club wasn't a match at all (isn't that what they tell you anyways-you can't find love in the club? No surprise).

And then you. You came back before you went away for good, and I just don't know what to do with that now.

January. Months passed and there you were. We made eye contact in the most dramatic way possible. It was so cinematic I can't even pretend it was anything else. We locked gazes with each other in a way that was so absolute I will never be able to erase it from my memories of you for as long as I live on this earth without you. I was standing in that same club from September, up on the second floor, gazing over the balcony. I always found myself looking out over the dance floor before me and assessing the crowd, simply because I liked to people watch, I liked to take it all in. And apparently you did too, because there you were, sitting in that same VIP section from September with a group of friends I didn't recognize.

You were sitting up on the ledge of the booth above everyone else, looking out over the dance floor of people packed in like sardines. And then you looked up at me, and my heart beat a little faster, and then I remembered.

I know you. I said to myself. You.

And then you smiled up at me and we stared immovably at each other. I couldn't help but smile, as a flash of recognition covered your face. I waved pathetically, a little unsure of what to do, looking down over the balcony at you in the overbearingly loud club. I was totally enraptured, confused on why it had taken me this long. You waved me down with an arm, as if motioning for me to join you.

You grinned and mouthed, Come here!

I remember making it down the stairs and pushing my way through the crowd to get to you, and once I found you, there was never any turning back for us, was there?

The truth is, I want to go back. Not to be with you, but to be with me. I want to go back in time to that sliver of space where I thought you were so perfect for me, and you thought I was perfect, and together we just existed so imperfectly but perfectly. I want to go back to that sweet spot when I was naïve and wild, to that moment of youth and laughter and comfort.

I want to take it all back and I want to go back, if only for a moment. Those are memories I will always cherish, but now I don't know where they belong.

"Where do I file these away?" I ask myself. Are the laughter and the arguments and the make ups now overshadowed with the fact that you are dead? Have all those memories-all that light-turned dark now? With death is the finality that I will never again see you or hear your voice or say I'm sorry. So, when I lay here at night and I reminisce as anyone would after hearing the news, I cannot help but to wonder where these memories now belong. Where do I hold them? In what corner of my mind and my heart do they belong? I am realizing that as time progresses, and I grow older, I often feel like I have less-and not in fact more-answers than ever before. It is as if the older I get, and the more life shows itself to me so unapologetically, the less I know for sure.

In the end, you and I never could sort ourselves out. We fought like hell, like a hobby. You were stubborn and fiercely independent, just like me. We always made up, but even after a short amount of time I could see so clearly how unhealthy we were. You were unhappy and I couldn't make you happy. I was dying inside to make you happy, but there was so much that you had to figure out for yourself, I knew I couldn't be your savior.

In those places where we aligned, we also repelled. In our commonalities we fell apart. You were heavy, you were burdened. You took on every responsibility in the world and carried it on your shoulders-your sisters, your single mom, your brother, your nephew, your finances, everything.

You, a financial advisor, and accountant at one of downtown's biggest banks, told me (a then-college student) to start paying for my own meals and drinks. You were so pressed about money that I would have done anything to ease the burden. So, I began paying for you when I could, because I wasn't going to let something so stupid ruin us. I felt so horrible that you thought it was about the money. That drove a ridiculous wedge between us, but it was never about the money for me. I think I got mad because inwardly I wondered if you didn't think I was worth it. You made plenty of money and I didn't need to ask where it went. But was I that much of a burden?

Our issues were only beginning. You refused help, you refused therapy and anti-depressants. You refused me at times...there was a darkness you wouldn't ever explore with me. A sadness behind your eyes. I could sense it all and I knew I wasn't crazy for seeing it. It was real then, and it is real now, hauntingly real. Your depression paired with your family history, our arguments brushed under the rug, the demons in the closet, my obsession with fixing people, and finally my realizing that I could not be the one to fix you. You were so drunk one night you cried. I had never seen a man do that.

"This can't be healthy," I thought to myself.

You would drink yourself into oblivion and then you would pick a fight with me and forget it by morning. Or maybe you would tell me you loved me, it just depended on the night. One summer night after an especially over-the-top blowout fight outside your house, I told you I was walking home. I can't even remember what our fight was about, but you chased me down. I was walking all the way down the street with absolutely no intention of walking all the way home, but my judgment was clouded by my cries for attention. I wanted you to show me you cared. I wanted you to run after me.

My learned pattern of behavior was that chaos equaled love and all of our chaotic episodes made me think that maybe we had a chance.

"Come on Sophia get back inside!" You were yelling after me at the top of your lungs. "You're not walking home! Get back inside!"

"No!" I screamed back, while I wiped tears from my ears.

In the end, you convinced to come back with you like I always did. And I thought to myself, "wow a guy who follows me, who chases me down and tells me to come back inside. We have a winner." Then we would laugh at how stupid we were for fighting and everything would be alright until the next night that you were drinking and wanted to yell at me for your own insecurities.

Why was I "entertaining" men at the bar? Why did I hug an old friend, did we used to date? What did I do this summer? Did I even care about you at all? According to you I didn't. You were constantly projecting on to me, your own fears of getting cheated on. There was nothing I could ever say to convince you that I cared or that I only wanted to be with you. Because maybe deep down you knew that I could do better and maybe I knew it too. In a sort of self-fulfilling prophecy, you pushed me away in the end. We were a mess.

We were toxic at times, but bearable. Fixable I should say. But never had a chance.

We only lasted a few months yet continued to return to each other over the course of almost two years after the first night we met.

You were threading in and out of my life in a way that meant we were stuck in a pattern that could only be broken once one of us started dating someone else. Some outside force would have to intervene in order for us to get rid of each other, because we certainly couldn't on our own. Months of silence would go by and then we would run into each other, and it was like we never left.

Weeks would go by, and my phone screen would suddenly light up with your name. Clearly, we both felt the same way because neither of us seemed to forget about the other. It was never really over. We just transitioned into that prolonged period of grey matter, that in between of "what are we?". There was an undeniable attachment between us that was labeled ever so clearly as "having history."

I left for the summer and came back. A day after being back, I saw you again. I couldn't help it. I missed you that summer and you told me that you did too. I will always care about you, I promise.

Summer faded into fall and winter then spring. We never saw each other, not once. Then the last time: St. Patrick's Day. You always loved St. Patrick's Day. I wish it could have been different, I wish that we never ended in the way which we did, but perhaps our ending was proof to me of my very own strength, of my own self-worth and self-love. Perhaps our last encounter was actually a very distinct time which I can clearly define that I trusted myself. And because all of my unstable and chaotic relationships had caused a severe lack of distrust in my own decision making and in who I was, I cannot ever be sorry for leaving you how I left you.

"Do you want to come see my friend's band play?" Danny questioned, scrolling through his Uber app. "In the Hills, they're playing in like a penthouse. It's gonna be a vibe."

I stood on the sidewalk outside of the three-storied nightclub that we had just escaped, as all of the people from inside came spilling out of the exits chaotically.

I mulled over my choices, while Danny warned me that the Uber was only three minutes away, so I had to think fast.

Just when I was about to agree, over Danny's shoulder I spied you drunkenly shuffling out of the double doors with a few of your friends.

I hesitated on my options, mentally kicking myself for what I was about to do next.

"Um, I think I'm just gonna meet up with my friends and call it a night. But send me the address I might come through if I change my mind."

Danny was relentless but I managed to slide my way out of the situation right as his car pulled up.

My phone dinged and I looked down at it to see the apartment number where the band was playing, as Danny's words echoed out simultaneously, "in case you change your mind."

And then he was gone.

Thank god, I blew out a sigh of relief. I didn't really want to spend the rest of the night with Danny and his random friends. I wanted to be with you. Or at least I thought I did. Did I? It was hard to say. It had been so long, so much had changed. Nothing was the same. I sauntered over to where you stood leaned up against a wall, debating with your friends on what to do-do we go home, do we keep partying?

I couldn't believe that here I was, back with you. I had just left you in the club thirty minutes earlier and said goodbye for the night after we had run into each other for the first time in six months. But I knew deep down that I missed you, and maybe I was just searching in my loneliness for that which was familiar and therefore comforting. I knew that you knew me. And that reassured me and made me feel safe.

"Where are you going?" you questioned once you spotted me nearing you.

"With you."

When we got back to the apartment, it felt like I was dipping my toes back into the memory pool. Except this time I realized that I was so far past this dingy two-story walk up on the mountain overlooking downtown, that I actually began to wonder why I had come back home with you.

We made it inside your bedroom and closed the door, climbing into bed. I didn't realize how drunk you actually were.

"I'm tired," I excused, fending off his attempts at affection.

Isn't it crazy how one day the only person who you wanted affection, love, and attention from, becomes a complete stranger? And you couldn't imagine that there was a time when they were anything but an unknown thing to you?

I rolled over and fell asleep. We weren't even touching. I realized in that moment that if it weren't so late, I would've just gone home. I realized that you weren't the person I wanted to be laying next to. That era had died, those days were finally over. I was relieved almost, like I could finally close the pages to an old, worn book which I kept reopening against my better judgment. You just weren't it for me. When I imagined in my wildest dreams who I wanted to be with, I wasn't quite sure who it would be, but it wasn't you. Not anymore. The next morning, we got up at 7 am for you to drive me back to my downtown apartment. I didn't know why we got up so early, but it was probably for the best. I was still wearing my all green get up from the St. Patrick's Day before.

When we pulled up to the twenty-floored luxury apartment building I had somehow managed to call home for two semesters, there was an uncomfortable and unsettled blanket of silence that almost suffocated me before I could even open the passenger door.

I looked over at you uncertainly and guiltily uttered words I didn't even mean, "I'm sorry I wouldn't really…ya know…" The words fell off until I blurted out, "I'm sorry I didn't have sex with you."

The old me was always apologizing to men, for all the things I never did wrong and everything I never owed them.

"It's okay," you looked over at me with an expression I couldn't quite decipher and shrugged, "I get it. You're too good for me now."

I tried to decide whether there was any bit of sarcasm in his voice, but I didn't think so. Not this time.

I just couldn't bring myself to open the door because I knew it felt like the last time.

The silence that followed was agonizing.

Finally, I shattered it with four words, "I guess I am."

We stared at each other for a while; there was nothing left to say, nothing we needed or wanted to. We had officially said it all. We had fought like hell and now there was just nothing left to fight for.

I leaned over the seat and kissed you on the cheek and then I opened the door and got out for the last time. I watched your car fly down the dead empty streets of downtown after St Patrick's Day, as if my brain was silently etching it into the final pages of the book that I knew would close as soon as I walked into the lobby. And while I knew that it was probably the end for us, I never imagined you were going to die.

Exactly 11 months later-one year minus thirty days-you were gone. Just like that, in a blink. February 14th, Valentine's Day. What a bitter irony. That I once slept next to you and now you are dead is something rather unsettling. It stings in an unfamiliar way, it is a grief which I have never known before. At one point in time you felt like home and now you are something of long, long ago.

Isn't it wild, isn't it bizarre, how one moment-one minuscule, maybe even obscure moment in time-can change the course? It can override what was going to be and shift it into what now is.

If I had never been interested in your friend, he never would have invited me to his birthday. And if I had never showed up that night to your friend's birthday, I never would have met you. If we had never locked eyes in the club a few months later, we probably never would have spoken again, and I never would've had the chance to know you and adore you and then mourn you. And if I had never told you that you simply were not IT for me, then maybe I would have been laying in that bed next to you where they found you on February 14th.

Or maybe I could have saved you. But I have put that fruitless wish to bed: we cannot save others who do not even want to save themselves.

So, I trace it all back, I trace my life back every step and every indecision and decision and mistake and "accident" (for there are really no accidents) and blessings and curses. I end up finding myself back at that place where it all began.

I remember to forget, or something like that. I force myself to relive it, to remember it, to heal. To smile at it all and most importantly, laugh. To imagine your voice. It is all I can do or know how to do when I find myself at a lonely crossroads of both new life and also loss, of confusion and also cold stark reality.

There are no accidents, no coincidences, but it is ever so hard for me to fathom that this was the ultimate life plan for us. It is hard for me when I imagine staring down at you from that balcony and smiling at you and you smiling back at me, that you are gone. Imagining that irreplaceable moment-that spark-and then knowing now that we would find ourselves so far removed. That our paths would so utterly divulge, leaving me to ask myself, "where do I keep you now?" And I have to force myself to swallow down that inevitable lump in the back of my throat and answer, "put him where the good things go."

I collect my binders of information together, my mental stacks of photo albums and I gather everything up that I have left of you. I hold it heavy in my arms and then I sort it away in a dusty file cabinet crammed full of moments and memories. I don't have to bury you down where the forgotten things go, I don't have to erase you. I put you away somewhere that is easily accessible, but I do not have to visit it often.

To wash your hands of the situation, to dust yourself off is something that our culture promotes, but it is a kind of numbness that I can never manage. It is a kind of culture that caused you to work yourself into the ground, neglecting your mental well being and lending yourself some much needed grace.

Our culture says work to live but work until you are dead having not lived at all. It is a bizarre reality, one that you knew well each day you walked into that massive bank building at 6 am and walked out at 6 pm.

You shouldered it all, but what if society had been kinder to you? What if society didn't tell men how to grieve, but let them feel instead? Feel an entirely well-rounded base of emotions. Let them cry, encouraged open and honest communication. Spoke about mental health. Right back we trace ourselves to White Supremacy Culture which shuts down the exhibition of feelings and entwines this lack of self-reflective behavior with the very apparent presence of "toxic masculinity".

Six million men are affected by depression every year in the United States. Six million men in three-hundred-and-sixty-five days. Men are two to three times more likely to misuse drugs than woman. And men die by suicide at a rate that is 3.54 percent higher than woman (as found in 2017 via Healthline).

In upholding a structure of standardized masculinity, men often feel trapped in the inexpression or invalidation of their feelings. This burden is too much to carry. In grieving you, I can finally see that you were grieving your entire life. The stigmatization of men's mental health and toxic masculinity have presented a barrier for all men of all ages on what they "should or should not" act like. These gendered social norms paired with a toxic work culture of overwork and mental health neglect, lead me to many lessons learned in your absence.

I miss you, miss you in a way that one misses a warm and familiar childhood friend. Because although it was not perfect and not meant to be, I can chalk it up as only being that. I leave you with no feelings of ill-will or malice. I accept what I cannot change. I know I could not change you. I'm not angry at you, I'm not mad for the way that we left things, only sad that our last goodbye was laced with so much left unsaid. That your final words to me were an admittance that I was too good for you, and that all I could say pathetically in response was that you were right, I was.

I don't think that I was too good for you. You were good, too. I just think I wasn't for you, period. I wish I had said that instead. I wish I had known better.

But I'll always remember our best memories together. When it was good, it was amazing. And so, I put you in that place where good memories live on, and I am just thankful for that.

Lastly, and most importantly, I make room for the new memories coming down the line. It is all I can do now, and it is worth it.

I have learned in this life that death is but a thing.
Only a moment
On a timeline that never ends.
Merely a doorway from one space to another.
Death is but a second-
An absence
A temporary goodbye
A passing through from here to there
The closing of one book before we open another.
Every season ends
But in its place comes something new.
When the frost fades,
Flowers bloom.
And so, death is just a simple passing,
From room to room.

I acknowledge that yes, death is so much more painful than the simplified idea that we are only momentarily separated from the ones that we have lost. But sometimes to think these thoughts is all we can do to release the baggage. Death and grief are an excruciating affliction that never go away; we simply learn how to live with the loss. In time, the agony dissipates to something that we can exist beside. That's what healing is: the inevitable and unspeakable "thing" never really goes away, but we grow accustomed to the pain dulling.

We resolve it, we come to terms with it. We begin to understand that we are much more than it.

There are so many bits and pieces in life that become us, that become who we are. We are always becoming, stepping into, existing within, and carrying on towards. We are every scrap of every experience ever lived, ever human ever loved, every memory ever hardened into our brains. We are entirely a collection of what we know, what we have seen, and what we have felt.

Yes, it is immense. It is grieving. It is living.

"The world breaks everyone and afterwards many are strong at the broken places."

-Ernest Hemingway

(Furthered resources at the end of book).

Chapter Twenty-Six

An Ambiguous Aversion

"An aversion toward ambiguity. The illusion of seeing an incomplete stimulus as though it were whole. The act or process of closing something....an individual's desire for a firm answer to a question."

-Oxford Dictionary Definition of CLOSURE

"What is your perfect day?" she asks me.

This damn therapist, I think to myself. Another Tuesday and here we go. Should I lay down on the couch now with Minnie Mouse and sob into a box of Kleenex?

What is your perfect day? Her words echo in my head, as I gaze blankly back at her. I am calculating, quietly measuring up the white walls and grey couch as they stare back at me. I must have studied the floor lamp a hundred times over before I open my mouth to speak. How long have we been sitting here in this stillness?

It has taken me a second, but unwittingly I answer.

I have no idea.

That is all I say. But truthfully, I do not know. I have never had one planned in my mind. A bungalow in Bora Bora, swimming with elephants in Thailand, marrying the love of my life in the middle of Paris...what am I supposed to say? I do not think that faking some extravagant scenario is going to improve my mental health journey.

I am sure that she is getting at something deeper here, but whatever it is evades me. Have I lived out a perfect day before? For something to be categorically perfect, doesn't it have to be as good as it possibly can be, the day that can't get any better because it has all the best components? I rehash days from my childhood: warm hugs, still walks on the beach, listening to the roaring applause of an audience as I stand onstage in awe. Or is my most perfect day to come? The day when I have children, get married, or look back on a career which has fully bloomed the way I envisioned? What constitutes perfection-and are we ever perfect anyways?

No one has ever asked me this before.

I have been working a lot with my therapist on the idea of "closure." My Tuesday lunch breaks between college courses are devoted to the twenty-four floored building downtown where Theresa helps *fix me*. The word closure races through my mind every time that I feel a burning pit in my stomach, an ache in the place where my heart sits. We throw the term "closure" around as if it will provide us with our answers, our destiny, and our future. Truthfully, I am waiting for my therapist to tell me how I can attain this fictional "closure" and how quickly I can manage it. I am more than ready to slam this book closed, brush my hands of it, and mark a tiny check in the box next to "all healed!"

"If only I get closure..." we tell ourselves.

"Did you get closure?" they ask us.

But what does closure look like, and can we still attain it even if it is not on our own terms?Or what if I dared to pose this thesis, that perhaps closure in fact is a myth in itself, as the very dictionary definition would elude?

Do we really need this fantastical, mythical closure to heal, or do we simply heal ourselves?

What is closure anyways? The dictionary definition even refers to closure itself as an illusion, "seeing an incomplete stimulus as though it were whole". Is closure truthfully an illusionary idea of making peace with one's past and have we managed to misinterpret closure to what could actually be labeled as healing? Because the facts of life are that while we believe closure to be the literal closing of one chapter in order to freshly open the next, isn't that what healing actually is? Mending that which is broken.

The incomplete stimulus which we try so frantically to make whole will never be whole. We must make ourselves whole. We cannot make our past whole and we certainly cannot rewrite history. Maybe, just maybe, we have mislabeled healing as closure, perhaps it is not in fact closure that we are desperately aching for, but rather an admittance and recognition of what has happened, the knowing that we cannot change it, and the ability to heal after.

The reality is that I am never fully at peace with the things that I have seen and what has happened to me. Perhaps this societal idea of achieving closure is too neat and clean and does not account for the non-linear and often messy way in which we come to terms.

In a reality that some may find harsh (but really, this is just how life operates) I acknowledge that closure with every single person who caused me pain is unrealistic and unattainable. Therefore, I have to turn within.

Maybe closure can be found within myself, maybe it is not a myth in the sense that I can tell myself, "This no longer controls or defines me". But if we hang closure onto the inclusion of the other person, there will never be closure; therein lies the myth.

This reality may feel cruel, but it is a fate we are bound to meet in the achievement and realization of healing. We will never gain closure in the picturesque way that we imagine it, because life is anything but picturesque. Why would we place false expectations and pressures on ourselves for feeling pain, instead of simply letting ourselves feel and just be?

We cannot neatly box up our lives and tie it with a satin bow. Healing is like a children's coloring book that often gets filled in haphazardly and far outside of the lines. The pages are full of color, and although messy and disarrayed, it is life. Like humanity, it is imperfect but there is something special in this.

My father once told me that the old Biblical saying "turn the other cheek" doesn't mean "keep injuring me."

If you are injured on one cheek, turn the other cheek to the side which does not hurt. Metaphorically, this means that internally we have overcome.

Yes, I was injured, but I am at peace.

I do not need to do to you what you inflicted upon me.

When I turn the other cheek, it says that I can move on with my life-that I deserve to.

Usually, our human nature tells us to associate the promise of closure with revenge, justice, or retribution and an attempt to get even. We never get it. And not everyone is deserving of it anyways. So then do we not ever have closure? When does this harbored resentment subside?

This is why a false sense of the very word feels to me, like a "self-help-book" lie. Closure has nothing to do with the other person. Call it what you will-healing, resolve, peace-but it is only on us. Can you resolve that you were injured, can you admit that it was wrong but that it does not have to control your life, your responses, or the outcome of your story?

Turning the other cheek means I am looking in a different direction, gazing to the other side. I am moving on, what happened to me does not have power over me. I have turned the other cheek, quite literally turned the page, closed the chapter. These realizations are a necessity, and perhaps we could call it closure. But I admit this label only with the full knowing that this pathway to healing has nothing to do with the other person.

The Merriam Webster Dictionary refers to closure as "an often comforting or satisfying sense of finality." Finding finality within closure means that an event has irreversibly ended, that we have put a period on one sentence in order to write a new story. But I would argue that some sentences never require or obligate a period, but rather three small dots in a row.

With this idea of having reached the dénouement known as closure, we assume that we will have fully recovered and be able to release our balloon of turmoil to the heavens, pack the box up to send off to Goodwill. But this false sense of finality that we grasp for may actually make our healing and our suffering even worse because we try to put a timeline or an expectation on a journey that has none. Realistically, there is never an actual end in sight to any of our grief or our pain, only the dimming and dulling of said pain, which becomes tolerable and livable over time. There is never an end, only a beginning: a fresh start, a new life…healing.

Healing does not mean that I am okay with what has happened, only that I am okay with living a full life, after.

Healing is like a deep, spring cleaning.

Healing is only doled out through the achievement of peace, something that feels of an impossibility for a soul this angry and broken down.

Healing is attainable for every individual, but only for the one's willing to do the work.

You don't need closure, but you do need healing.

Often times we never got to say exactly what we wanted to say, exactly when and how we wanted to say it. The words never poured out and the opportunity never presented itself. We walked or ran away without ever having our time. Perhaps we left or we were left. Maybe even both. We never got even, we never drew out our sword to inflict the sort of pain that would level the playing field, we were never able to erase the memories entirely.

In life, we fall into the most human moments that bring about fruitfulness. We are fed and whole, we experience pure humanity, and some may even call it love. And other times, we are reminded yet again of the aspects that make us truly mortal. We endure and encounter moments of pure drought and starvation, often times in place of where we once sat at the table with a plate full, a glass overflowing. I acknowledge that my coping mechanism and responses produced out of trauma and pain have been to remove the memories entirely. I have operated for years on the sole pathway of forgetfulness. I find that repressing, suppressing, and erasing are my most promising pathways to the future. I fool myself into thinking I may live a life whole and wholly, through the erasure of my most defining moments-the ones that hurt the most. These memories are long gone, dissipated into mist. Names are forgotten, the bad goes away and with it the good.... I have managed to eclipse entire months and years out of the short twenty-some years that I have lived.

In the moments like tonight where I even begin to unpack this dreaded theory, I dare to ask myself, "why?"

Why have I forced myself to forget without even trying? What do I remember? If I dig and dig and dig, will it come back? What have I to unearth? What healing is hiding underneath layers of dry soil? How does burying it all away in the back of an overcrowded closet equate to healing? Should my disassociation worry me? Surely, I cannot carry on with my days in this mode of survival? Survival. That is exactly what it is that I am doing.

Surviving.

I am so exhausted and limp of surviving. I am so tired of being patted on the back for how well I shoulder the ugliest bits of life that I have had to see and feel. I am numb to you telling me how strong I am, how well I take it, how powerful I am for making it through "so much." I am applauded for my resilience; this only drives me to be colder and harsher and firmer and harder-to live up to your version of "strong and brave." This is not closure to me. I do not feel settled and secure, only hollow with the knowledge that I have managed to trudge on. Good for me.

I continue to mentally thumb through the pages of my very own life and past. Conversations and laughter and tears. Men, relationships, cheating, abuse, more tears. Danger. Assault. Attack.

Fear. Anger. Lies. Deceit. Goodbyes, one after another. Threats. So much anger, boiling inside of me, foaming at the mouth. I never said what I wanted to say, I never really won. I never got justice. I've never had justice.

If having closure with others is an impossible myth, can I not find it within myself?

I think about that day downtown, on the second floor of the police department. I think about how the system failed me, how no one really saw me. Ever. I wanted to scream. Please look at me, please listen, please for the love of God believe me. But don't just believe me, DO SOMETHING about it. Somebody, anybody.

They failed me.

I think about sitting there in anticipation in that waiting room on the third floor, the stark white walls so sterile and uninviting. And there was little old me, a splotch of blank ink on white paper, sticking out like a sore thumb. I think about the smallest details and although they were minuscule, I have managed to recall them all. The woman at the front desk and the way her eyes bore into my soul from over the top of her computer screen. The silent buzz of the elevator coming and going, a tiny ding as it reached our floor. The only SVU detective in the building, stepping off the elevator and breezing past me.

He whisked me away to a small room in what I can only categorize as a blur.

I remember thinking how it was nothing like the Law and Order Special Victim's Unit episodes I watched on Thursday nights. There wasn't a multitude of detectives buzzing around, only a single quiet room with a couch and a small plaque by the door that read "Special Victim's Unit." There were no phones ringing off the hook, no abundance of police ready to take a statement. It was dead and silent and empty; it was nothingness just like everything else had been. Truthfully, I felt as if I were inconveniencing this man, taking him away from his lunch hour.

I remember asking myself, "how did I get here?" And that question once more, three letters: "Why?"

He told me to walk him through the story; start from the beginning. He told me it was too late; we were completely and utterly helpless and without hope. No one would listen, I couldn't go to court, I didn't stand a chance. He told me he could send in a victims advocate to help. Would that make me feel better? Her name was Skye, she had resources.

Resources. I wanted to laugh.

I didn't need an advocate, I didn't need help, I needed my rapist's life to be over in the same way that I had felt mine was over, so many times since that night. I needed him to suffer. I didn't need another person to tell me it wasn't my fault. It was a useless comfort. I don't even remember the detective's name. John? So much has eclipsed me in the years since those moments....

I think about throwing the glass bottle at his head. I grabbed the first thing I could find and swung. We were standing on the back deck the night that I stormed Harvard and Harris's house. I think of Gordon holding me back, I think of the look on Jake's face. I think about crying in Lewis's arms that night in the guest bedroom. I think about that little brown room with the couches in B's freshman dorm. I was crying because I realized I had been raped and because I knew I could never go back to before.

I think about the weddings and the funerals, I think about my ex being found dead on Valentine's Day.

I think about all of the relationships which came after what had happened to me and how they had made me lose trust in myself and my sense of safety in this world.

I think about why you did this to me, what was the point? Did you get drunk and do this a lot? Was I the first or the last or somewhere in that disturbed in between known as the middle?

Did you know that you took something away from me that night never to be regained, or did you forget?

I think about closure. That ambiguous aversion which never really goes away. And I think about where it belongs in my life. And I think about where do I belong in this cold, cruel world? But she is also beautiful.

Me...and this world.

That to me sounds a lot like healing. Finding something that once upon a time could not be found.

So, what did I do with that? Where did I put all of that, where did each broken bit get filed away? Or did it all mesh together like one giant volcano erupting and overflowing with all of life's messiness and orderliness and love and hate and beauty and ugliness?

Did the good and bad manage to coexist and was that the beginnings of healing-admitting that I couldn't have one without the other? Believing that even if it was ugly, the other-the opposite-would soon come?

I think about the days which I have lived both vigorously and painstakingly. I am brought back to a time where I craved but lacked the ever-elusive myth of closure. I begged my body to let it go, but she couldn't. I pleaded with my mind to lay it down, but it was an impossibility. I couldn't possibly define closure enough to understand it, let alone take hold of it and live by it and through it. I had some major problems with letting go. The injustice of life had crippled me, the way that I had never had my day in court or got the last word. The pure unfairness and unkindness of the planet Earth infuriated me to my core. How could I possibly go on living knowing that I never received that which I so deserved?

Is this life?

My mental illness is a liar, it has slowly begun to deceive me into believing that I need it to get by, that I need it to survive, that I am unable to exist without my imbalances keeping me afloat. It tells me that without my textbook idea of closure-seeing the man who did this behind bars for the rest of his life or dead-I will never be whole again. I know now that where I stand today is not quite where I want to be, but that beginning on this path is always the hardest part of the journey.

I am beginning to understand that my mental illness has enough power to drive me into darkness as I am able to identify that it has in various stages of my early adult life. The impulses, obsessions, compulsions, and anxieties that rage within me are hell bent on destroying my chance at a wholesome happiness, one I believe I have finally earned in this lifetime on earth. Neglecting my anxiety/panic, my PTSD, my depression, and my obsessive compulsive disorder leads me to believe that I can only gain the closure that I want, in the way that I want it. If I cannot have it exactly how I want it, then I cannot have it at all. In reality, closure is an open-mindedness with one's past. Without it, we will surely crash and burn. I am learning this in time. You can too.

Do I forgive him? No. But I don't need to. I don't hate him anymore; it feels so long ago. I cannot hate him because it will physically kill me, I will be so destroyed and crippled by my thirst for retaliation. I haven't needed to fully forgive him to move on; I think just maybe that is a myth. And while we are all worthy of forgiveness, forgiving him has not been part of me chasing after closure. I will never have closure with him, I don't need it. I need to heal myself. Closure with this soul if I can ever have closure at all.

It has meant forgiving myself: forgiving myself for being there that night, for drinking, for meeting him…forgiving myself for the outbursts, the tantrums, the screaming, the punching, and all of the aftereffects. Forgiving myself for everything I did after.

That is healing to me: showing myself an insurmountable yet deserving grace. He doesn't need nor does he deserve my grace, because he is now nothing to me, he is nameless. I don't have to go back to that place in my mind ever again, although it has taken much practice to explore this new territory of living. I have turned the other cheek because I know I will never get even, but I know that I am headed somewhere much better.

Naturally I wish it never happened as we all wish but wishing isn't the same as closure. When I look back on my relationships that have crumbled, my sexual assault, and all of the moments in life that have added one more scar to my skin, one more tatter to my heart, I wish that I could have a final say. I wish that I could have a choice in place of where my choices were taken from me. I wish that I could divvy out punishment to fit the crime. While I may never have these edifications, I have this book.

So perhaps, if closure does indeed exist, that is a taste of closure. The taste is sweet.

But if it is surely closure at all, it is closure within myself, a peace found within that means I can write this story and put it to bed. I don't have closure with anyone else, but I don't need it. I am healing.

Healing is not the erasure of our traumas, but rather the acceptance that this is part of our story and that we can still navigate a future past it. And we will get there.

I think about what a perfect day would be to me, and why my therapist is asking this. Perhaps she is forcing me to open my mind and to think about that which I always seem to neglect: the good. Maybe, just maybe, she is trying to prove to me that I am still capable of achieving a perfect day, and maybe I already have a few tucked under my belt. Maybe she is trying to remind me that my traumas do not affect my ability to enjoy life, to love, to lay under the sun and bask in the light.

I think it is important to acknowledge that we are all lost, and that healing or the myth of closure are never linear. If we were to chart our expectations for both out on a graph, it would look like a million squiggly lines zigzagging up and down, never a singular neat curve or clean line.

I think it is crucial to life that we pursue this acknowledgement of our tendency to lose our way and perhaps it takes us entire lives to embark on the journey of finding our way home.

Is that all life is-coming home? Coming to terms with home, finding it? Maybe not. But it certainly defines our path and where we end up along the way. Our endings remain undefined and unwritten-but so many times all we want-all we look for-is the chance to be loved, to be forgiven, to forgive ourselves, to find a place of belonging and settle into the safety of knowing. We want freedom so desperately. We want to get back what we lost, or what we never had in the first place. Our lives are utterly unlike, and yet in this we share similar desires, reaches, and struggles. We all dream of being content, we all dream of existing in a life without shame, we ALL envision the time in our lives when we are finally home-and never have to leave or be left ever again.

I think it is important that we acknowledge that we are all lost. I think it is important to acknowledge that this human condition is finite and does not last. And that the warmth and understanding of being known and of being seen is something we all long for and one day will find, as so often those that are lost become found. Finding our way, forgiving ourselves, putting it to bed.

And again, I think back to that day at my therapist's office, that one unruly question. The question of all questions, the hypothetical that I had never allowed myself to explore. I was so used to thinking with a negative mind, boxing myself into all that was bad and wrong about the world, reliving what angered me, and picking apart the flaws of both myself and others. Each time I met someone, I always viewed them through a lens of potential...and what I could fix about them. The *do's and don'ts* of life were much more apparent than the actual living itself.

This is proof to me that I had not allowed myself healing in the way that my body, mind, and spirit required. It was an essential and often neglected piece of completing my devoid puzzle.

If I've proven one thing to myself, it's that I CAN. I can do anything. I can do healing.

I have survived. And not for anyone else but for me. Not simply to stay afloat in this humdrum, ever churning world that never seems to take pause. No, not for them. Not for the workaholics and the ones who praise my superhuman strength through turmoil. Not even for my family.

I have found that I cannot shoulder the world. And so, I survived simply and only for me, I healed simply and only for me. For the little girl I once was, and even for my future children.

I miss that little girl; I want to know her again. I want her to be proud of me. She always has been, but I never saw it.

The beginnings of healing. Call it if you will, closure within oneself. It's happening, I can feel it.

Self-acceptance, forgiveness, showing myself grace, granting myself the one thing I have never allowed: time.

Beginning again. Coming home.

What is my perfect day? I think to myself. I think perhaps I have probably already lived so many.

What does your perfect day look like?

Tell me about it.

Sinking deeper into a moment,

Sinking deeper and deeper.

Time does not exist,

Everything is still.

Feeling alive again,

Photographing each feeling with my mind.

Catching my breath,

For once, breathing out.

Never. Having. To. Say. Goodbye.

"Where have you buried your best days? Have you lived or not? Look, one says to oneself, look how cold the world is growing."

-Fyodor Dostoyevsky, "White Nights"

Chapter Twenty-Seven

You Are She

Sojourner Truth said in her "Ain't I A Woman?" speech over a hundred years ago: "If the first woman God ever made was strong enough to turn the world upside down all alone, these women together ought to be able to turn it back, and get it right side up again!"

In women, in femininity, there is an unending powerful energy, a cosmic strength, and an infinite potential. Women are needed.

For Christmas, I opened a large coffee table book given to me from my mother. It was simply titled "SHE" a book printed by Kate Spade's company, a compilation of powerful women, and their quotations and their photographs. Everyone from Gloria Steinem to Elizabeth Taylor. It was the perfect book for me, my kind of art-filled, photography packed, "hail to the women" text.

As I flipped through it, my mother smiled and said, "there's an inscription!"

I peeled back the pages to the very first one: "You are SHE. Love, mommy."

In blatantly laying my ugliest truths out to my mother, she had in turn lifted me up and told me that I was the strongest woman she knew: her daughter was a survivor, brilliantly strong, and she never underestimated that in me.

It had taken my mother a few months to bounce back after knowing the truth about my assault, it had pained her so deeply to know her daughter had suffered through this alone. Parents often ask themselves what more they could have done, or what they didn't do. I am sure my mother probably asks herself, "why didn't I make her stay home that night?"

I am proud of the parents who stand by us. This hardship is so much for them to bear too. Just like families who cope with a loved one being murdered, my grieving process would be one that belonged to them as well, a journey they would embark on both with me and alone.

My mother has become my biggest advocate and everything I could ever ask for.

In giving me this hardcovered book, she was reassuring me in a simple gift. She was steadily reminding me, that I was SHE. I was the strong and brave. I was the wild little girl turned wildly resilient woman. Thank you, mom, for these gestures of support that never go unnoticed. I tuck them away from when it rains.

"Strong women raise strong women." You are the strongest of them all Mary Kathryn. I am constantly being surrounded and supported by unbelievably strong "she's."

My mother was my first greatest and bravest display of a powerful woman. She lost her father a week before her first day of college. Her childhood had been hectic. Her father had left her mother and three children, for another woman with three children. He was an alcoholic. Her brother turned to substance abuse also. My mother has been through hell and back, lost both a dad and a stepdad and countless others. She had her series of failed relationships and being cheated on, before she met my father. She dated Joey the twenty-four-year old DJ when she was seventeen and watched night after night as he worked crowds of women and groupies. She dated Jon who had a great family, but was emotionally abusive, always falling short.Her mother now has dementia and is in hospice. I have watched as the last few years, my mother has become her own mother's caretaker. My mother is unbelievably non-human. She is extraordinary in every way.

My mother was at a woman's Bible study sometime last fall, when she suddenly broke down and started sobbing at an unfamiliar woman's kitchen table in front of a group of strangers. Through the tears, she repeated the same words that Bethesda had just a couple years earlier: "It is not my story to tell."

I realized how sensitively and delicately the women in my life handled my story. First, they acknowledged that I was the only one who had the right to share it, and secondly, they let me lead the way. Meanwhile, my truth had been trampled over by men.

As the women tried to console her, my mother said the words I had never thought she would have to say in a million years. "My daughter was sexually attacked."

I imagine the words must have felt like chalk coming off her tongue.

The leader of the women's group looked around at the age range of women gathered around the table and asked this question: "Have any of you ever experienced this?"

Every single woman raised their hands.

Every. Single. One.

My mother now found herself sitting at a table of various women, who all had this happen to them, had all been assaulted at some point in time, in some way. My mother was the only one who had never had this happen to her, but it was affecting her life now in ways she could never imagine.

When I asked my mother why she had waited months to tell me all of this, she said it was because she didn't want to upset me. "No mom, this does the opposite," I explained to her. It made me brave.

Women are ultimately the people who raise their hands at the table.

These women are everywhere, they are all around me and you.

When they raise their hands, they hold power to tell their stories, their way, and to encourage others to do the same. I sit at that table everyday of my life, I just hated that my mother did now, too.

A dear friend of mine in college disclosed to me that her abuser had led her to question her sexuality. She began only dating girls, and then every now and then, when a boy would catch her eye, she would feel ashamed. She was supposed to be gay, she thought. She could not flirt with guys or find them attractive, could she? Then one night she realized maybe she had been driven so far towards girls because of the hurt that had been inflicted upon her by men. For so many of us, being raped leads us to believe we may never be able to trust a man again.

She has since concluded that maybe, just maybe, she likes both, and she is okay with that.

Bethesda watched her father wither away until there was nothing left. For four years, her doctor father became the helpless patient. She lived life on the edge, never quite knowing what tomorrow held. And piece by piece, she lost her father, so slow that it tore the life out of her. I always thought she had the best life because her dad would bring her home Juicy Couture necklaces and had impeccable taste in designer. I never could have imagined how dim her house would turn, how black it could be after the light of her dad was gone.

The drawn-out suffering of her father's cancer was the ugliest part of life I had experienced before this happened to me. I watched my best friend, knowing that there was nothing I could do to bring her father back, or to save him from the debilitating disease. I felt as if my hugs and words could never be nearly enough. I learned from her that you can still have a life "after." That you can still love, and learn and grow and hope, but these things are hard to do. I learned that you can forgive, that you can show grace, that you can continue onwards, no matter how painstakingly slow or heavy the trenches. Bethesda, while your guardian angel watches over you, I consider you an angel to me. Theo would be so proud of the daughter you have become, exactly in his image, just the way he raised you to be.

One of my closest friend's named Kat, has a story much like my own mother's: an addict for a brother. Kat's older brother was more like her younger brother, and she took it upon her own shoulders to shield her little sister from the effects his addictions had on her family. Kat's brother got the help that my mother's brother never did. Kat, you are strong, and I love you. A man will never define the unique perception you have on life, the laughter you have brought me, and the light that you have immersed me in for the past three years of college.

Another very close friend of mine was given herpes by the man who told her he loved her, who she shared her virginity with. Now she will have to live with this for the rest of her life. The broken heart will subside, but the trust issues will not, nor will the serious condition that has become her reality and will deeply affect how she has children, her dating life, and her health forever. I think most importantly it affected the way that she currently views herself; she now harbors feelings of disgust and disgrace against her very own body, which should be her most sacred place. Walt Whitman (who, if you could not tell by now, is my favorite poet) tells us that "if anything is sacred, the human body is sacred." I just hope that she sees how valuable she is—to me, to herself, and to the world that is waiting for her impact, because a heart as big as hers is a rare find.

I once had a roommate who was raped on the Fourth of July. Something as celebratory to most as Independence Day traumatized her. She would lay in bed listening to the fireworks outside of her window, remembering every detail. In our apartment there were small glass windows, above each doorway. Something that I thought nothing of triggered her into remembering the boy who had climbed up to video her rape through a similar window.

Women work full time jobs, birth babies, run corporations, breast feed, have periods, and live with tragedy and trauma against their own bodies. Women are mothers and comforters, but also warriors and heroes.

I am surrounded by these "SHE"'s every day, and together we push on.

I have since changed a lot from who I was "before." If you knew me before, you can probably sense it in my eyes. The eyes reveal all, and they tell you that I am so much unlike the girl you used to know. The girl from before, who is SHE?

Shall we meet her?

Healing, not healed. Scattered, broken, despairing, mistrustful, hateful. A girl of many talents and much hurt. Cuts that ran so deep they were on the brink of infection.

This girl didn't deserve any bit of ugly from the world, but she got it all. No one special enough to be exempted from dealing with the same things that everyone else must deal with.

I suppose our lot in life, in fickle humanity, is struggle and survival, and finding purpose even to our pain. I have been given a chance; this I know. A chance for a better life, a chance to disregard the old me for the new me.

If you ask me who I am today, I suppose a lot is still up in the open air. I can tell you that I am a dancer, a daughter, a friend, a teacher, that I am in my last semester of college. I can explain how I am single, with no man in my life to buy the time. I may even describe my family for you a little, and how much I adore them. But the words that I will not type, are perhaps the most valuable, they appear in between the lines. They are the thoughts and ideas that I am still pondering, the open-ended future I am still pointed towards.

I write this not because I have all the answers. I write this because I have learned to survive through the questions, and you will too.

"Who is she? I wondered.

Does she want to be in love?

Does she want to be alone?

Does she want both love and loneliness at once?

Does she crave independence or nourishment?

Does she want to care or be cared for?

Does she feel fed by her art?

Does she let the humans she is surrounded with, take her in and hold her?

Do her most vulnerable points make her strong?

Is she okay, with being she?

She should always be enough for her."

The dictionary definition of SHE is simply a female, a woman [Middle English: probably a phonetic development of the Old English feminine personal pronoun hēo, hīe.]

The dictionary leaves out a few crucial synonyms: energy, power, influence, voice. Daring, wild, intellectual, soft, sensitive, strong. Beauty, pain, beauty.

I asked my dearest friend Jordan, "what do you think of when you think of a woman?"

"The source of life, the source of everything." He responded without a bit of hesitation. "According to the whole Adam and Eve story, they came second. But really, life is created from female. So, they are quite honestly the most powerful juxtaposition we have on earth."

Without your mother or my mother, we would not be here. Females are strong life forces who we also must thank for producing life itself, carrying out the very thing of God. Women and mothers might just be the closest thing we have to the powers of God, superheroes on earth.

Salma Hayek's 2017 New York Times article still hangs in my mind, with one of the most prominent phrases being this: "We are finally becoming conscious of a vice that has been socially accepted and has insulted and humiliated millions of girls like me, for in every woman there is a girl."

In every woman, there is a little girl just wanting to be loved and understood and heard. When they speak, they want people to take note, not just dismiss them as being a child. Even now, I still feel that in my soul: I want to be heard, not dismissed, because I "know nothing" or because I am a woman stepping into a male-dominated light.

Little girls are seldom afraid, but rather made bold from their lack of experience. Being naïve often means you are not afraid, because you have not experienced enough to make you fear. This freedom remains in us but diminishes over time.

When horrible things happen like being sexually assaulted, the little girl in us reappears once more.

Little girls need to be fed both emotionally and physically, a smile from mom and a hug from dad can go a long way.

Not much changes when fierce little girls grow into becoming women that influence the world.

As a little girl, I was stubborn, bold. I wanted to be wholly myself: expressive, wild, and accepted for who I was, fiery spirit and all. I fought hard, I punched a little boy in Kindergarten for hitting me and knocked him right off his chair in the middle of class.

I punched my rapist too.

Three months after he attacked me, and right in the nose. Made him bleed, made him scream, caused a stir of shock in a crowd of people in a bar back in my hometown.

In every woman, there is still that little girl.

When I was in preschool, my mother used to pick out at least three outfits for me every morning and lay them out on my bed. I would scrunch up my nose and shake my head, directly go to the closet, and select a mish mash of clothes: a pink feathered sweater, striped rainbow-colored tights, a polka dotted long sleeve shirt. This was my earliest memory of being SHE. Of being me, of holding out my arms and saying, "this is my world, welcome to it." Of being creative, of being open and unapologetic, of saying "I am going to mix patterns and be fabulous anyways."

For me, being SHE means saying, "…and be fabulous anyways."

Despite everything I have been through, I am still valid, I am still beauty encompassed, I am still me and she and everything that I want for myself.

I have been through hell and back, but also glimpsed pieces of heaven in the people I have been lucky enough to cross paths with just when I needed them most.

I have fought tooth and nail against a society that pushes back against me and attempts to silence a voice that can never. be. silenced.

I have been through hell.

I have been through deserts, and then tundras.

I have been on the rockiest of ships, nearly drowned in the darkest of waves,

And created a shelter for myself in some of the worst storms I have ever known.

She is self-sufficient, but still open to love…

And worthy of love, love through in and through-out.

But not defined by being in love,

But rather who and how she loves.

Perhaps I will always be a little more paranoid than anyone else that I know. Perhaps I will always be more prone to skepticism. Perhaps I don't quite trust men, until they prove it to me. But my rapist didn't take away my ability to love. She still loves.

And thankfully for me, love has no expiration date, no slough of questions that follows in its wake, no pretenses, no unbelief.

I love my mother, Mary Kathryn.

I love my father, Michael.

I love my sister Lauren.

I love my best friend Bethesda…

And all my college friends.

And my dance friends.

And my childhood friends.

I love my little gray cat Prada.

I love my family's five dogs (and the four that passed away throughout my childhood: Lilly, Rosie, Ashley, Bree).

I love my students.

I love my mentors.

I love moving, dancing, experiencing, expressing.

I love a forgiving God.

I love when the sun rises because it always does.

I love myself, because I always survive, I always win.

I love myself because I AM she, and she is so damn hard to be.

Chapter Twenty-Eight

More Blue Days

"Here hath been dawning another blue day; think, wilt thou let it slip useless away? Out of eternity this new day is born, into eternity at night will return." -Thomas Carlyle

Today it is Blue Monday. This is the first year I have ever been privy to this phrase. Tonight, will be the first full moon of the year, also called the Wolf Moon. In 2005, a United Kingdom press release company labeled it the most "depressing day of the year." And although the pseudoscience is unproven that this early day in January is indeed the worst of our entire cycle around the sun, I do believe it is interesting that today has been labeled Blue. Not grey, not black, but blue.

For someone so used to the soundless black and white moving pictures, the concept of color is foreign yet necessary. To imagine blue for someone like me who has been bereft of anything colorful, is revolutionary. It is incredibly unlike my brain wiring to imagine a word that is traditionally connotated with a nagging sadness, as that which can be bright and light.

I don't think Carlyle meant that our blue days were ones full of thunder and rain. Often, we describe saturnine feelings of melancholy as feeling blue. But now, I don't imagine the blue that is depressing and lonely and full of longing. I don't envision myself as a little girl holding the pale blue Care Bear "Sadness" with the raincloud on his stomach.

I don't think Carlyle saw the blue days as the rainy days when we feel lousy and curl up in bed because there's nothing else to do but watch the rain patter on our windowpanes. And I think that's the point: words often have two meanings. And sometimes the things which we have painted to look dull and ugly, are actually everything but. Blue which is sadness but is also stillness, softness, coolness, and silence. Red which is love and passion but also anger. Heartbreak which is just as much pain as it is a lesson learned. Suffering which is just as much hardship in the beginning as it is reward in the end. Black which is just as much darkness as it is depth. White which is just as much bright light as it is blankness.

Perhaps something doesn't have to be all bad, perhaps there are nuances and shadings (perhaps there are grey areas like I learned in my chapter Living In Black & White).

Perhaps there are two meanings to blue and perhaps I have only befriended one.

In my life, I refused to think that any life event could ever hold more than one meaning. Lewis hurting me in the way that he did could only feel like a stab to the gut for my eighteen year old self on that hot summer night. It didn't feel like a learning lesson or a crucial life experience of knowing my own self-worth and what I deserved. All I knew was the hurt that I was feeling, and that hurt in the moment was loud enough to drown out anything else. When I was assaulted, all I knew was the days that I counted after that spring night. Each day was one day further away from the day that it happened to me. I couldn't wait for it to be a week in the past, a month in the past, six months, a year. I willed the days away because I knew that if time passed, maybe so would my pain.

Pain often feels one-dimensional, when in actuality it brings forth various levels that we are often unequipped or unready for. To my pain there has been layers of knowledge, of knowing myself better, of healing, of closure, of closeness to others, of seeing the world for what it is in all of its shades and colors. And understanding that words, like pain (or blue), can have two meanings.

And I am not saying that all pain is for a purpose, but I am determined to bring purpose to mine.

I think of the brightest color blue. I think of the calmest color blue. I think of every color that surrounds me that I have been both numb and blind to for so long.

And I think that if one day I can wake up to blue skies out my window, and feel not only an absence of dread, but an actual curiosity for living life in place of where an ache once lulled through my body, then I know that I will be alright. Those days always felt so far out of my reach. The days where I could not bear to even peel myself up out of bed but do so anyways because I was without choice. And it didn't matter if the skies were blue or the sun especially bright, because I couldn't see far enough past my own pain to acknowledge that anything could be beautiful.

When you're in pain, time moves slow.

Sometimes it feels like the world is moving on without you. Like all you can do is put one foot out in front of the other and barely slip out from under the covers.

People celebrate birthdays, they celebrate babies being born and their friends falling in love. Couples get married. Families take vacations. They blow out candles, they light up Christmas trees. Teenagers move into their dorms and graduate college. Parents become grandparents. But when you're grieving, you become accustomed to forever being stuck in the past. Life, then, isn't for living but for surviving, and thus it seems that while life happens all around you it never happens to you. Or perhaps it does happen to you but you were too unaware, too out of your own body, to notice any glimmer of beauty or of liveliness or of light. And so the ones that grieve trudge on, painstakingly, and wish the days away.

I think of my childhood. I think of a time far before the days which I had grown so accustomed to wishing away. I think of the days before I knew words like anxiety or depression, words that I not only knew by their dictionary definitions but also came to call my unwanted companions. I recall days of naivety and innocence, where I was blithely unaware of politics, of wars, or of pain. Days where I never learned words like rape or incest or abortion in school.

At what point did I come to understand words like assault, grief, or suicide? What was the day where it all changed, the day when I grew up? When did the blue days turn black?

I recall a childhood that was less than perfect but never lacking in color. I imagine my favorite blue ice cream when I was a little girl. I can see the baby blues and electric blues of my youth.

I think of the color of the clearest summer skies and how we used to play kickball in the backyard underneath that blanket of blue. Or being seventeen years old again and swimming through the ocean. Sneaking into the lake late at night. His blue eyes. I think of the sky when it hits about 8 o'clock in the summertime. I think of the slate blue house I always wanted my parents to buy in the neighborhood next to ours. I think of tranquility, sweetness, and quiet. I think of that blue ice cream from my childhood turning my lips purple. For some reason I think of my dad, because we would always beg him to take us to the ice-cream walk up window. I think of blue like a newborn baby's nursery. Blue that is pale and subtle, gentle yet welcoming.

I think of improvisational dancing in college to the color blue. I never knew that color could be translated into dance until I studied the movement of wavelengths on the ultraviolet color spectrum at my arts university. It was a reiteration that color is everywhere. There are a lot of blue things to love that bring both silence and serenity, nostalgia and contentment. A life that is cool and still. I would love to live a life like that. There are so many shades of blue.

I think of all of the blues which prove that words always have two meanings. The Tiffany blue bedroom I had in high school that I insisted on roller painting all by myself. I remember the way that those bright, freshly painted walls made me feel. And I remember just the same how I felt when I came home on break from college and saw that those walls were no more. I opened the door to see that those walls which I had labored so lovingly over and pridefully painted all on my own, were covered in slate blue and that all of my sister's furniture now filled the room. And I wondered to myself, "why do I care? It's just a room." I thought that there must be something wrong with me for wanting to cry in that moment.

I was living in an off-campus apartment by that time. I didn't need a bedroom at my parents anymore. It was silly really, it was just paint. But now I recognize that nagging ache. I can understand the hurt which I felt when I opened up my bedroom door unknowingly to see that it was no longer mine. It was the palpable grief of life moving on without me, of my childhood coming to an end.

As silly or unreasonable as it felt then, thankfully I can label it now. I was scared that while I had moved away to attend university, everything was happening all around me and without me. I was getting left in the dust and maybe I wasn't even really living at all.

I think of my favorite blue sweatshirt, the one that belonged to my mom's stepdad Joe, whom I never got to meet. It's the coziest and most comforting piece of fabric I own. But I never got to see him wear it.

I stare down at the photograph of little me propped up against my computer screen. Blue headband, straight across bangs, and white peasant shirt. And I think of what I would say to her. Or how maybe beneath it all I feel a guilt that I couldn't protect her. That all naïve innocence has been long stripped away, that her thoughts on love are plagued with the experiences which have jaded her, that she's not as trusting or neighborly or wholesome as she once was, that she doesn't yell to turn the song off because it says a bad word. Because I wish I could've kept the skies blue for her forever and kept them from ever clouding over. The more I have considered the study of my inner child, the more I have learned the art of forgiveness, of courageously and boldly summoning up those five words which never seem to flow off my tongue: "It is not your fault."

If little Sophia could have learned and understood this concept, perhaps she would have saved herself from a young adulthood of people pleasing and swallowing down the unkindness of others, especially by the ones who claimed to care about her the most. Maybe she could have learned to speak up for herself much, much sooner.

The blue of my childhood days turned grey a long time ago.

I think of my darkest days, the ones I used to label as "blue"; blue which has two meanings. I think of how many times my bones have been plagued with a dull melancholic "blue" feeling. I think of when it hurt. I think of the navy black sky, and I think of the terrifying yet familiar night. I couldn't wait for it to be night, because then that meant that the day was done, and I could mentally tally off another day that I had lived "after". I could close my eyes and pretend it never happened, cocooning myself into a dream world-a parallel universe where bad things didn't happen to good people.

The thing about the blue days which I have known previously, is that they are always entrenched with a much darker hue than Carlyle's. The blue turns to black, and not the kind of color black which adds shade and depth, but the black of nothingness.

I suppose my purpose in writing this chapter isn't really to recall all the shades of color in my life and to reminisce on pretty prairie blues, but instead to convey the actuality of survival from a sexual assault. This chapter has various meanings, like pinpointing the lack of color that often exists in a victim's life, making bright blue days feel like nothing, or good days an impossibility, making us see life through a clouded lens of negatives where only bad things happen to us and nothing wonderful or pure will ever come our way. This chapter speaks on the way in which trauma survivor's depressive and all-consuming emotions can come often become addictive and safe to us. For example, I have found that it is indeed easiest to write when I am down, when I am searching…when I am "blue." But I also note that there is always two stories to be told: how something bad can also be good, or how something painful can also grow us instead of defining us.

How strange and silly that we have managed to associate emotions with color, to transcribe that which is visual to that which is verbal and emotional, much like life. It seems that all is always felt.

When I feel blue or melancholy, when I feel those subtle reminders of my own pain and grief or the unfairness of a world around me, I turn to these pages. I write on the blue days. I have become dependent on this and find it nearly unimaginable to write about happy things. The happy things come and go and I forget to write them, but the bad things I always somehow set in stone.

So perhaps in acknowledging this, I have found my next mission, my next efforts in life through this self-reflection. I am going to try to dissect my own feelings so that I will be able and willing to write in any and all conditions. I no longer wish to sink into the comfort of saving my words for a day that is shaded with blue and sadness. I don't want to rely on my pain just to "feel something." I don't want to sink deeper into my sadness because it feels good to cry. I don't want to only write when it feels there is nowhere else to turn.

Instead, my hopes from this chapter, are that I may be able to write when I am happy too. That I could celebrate and memorialize those days, and in inking those stories down, set them into stone. Because those days deserve to be told too. I can't be a writer who doesn't know how to write about anything else besides my own utter pain and sadness. People have enough pain of their own. They can read about the pain, sure, but they also want to read about the better blue days, the reassurances that it does get better, the push to go forth and try and live them out. And while the darker bits of my story are crucially important to tell, I'm going to try Carlysle's way too.

If life is truly about perception, then even we can change the meaning of color. And we can acknowledge that while we may not be able to erase our past, we can indeed rewrite our own history in a way that fulfills our desires for the future.

I think of all of the beautiful shades of blue which I have ever known, and I make that a single day and I file it away for when I forget what color looks and feels like. I think of all of the blue days we have ahead of us that we've already written off in our minds and I pray for those days. I try to imagine a time "before" where I didn't know a sadness that never seemed to end, a sadness that was so constant it became nearly addictive. I didn't know who I was without my armor of pain. I imagine a time "after", where such pain will no longer exist either. This must be the place which I have dreamed of for so long.

A place of quiet and beauty. It might be messy too. But I am accepting of the imperfections that life holds for me. Nothing is or will ever be picture perfect. I have learned to put down my need for perfection long ago. That is what makes life art, that is what makes life exciting: it is unpredictable. It is imperfect yet fascinating, it is ever progressing never stagnant, it is light and softness and hope and rest and recovery, it is about prevailing through suffering. It is simplified and transcending.

It is blue. The sky is transparent cornmeal blue, the fields are coated in little blue wildflowers, your eyes are the most beautiful blue I have ever seen. I admit there are beautiful things in life. They make me feel as if I can breathe again.

Here hath dawned another blue day.

Shall you let it slip uselessly away? Or will you too come to find that words have two meanings?

"Out of eternity this new day is born, into eternity at night will return."

My life is colorful and full.
It is a lot of blue,
But it is a lot of everything else too.
Etched into the memories and moments

Are colors and saturations
That make me remember
What it feels like
To be back in those days.
I try to make my today
As vibrant as possible
Even on the days that it rains,
To make up for the days
Which I have lived so colorlessly.
To make all of my blues electric
And all of my reds fiery,
Or I would have wasted away by now.
Wasted away like I once remember
In my own bluesy melancholy,
Of days long gone
That are never coming back.
Caught up in what ifs and has beens
Trapped in a life of guilt and regret,
Loneliness and numbing
Ache and pain.
But what I have come to find
Is that pain is a necessary component to life.
However unjust and unfair
It's presence is to us,
However wrong it is that we be wronged,
Pain teaches us
To see that which is beautiful
And to recognize it as so,
In stark contrast to the ugly.
One without the other is useless.
Because,
Even the most special and bluest of days
Would look pale and insignificant

If it was all we had ever seen before.
So it is through my pain
That I have come to see
That colors like words
Have two meanings.
And my experiences
Which seemed to bring about
Nothing but darkness and suffering,
Have birthed bright life and a gratefulness
To be here.
"Coming Back To Life"
Words by Me.

"The world is blue," Yves Klein
"When I don't have red, I use blue," Pablo Picasso

Chapter Twenty-Nine

In Hell, There's Heaven

What is my light at the end of the tunnel going to be, and where oh where will that little big light be?

More people need to be told they are loved. To verbalize love, to emanate love, to show love, is perhaps to show a glimpse of life past this earth. Like finding heaven in hell or light in the darkness. Liz Milani writes in her book: "The longer I live, the more I experience, the more gray and unsure life becomes. Except for one thing. This ever becomes clearer to me, every hour, every day, every year. Love is truth. Love is what I believe."

Love became my light at the end of the tunnel.

Love became my reassurance in the murkiness, my drench of color in the black and white.

I have never been in love, but there are plenty of people whom I love so deeply and pragmatically, who valued my story and emboldened me to shout it to the rooftops. I have never been in live, but I am still surrounded by the special few that I consider to be my soulmates. I have so many humans that I say "I love you" to at the end of the night, that I can't help but be washed over in it.

Washed over in love and acceptance, when all I was feeling was dirty and ashamed and disgusted and angered, and all I was seeing was red.

I suppose all that is left now is the many questions I have for myself.

I sit here now, and I wonder, where will I go?

Will I ever actually have fully, one hundred percent forgive him?

Can forgiveness be an attainable pathway for me? I pray and pray and pray…

Dostoevsky once wrote: "If a man has a conscience, he will suffer for his mistake. That will be his punishment as well as his prison."

I can't keep punishing you in the innermost corners of my mind. Every day I punish you and in doing so I punish myself. If you have any knowledge of right or wrong, then you will know that you are wrong. And that will be your cruel punishment…getting to live with your choices and going to sleep with that every night that you lay your head down on your pillow.

Do you see my face in the darkness?

Do you look up at the ceiling and feel my fist connecting to your nose?

As you lay there, do you remember us laying on the tile floor?

Do your choices make you sick?

Did you do it again…

Are there more girls out there?

Do you parade around as if you have done something-anything-good with your life? Because you will never be good unless you drastically change your entire existence.

For my last semester of college, and to no coincidence, I had registered myself for a course about the psychology of evil. The first day we talked about M Scott Peck's psychological criteria for an evil person, and one of the lines etched itself into my mind: "is unable to think from the viewpoint of their victim."

I have tried for so long to understand you, to hate you, to deny you, to feel sorry for you, to forgive you. You were a monster to me, the epitome of evil that had entered my life as most evil does: slowly and yet all at once, and then gone as quick as it comes. It leaves only destruction and damage in its wake. If you are the evil that I think you are, then you would never repent from your ways. If you are the evil that I think you are, then you must be stopped. If you are unable to think from the viewpoint of your victims, then clearly you will never see your wrongdoings. If you are the evil that I think you are, then you are damned.

For you, it was just another night out, another bender, wasn't it?

Another night beer drunk and hopped up on the cocaine that you sold to all the preppy private school students of the college you had dropped out of. For you, it was just another drunken, sloppy, fractured "interaction" with a girl. For you, it was just another "kiss" since you "remember the girls you have sex with" or so you say.

But what about me?

What about eighteen-year-old virgin me?

What about her?

You never stopped to think about her, but I can't help to wonder, do you now?

And does that make you any better?

Or me any better off?

You take and take and take, but at what point does that take away from you? What are you left with?

Do you know what you have done?

Is your life an empty shell?

Are you fulfilled?

Do you remember my name?

Are you in your own personal hell of a prison, the one you spent years building brick by brick? Have you yet grown used to curling up inside of it, cowering away in that dark, comforting space?

My own personal prison was you.

That is until I formed these three words: I forgive you. My light at the end of the tunnel will be these three words.

I wonder if I will ever actually be able to say, "I Forgive You" and mean it. I am still so uncertain. I am still a nomad on this journey, pressing on with purpose, no longer wandering aimlessly. But I have not reached my destination yet.

I am not home just yet.

I am not at the top of my mountain just yet, but it is no longer storming.

I forgive you because I am sick, so sick sometimes, of always writing about you and thinking about you and wondering if maybe you think about me too?

I am angry, so angry, that you have found an impervious place in my mind-the place you don't belong.

I want nothing more than to relinquish myself to these three words, to set myself free of these hateful feelings I have for you. I want to forgive you for my sake, not yours.

You invaded this body, this sacred temple, but you have managed to seep into my mind, also a sacred home you don't deserve. You have no right to live here, to live in my memories, but you do. You inserted your dick inside of me and inserted yourself into someone's life who never asked for you to be there in the first place.

By the way, you are not the reason I write this. I am the reason I write this.

Don't mistake this open conversation I have chosen to have as a conversation meant for you. Rather, this form of communication is one sided.

For once, I will talk.

And you will listen.

When I say I forgive you, I want to mean it and I think one day very soon I will. I don't harbor the wrath I once had for you. I will never live unbounded and free if I continue to say your name and never forgive you. I have not thought of your name in a long time, I have not seen your face in my nightmares in even longer. I assume this must mean I am making bigger steps than I give myself credit for. When I feel at peace, I realize that must be in some lengths, due to my ability to forgive. I forgive for my own sanity. I will never be me again if I don't forgive you. My ability to forgive comes only from my very own process of healing, and the forgiveness I have been lent in life. My forgiveness stems from the undeserving forgiveness I have seen and experienced from the people around me. I forgive because I am forgiven. I forgive because I want so badly to be the girl from before, not "after". I forgive because I can't let you change me even more than you already have. I forgive because I want to see a tomorrow that doesn't look like that night with you.

In writing, I find myself asking so many questions I have never been able to vocalize out loud. I type out these questions with thudding pulse and mouth them out into open air for the first time in nearly three years. I often think of the incident, but not of the human. When I begin to ask these questions, he turns from monster to real flesh and bone, a person living day to day just like me.

And I ask myself, where will he go? Will life ever take him out of the darkness? I don't worry much about how far down he will spiral, as long as I am not taken down with him. I can't afford for my spirit to spiral down into that dark godless place, riddled with unforgiveness and bitterness, lacking in all hope or light.

I cannot turn back the clocks of time.

I cannot live in a world where this never happened to me.

I cannot go back to that time and place labeled only as "before."

I cannot choose to stay home instead of going out that night.

I cannot unmeet you.

I. Forgive. You.

This time, these words were targeted towards my very own heart.

In this, I found more self-forgiveness than my therapist ever could have warned me for. I have unrelinquished the blame, I have finally laid down my body at rest and taken off my muddied boots. I have left them outside on the doorstep, for the rain to wash away all dirt and soil and imperfection. I forgive myself for the things I never choose, I forgive you for taking away my right to choose in the first place.

I am an imperfect human, with still so far to go and so much to give. And some days are easier than others. But other days are quite literally the most wonderful of days and that is all I can ever ask. All I could ever ask was to laugh again.

In writing, there holds much healing. You turned me to stone, but I choose the fluidity of words on paper, of body moving again, of toes curling and uncurling as they touch the floor for the first time in the morning. I choose to feel the first spring rain, to bike over bridges and laugh until my stomach aches.

I choose to speak, regardless of who listens, simply for its own healing powers.

There is weight in words, in these words, sometimes too heavy to bear, dark to read.

In writing, there is much power. And there is power in truth. This world needs more truth.

I abide by truth, I live by the honesty that comes with having a voice, the vulnerability that comes with total uncomfortable transparency.

My ugliest parts have made me the most beautiful, my weakest moments have made me the strongest.

I have seen the absolute worst in the human academy, my faith has been dashed and then restored. I consider my past circumstances untimely and cruel, yet my story to be incredibly redemptive.

I thrive on in light, and I recognize it for its greatness, because I have been blind in that navy-black darkness for so long, and it makes claiming the light change your life.

There is power here, I have often thought to myself like I did that night in the room where we sat with our eyes closed. There is power in every one of our stories, and I wish we would use that power to share them more.

In hell, there has been so much of heaven. In my own personal black, I have found the warm lights of home pushing me onwards, leading the way.

December 18, 2019:

There are certain kinds of feelings whose feeling cannot be placed.

Cold toes under warm blankets

Belly laughter at just the right time

Cuddling up to your best friend

And falling asleep on a human's shoulder.

Opening up a gift picked out specially for you,

Feeling the heartbeat of someone else.

Knowing that your tears are not unaccompanied.

Holding on to new life, with all pudgy ten toes and ten little fingers in your arms.

Your mother telling you she is proud.

Hearing the one's whom you love, validate you

Or tell you it is okay to cry…

It is warmth.

Another unknown word for it

Perhaps may fit better

But warm heart and warm body

Will suffice.

The warmth of feelings that can't be named is much better than the feeling of that which is unwanted…

I look back on old journal entries and see that even in those unwanted days, I still had hope. My very own words, some now five or six years old, still surprise me…that in some of the darkest hours, I was still writing, makes me proud.

It reassures me that I have in fact always been strong, I just was not looking close enough to see it. But all the time, I was writing.

Taken from the pages of my journal some 4 years ago, reflecting on the death of my best friend's father:

August 19, 2015:

"But even when things get ugly, we still have beautiful moments too. And the future- the promise of one-can be a beautiful thing.

the day my best friend's father passed away from us it was the most beautiful day we had all summer- that is no exaggeration. I still remember it. I feel it, I see it. the sun was almost too bright for stinging eyes, the warm wind drying our tears as they hit our face, the air smelled like flowers, the sky looked new...and I just kept thinking how much he would've loved a day like that day. I would've pulled my jeep into the driveway and seen him gardening out with his wife. It was the most beautiful day of the summer and possibly the ugliest I had ever had in my life. it was a beautiful day, for him. In the movies it should have been raining, the sky should've been gray, but the unusual sunshine & the summer breeze were like God's little reminder to us not to cry, to take heart. Because this great man that had given me the best & greatest friend, I could ever ask for was out of his suffering and his pain was no more. Now, the pain was hers to bare. And yet, in heaven he was surrounded by a thousand angels, and he was dancing, and he was waiting for when we grew old and rejoined him, and I imagined he looked just the way we remembered him in the time before, I am sure of it."

Is this not life?

"If there is meaning in life at all, then there must be a meaning in suffering. Suffering is an eradicable part of life, even as fate and death—

Without suffering and death, human life cannot be complete."

-Victor Frankl

Chapter Thirty

Look How Far We Have Risen

Walt Whitman once said, "It is not far, it is within reach. Perhaps you have been on it since you were born and didn't know."

He speaks of the journey that we were sent on long before we had any say so in the matter. He reminds me that the finish line is near, that I am coming ever closer to the top of my mountain. It is within reach; it has always been even when I could not see far enough ahead to know this.

I am a mountain

I stand my ground.

But I am a river

I am always changing.

Turning

Tossing

Flowing

Settling.

I am a current, I am a breeze,

But I am also immovable.

I have managed to do both

And be both

Perhaps since the day I was brought into this world.

I have been brilliantly bold since the moment I got here.

And so, I release this.

I put this one down.

I am capable.

I am strong.

I can leave this one behind me now.

I know one day.

One day soon,

I will reach my highest place.

And maybe these nightmares turn into dreams.

Every now and then, I catapult myself down memory lane by digging through old thoughts in my iPhone notes section. When I could not get my hands on paper and pen, I would jot down the words as they came.

This, taken from my iPhone notes section, is titled: What Is It That I Want? What Do I Want?

"Do I want to be with someone, or do I want to be alone

Or do I just want to love someone

Because I already do love

So many people that my heart is so full

And is it that someone that will fill the void

Or maybe just the ability to smile when the sun comes out

And the chance to breathe again after a long day, A bad day

Because the bad days always end

What is it that I want?

To be happy.

But what does happiness mean?

Where do I find it?

In movement? In music?

In hope? In faith?

In family? In friends?

In nature and all of its abundances?

To have peace.

But where do I find it?

Within my soul?

But I am more tumultuous than the sea.

So how do I find that within me?

Do I find peace in the quiet?

The sacred moments of silence which breathe light?

The times when I stand on a stage

Or behind a wooden pew

Or on a sandy shore watching the sun set

Or the full moon dance above the waves?

What is it that I want?

To enjoy moments just like these."

I am lacking in nothing, I am made whole again in my brokenness, I am as resilient as the

bravest warrior, and soft like the gentlest of souls. I celebrate in my survival, in my second

chance to live…I am the murder victim who lived, long and hard and beautifully.

Whose blood is on your hands,

Whose face you will never be able to get out of your head.

Whose story will be read for years to come,

Whose crime could never be proved, but rings real as the sky is blue.

You could not make a victim out of me.

I am sorry you cannot succeed in making me weak.

Because I live, and live, and live…

Freely.

If there is only one thing that I have realized then it is just this: I know that somehow God allows these things so that one day they can all be stories that we tell, stories about how we made it out, stories of pain that we want to make sure no one else ever has to feel. write this so you don't have to.

I write this so that my story doesn't become yours. I also write so that if your story looks like mine, that you too will find the courage to do so.

The truth is, I don't know. I don't know why our fathers died and boys raped us, and we drank our lives to death when we were seventeen and got our hearts broken and watched our brother's struggle with addictions and lost our faith in people being good. All I know is that we went on, we held on to one another, and we lived wonderful lives for ourselves. We found purpose even when they told us we couldn't. We acquired the ability to show people our hearts and the chance to learn theirs. We grew to understand forgiveness, and to never go backwards. Maybe when people see these things and hear these things-maybe when they see us-they will see the light we never could.

"Nothing that you have to say is too much," one of my old college friends reminded me late one night. That was her answer to me when I explained what I was writing and expressed my fear that it may be too much for people to handle. I admit, these words often feel unsettling even to me, mostly because I feel so pointedly on display. My soul has been exposed and is at the mercy of strangers. I have asked myself so many times, "is this too vulnerable for people to hear, too bitter of a pill for the people that knew me to swallow?" Will I be viewed differently; will people see me as strange? Will they take pity on me? Will people receive it at all? Automatically, I was fearful of what other's thought. I was already boxing myself in at a time when writing was supposed to do the opposite for me: free me out of my self-imposed prison. So, after much mayhem of the mind, unapologetically, I wrote. I convinced myself that my opinion was the only one that mattered, because it did and does. Still, I worried that my words were going to be a lot to take on. I know they are. But it is often the hardest things to be said that are the things most needed to be heard.

Whenever you are between a rock and a hard place, asking yourself what to do with the thoughts that are too heavy to hold, both quietly and loudly tell yourself "Nothing that I have to say is too much."

Telling a story that feels so deeply personal to my soul has held its own complications for obvious reasons. But mostly I am so exhausted of being afraid and of fearing judgment, or of gripping on to an unrelenting shamefulness. I am so tired of staying quiet as a means to protect myself, as most survivors do. And many survivors may never come forward. I acknowledge that each person's story is solely theirs, and no one is obligated to share. I am not trying to be inspirational; I am not trying to glamorize my pain. I am merely expressing words four years in the making, so that maybe if just one person reads this and feels a sliver of hope, or feels a little less alone in this world, then all of it was for something. And it only takes just one.

But know this: you matter to me.

Let your words be your freedom and know that people will take away only what they can carry. Remind yourself that although it will be hard to hear and painfully complex for others to read, it is a necessary component to your healing. Acknowledge that not everyone will understand and perhaps even fewer will listen, but the ones that love you unconditionally, will pull you in closer and make you feel more seen, heard, and known then you have ever felt before in your life. It was these simple reiterations from the people most important in my life, which reminded me that the journey to healing was not a path I could walk alone. There was a certain restoration and affirmation that I never knew I needed until it was happening right before me and to me. Most of us shoulder the world alone not out of choice but out of mere survival. Out of a need to protect ourselves and the ones around us, we suffer silently. We brave a smile and settle into our armor day by day. The facade which we have built up piece by piece, brick by brick, becomes our reality.

As the days turned to years, I always pondered on the assumption that in this, I would have to walk alone. And perhaps to a certain extent, I do. But just because people have not lived it, does not mean they won't understand. And in this, I know now that my journey is not one of isolated despair, but rather support and acceptance as I choose to heal.

I am strong and unapologetic in knowing that my responsibility is only to my words and not the manner in which they reach others or how they are received.

I am strong and unapologetic in knowing that while others will take away only what they can, it is us-the survivors-who are ultimately the ones who took on far too much to bear single-handedly and carried it on our backs for an eternity too long.

We should not be inhibited by the fear that we are inconveniencing someone with the ugly truth of a story our parent's never thought we would be telling.

Who ever thought we would make it here to begin with?

I am here to tell you that you will make it, and that you will do more than just make it, you will live and thrive. You will bloom. You will laugh. You will laugh so hard that your stomach hurts. You will love. You will be broken down and built up. There will be days which are ugly, but also days which are so beautiful that it will almost feel unreal. Life is damn hard, but it is good. The road is long, but you were built for this. The people that you will meet along the way will make it so worthwhile, so try not to go through the motions. Nurture yourself. Heal your inner child. Read books, dance, and make friends. Indulge in the small and simple joys that life beholds you, because it is all we have on this earth. Mostly, just heal. Don't be afraid of what awaits you when you do. You have so much to be proud of.

We are the murder victims who lived. Onwards, upwards. Despite of. Inside of and outside of. Forever, and infinitely. Survivors who lived and live still, long enough to write the words some victims never could.

CHEERS TO THE STRONG AND POWERFUL,

The soft and vulnerable.

IN YOU I SEE MYSELF AND EVERYTHING I LONGED TO BE ON THIS JOURNEY.

You did not break, you did not let your flame diminish, you did not let life harden you or dwindle you down to nothing.

CHEERS TO YOU.

Cheers to your commendable bravery.

CHEERS TO THE ONES WHO SURVIVED.

I cannot thank you enough. You got me here.

We do not go unnoticed.

My peace I leave you with,
My peace I give you,
I do not give to you as the world gives you.
-God.

~~THE END~~…TO BE DETERMINED

BEFORE YOU GO…

"Because my words could never be sufficient…"

What I feared has come upon me, what I dreaded has happened to me. I have no peace, no quietness, I have no rest, only turmoil. (Job 3:25)

When you pass through the waters, I will be with you.
And when you pass through the rivers, they will not sweep you over. (Isaiah 42:3)

The Lord is close to the broken-hearted and those who are crushed in spirit. Blessed are those who mourn for they will be comforted. (Matthew 5:4)

"Come to me all you who are weary and burdened and I will give you rest." (Matthew 11:28)

Although he brings grief, he will show compassion. For he does not willingly bring grief or affliction to anyone.
Now is your time of grief.
But I will see you again, says He.
And no one will take away your joy. (John 16:22)

You will lift up your face;
you will stand firm and without fear.
You will surely forget your trouble,
recalling it only as waters gone by.
Life will be brighter than noonday,
and darkness will become like morning.
You will be secure, because there is hope;
you will look about you and take your rest in safety.

You will lie down, with no one to make you afraid.
Job 11

He will not ask who we are
He will not care where we have been
He will not see all of the goods of earth we owned
He will not turn at whom we knew
He only asks that we know (Him).
James 1:12

He will wipe every tear
From their eyes
And there will be no more death
Or mourning or crying or pain
For the old order of things have passed away.
Revelation 21:4

Psalm 23:
The LORD is my shepherd, I lack nothing.

He makes me lie down in green pastures, he leads me beside quiet waters, he refreshes my soul. He guides me along the right paths for his name's sake.

Even though I walk through the darkest valley, I will fear no evil, for you are with me; your rod and your staff, they comfort me.

You prepare a table before me in the presence of my enemies. You anoint my head with oil; my cup overflows. Surely your goodness and love will follow me all the days of my life, and I will dwell in the house of the LORD forever.

Acknowledgements

To the People That Made Me Strong:

A simple thanks,

I am so indebtedly grateful to the humans that held on to me through the harshest winds and waters.

I stop to wonder, where would I be without them? Nowhere.

I would be surrounded by nothingness.

I am so thankful for the numerous people that pulled me out from that place that I will never go back to again, people who I could confide in, and be met with sanity, safety, and stability. You provided me with the relief I needed in trauma.

To my mother, you are my earliest example of strength, you are my balance, you made me braver because you believed in me. You are the greatest daughter, mother, and wife, and also my best friend. To my father, you are the only man I have ever met that has not disappointed, thank you for always being my safest ride home. Thank you for dinner dates just us two, for giving me great taste in movies. Thank you, mom and dad, for all the tears and all the belly laughter and all the homecooked meals. Without you, I would die.

To my Bethesda, where would I be without you? I am so beyond blessed to call you my best friend of over ten years. You held me when I needed to feel safe in the arms of someone. You were patient with me as I struggled through the telling of my story, supportive of my words. You fought for me every day, in the same way that I promise to fight for you. You listened to me and heard me and believed me. You saw me for who I really was. You watched your father die and are somehow still the most single-handedly resilient and brave woman that I know. To Bethesda's older sister, Menna—my honorary big sister—I love you I love you I love you. I write this for the both of us.

To my sister Lo, you are every bit of good that I needed to be reminded of. A beautiful life is one that a beautiful human like you so deserves. You steady me. You are the song I needed. I love you much more than I could put into words on these pages. You're one of the main reasons I'm here, writing this. I thought I could never even say the words and now I'm writing them.

To the girl that sat with her eyes closed on the ground in a circle with me, yelling out "me too," I thank you. To my friend L who shared her "me too" story with me late one night and recommended Channel Miller's story to me as well, thank you. To Jordan, you are light embodied, you are everything. To Kat, you have made me laugh in the darkest times and been patient with me while I cried…you are so beautiful to me. There are many more names; thank you all.

To my male friends who championed me and said, "I believe you," the world needs more men like you. Thank you for being a safe place for me, for reading these words. Thank you, Landyn, for creating this cover and being my family.

Thank you to the men who have come in and out of my life, thank you for teaching me lessons about life and love…ya live and ya learn.

To Christine Blasey Ford and Chanel Miller and Tarana Burke for founding the "Me Too" movement, you emboldened my voice and reminded me that I have a chance. To Alexandra Waterbury, I am in this fight with you to end the abuse that has damaged the dance world.

To my previous therapist Tracy, thank you for helping me understand that only secrets could keep me sick, never safe, and my best bet was in acknowledging my own voice. To the four therapists I have encountered in the past four years, thank you for each teaching me something.

To my victim's advocate Skye, thank you for listening to me two years too late, for telling me that you knew it had happened. I have learned to live regret free thanks to your gentle reminders, but I still wish that you had been there the morning after.

To the artists I have surrounded myself with over the years, thank you for sharing your heart and your movement with me every day. Thank you for existing in the same space as me, thank you for existing. Thank you for being brave and open and willing to be uncomfortable.

To the thousands and hundreds of men and women that marched beside me in countless Women's Marches and Human Trafficking walks through our city, I salute you. In this solidarity, I was met with more safety.

Thank you, Kurt Cobain, for your outspoken support of women and your fight against rape, for inspiring the title for this book, for being so blatant and shocking that you dared people to listen up.

Lastly, thank you to my original publisher Diane, for believing in me and taking a chance on this manuscript. I am eager to carry these words on in it's second edition. Rest In Peace.

If this experience has taught me one thing, it is that I underestimated people. I underestimated how horrible and depraved people can be, especially underestimating that I would in fact meet people like this. But in this, I also underestimated how strong the one's are that I love. I underestimated how wonderfully brave and soothing people could be. They cancel out all the bad in the world.

For all the ugly and bad I have seen and felt, the people in my life are doubly good.

Thank you for walking me through, and lifting me when needed, and backing off me when needed, and carrying me when needed, and running with me when needed, and sitting quietly with me when needed, and listening to me when needed, and falling asleep with me when needed. Thank you for your patience, strength, and love. Thank you, all of you.

You made me value my voice and my purpose.

I think we are all a collection of the things we never got to say, or never could say. And I could say so much more about all of you. But from the bottom of my heart, I just say thank you, my loves.

With you, I survived the storms, and braved the waters, and more than that, I really, truly, freely, unabashedly, limitlessly, joyfully lived, unbounded. And loved.

And love, still. And live, more.

Resources

Some accounts to follow:
Instagram:
@wearethemurdervictimswholived
@thefemalewarhol
@paar.pgh
@the.holistic.psychologist
@ourfacess
@deconstructingpurityculture
@chanel_miller
@taranajaneen
@metoomvmt

Help to Survivors:
RAINN: (Rape, Abuse, Incest National Network)
www.rainn.org
National Sexual Assault Hotline: 1-800-656-4673
National Sexual Violence Resource Center:
www.nsvrc.org
Victim Connect Resource Center
www.victimconnect.org
"A Guide for Friends and Family of Sexual Violence Survivors."
www.pcar.org

Locally (Pittsburgh):
PAAR: Pittsburgh Action Against Rape
(866)-363-7273

Supplementary Reading:

Books on Sexual Assault:
Know My Name: Chanel Miller
She Said: Jodi Kantor and Megan Twohey
Catch And Kill: Ronan Farrow
Milk and Honey: Rupi Kaur

Others (Books I Read While Writing This):
Atlas of the Heart: Brené Brown
Leaves of Grass: Walt Whitman
What We Talk About When We Talk About Love: Raymond Carver
White Nights: Fydor Dystoesvsky
The Collaborative Habit: Twyla Tharpe
The Sun Also Rises: Ernest Hemingway
The Book Of Job, The Book of Ecclesiastes: The Bible

Statistics:

One out of every six women in America has been
the victim of an attempted or completed rape in her lifetime.
One in six.

Over 40% of women in the U.S. have encountered sexual violence.

College women aged 18-24 years of age are at three times more risk for sexual violence, while women in the same age category who are not in college are four times more likely to have a crime committed against them.

11.2% of all students experience rape or sexual assault.
 Among undergraduate students, 23.1% of all females and 5.4% of all males experience assault or rape.

21% of LGBTQ college students have been sexually assaulted.

Every 68 seconds, an American is sexually assaulted.

On average, there are 463,634 victims (age 12 or older) of rape and sexual assault each year in the United States.

The majority of victims are under thirty.

On average, there are 463,634 victims (age 12 or older) of rape and sexual assault each year in the United States.

Females ages 16-19 are 4 times more likely than the general population to be victims of rape, attempted rape, or sexual assault. I was five months away from turning nineteen.

21% of TGQN (transgender, genderqueer, nonconforming) college students have been sexually assaulted, compared to 18% of non-TGQN females, and 4% of non-TGQN males.

Long-Term Effect Statistics:

*I still often go through life wondering what is wrong with me, why I react a certain way to situations, why I get angry, scared, paranoid, or skittish. I know now I am not alone.

94% of women who are raped experience symptoms of post-traumatic stress disorder (PTSD) during the two weeks following the rape.
30% of women report symptoms of PTSD 9 months after the rape.
33% of women who are raped contemplate suicide.

13% of women who are raped attempt suicide.

Approximately 70% of rape or sexual assault victims experience moderate to severe distress, a larger percentage than for any other violent crime.

37% experience family/friend problems, including getting into arguments more frequently than before, not feeling able to trust their family/friends, or not feeling as close to them as before the crime

Citations:

Rainn.org

Department of Justice, Office of Justice Programs, Bureau of Justice Statistics, Rape and Sexual Victimization Among College-Aged Females, 1995-2013 (2014).

National Institute of Justice & Centers for Disease Control & Prevention, Prevalence, Incidence and Consequences of Violence Against Women Survey (1998).

Department of Justice, Office of Justice Programs, Bureau of Justice Statistics, Female Victims of Sexual Violence, 1994-2010 (2013).

D.S. Riggs, T. Murdock, W. Walsh, A prospective examination of post-traumatic stress disorder in rape victims. Journal of Traumatic Stress 455-475 (1992).

DG Kilpatrick, CN Edumuds, AK Seymour. Rape in America: A Report to the Nation. Arlington, VA: National Victim Center and Medical University of South Carolina (1992).

About the Author

Sophia Menelle is not just an author, but also an artist. Dancer, choreographer, dance teacher, and performer.

Graduating high school at the young age of sixteen, she went on to pursue professional dance at the Dayton Contemporary Dance Company II for over two seasons.

As a 2020 graduate of Point Park University with a bachelor's in dance, she hails from one of the top five dance programs in the country. Menelle returned to Point Park to complete her master's degree in arts administration the following year.

Sophia is an artist both on and off stage; she has spent many years developing her creativity through movement of the body but always returns back to paper and pen. She often journeys through various forms of storytelling based on personal experiences and spiritual awakenings, whether in her own choreography or her writing. She considers herself a women's advocate on issues such as sexual violence and abuse. Nowadays Menelle is busy juggling motherhood, dance teaching, and writing. She has recently returned back to Point Park University as a faculty member and is raising a son that she will one day share her story with.